RETURN TO GLORY:

The Leafs from Imlach to Fletcher

OFFICIAL HOCKEY PROGRAMME
ARENA GARDENS   PRICE 10¢
FASTEST SPORT IN THE WORLD.

HOCKEY HALL OF FAME

Andrew Podnieks

RETURN TO GLORY:

The Leafs from Imlach to Fletcher

ECW PRESS

CANADIAN CATALOGUING IN PUBLICATION DATA

Podnieks, Andrew

  Return to glory : the Leafs from Imlach to Fletcher

Includes index.

ISBN 1-55022-242-2

1. Toronto Maple Leafs (Hockey team) 2. Toronto Maple Leafs (Hockey team) – History.   1. Title.

GV848.T6P64 1995   796.962'64'09713541   C95-930404-5

Front cover photos of Burns and Gilmour by Graig Abel, Fletcher photo courtesy Doug MacLellan/Hockey Hall of Fame. Back cover photos courtesy the Hockey Hall of Fame.

Design and imaging by ECW Type & Art, Oakville, Ontario. Printed by Kromar Printing, Winnipeg, Manitoba.

Distributed by General Distribution Services, 30 Lesmill Road, Don Mills, Ontario M3B 2T6. (416) 445-3333, (800) 387-0172 (Canada), FAX (416) 445-5967.

Published by ECW PRESS, 2120 Queen Street East, Suite 200 Toronto, Ontario M4E 1E2.

Contents

Part One

Keon and Pulford celebrate Cup victory.

I

1967:
The Last Taste
of the Cup

Maple Leaf Gardens. Tuesday night. May 2, 1967. Game 6 of the Stanley Cup finals. The voice of Foster Hewitt.

"There are only 55 seconds of regulation time remaining. Toronto leads two goals to one. The hometown crowd is anticipating a Stanley Cup victory, while Montreal Canadiens are using every strategy to get the tying goal and push the game into overtime.

"Less than a minute remaining, and the Leafs are called for icing; the referee calls for a faceoff to the left of Leafs' goal. There's a delay in play and Montreal goalkeeper Gump Worsley doesn't know whether coach Toe Blake wants him to come out of the net. Now Blake has decided to remove Worsley. He's going to the bench. With 55 seconds to play, Montreal will use six attackers and their goal is empty. Canadiens intend to shoot the works. Béliveau is coming on the ice; so are Roberts, Cournoyer, Ferguson, Richard, and Laperrière. It's all or nothing for them now.

"Leafs too are making changes. Imlach is making his stand with an all-veteran line-up of Stanley, Horton, Kelly, Pulford, and Armstrong. Sawchuk, of course, is in goal. Béliveau will face off for Montreal and Stanley for Toronto. Armstrong is still at the bench talking to coach Imlach. Referee John Ashley is becoming impatient. Ferguson skates over to talk to Béliveau. Stanley is hesitating; now he comes into position. This faceoff is vital. They're all set.

"The puck is dropped; Stanley gets possession; he snaps the puck to Kelly; Kelly kicks it to Pulford; Pulford passes to Armstrong; Armstrong is driving hard. Army shoots toward the empty net. It's on target. It's in! HE SCORES! Armstrong has scored the insurance goal! It's now Leafs three, Canadiens one. Toe Blake's strategy backfired and that shot has just about decided possession of the Stanley Cup. Canadiens had to gamble everything but lost. Time of the goal — 19:13."

There is something charming and even dream-like about watching the oft-replayed seconds that decided the 1967 playoffs when the

Chief scored into the empty net and assured the Leafs of their fourth and last Stanley Cup of the 1960s. It was Canada's Centennial year. The country's two great teams, Toronto and Montreal, were playing for "our" trophy. Our greatest players — Johnny Bower, George Armstrong, Davey Keon, for Toronto; Jean Béliveau, Henri Richard (the Pocket), Yvon Cournoyer, for Montreal — were at the height of their powers. The game was broadcast coast to coast on the CBC with the immortal Hewitt at the mike; the players appeared to be skating unnaturally quickly, funny-looking in retrospect. And the Leafs — yes, the Leafs — won the Stanley Cup.

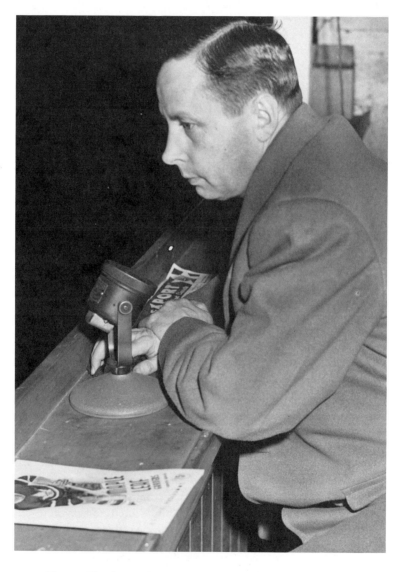

Foster Hewitt in the gondola at Maple Leaf Gardens.
HOCKEY HALL OF FAME

This was an age of romance, of naïveté, when sticks were straight, goalies barefaced, players toothless, hockey made of war-ravaged men of 30 and 40. It was a time when fans wore fedoras and suits to the game, when bench-clearing brawls were common, when equipment was simple and players small. It was an age before offsetting penalties and instigating minors and Tuuks, before helmeted referees and visors and video replays, before 7:30 games and flashy scoreboards and rinkside advertisements. A time when shots were blocked and defencemen defended and hip checks were in vogue, when plays "failed to click," rookies were 26 not 18, and players routinely stayed with a team for a dozen years or more; when a CCM was the stick of choice, and the Leafs and Habs played each other 12 times a year instead of twice. It was a time when the Gardens' faithful knew the skaters like they knew their own children, and the children used to recite the roster like a poem or the Lord's Prayer: One Bower, Two Hillman, Three Pronovost, Four Kelly, Seven Horton, Eight Ellis, Ten Armstrong, Twelve Stemkowski, Fourteen Keon, Fifteen Jeffrey, Sixteen Walton, Eighteen Pappin, Twenty Pulford, Twenty-one Baun, Twenty-two Conacher, Twenty-three Shack, Twenty-six Stanley, Twenty-seven Mahovlich, Thirty Sawchuk.

Then, hockey was a religion, the Gardens a Church, the players the Saviours, the Leafs the only team to brag about, the Habs the mortal enemy. A ticket to the Gardens sent shivers down any boy's spine and the hallways induced a palpable fear, awe, intimidation, inspiration. A player's stick or handshake was more coveted than a Rolex or condominium, and the simple dream of skating on Gardens ice was enough to keep a kid honest and passionate and loyal and determined. This was a time of strength called Howe and speed called Hull, class called Béliveau and courage called Bower. It was, in short, a long long time ago.

May 5. On a warm, sunny day, three days after Armstrong scored the clinching empty-netter, the team was given the traditional ticker-tape parade up Bay Street. The players wore blue-and-white carnations in their lapels and when they arrived at the new City Hall, the Mounted Police, 48th Highlanders, and Mayor William Dennison were there, along with a crowd of 30,000, to greet them. A blue-and-white Maple Leaf was hoisted up the flagpole and fireworks shot through the air in celebration. The Leafs were heroes, Stanley Cup champions . . . the best.

The 1966–67 season had been just like any other — six teams, 70 games — yet in retrospect it was unique. It was the 50th anniversary of the NHL, the year Turk Broda was elected to the Hall of Fame, the year Bobby Hull scored 50 goals, the year Sawchuk got his 100th shutout, the last year before expansion doubled the size of the NHL. But most important, it was the year an 18-year-old Boston Bruin rookie named Robert Gordon (a.k.a. Bobby) Orr, wearing the un-

poetic number 27, began to transform the very way this simple game of stick, skates, and puck was played.

For the Leafs, the season began in a manner befitting the paradox of the Punch Imlach era, which was reaching its zenith at the very moment it was falling to its nadir. Frank Mahovlich, whom everyone called the Big M, except for Punch who called him "Maholovich," sat out the first two games of the season in a contract dispute with Imlach. They were $500 apart. Mahovlich had scored 198 goals in the last six years at a time when 20 a season was like today's 40, and the Leafs needed his skill and character if they were to win. How Punch could have denied Mahovlich his trivial demands was unreason itself and served to underscore the end of the old régime, which Punch personified, and the beginning of the new, which he vilified.

Mahovlich had just completed a four-year contract that paid him $25,000 per season, and he was now asking for $40,000. Four years earlier, Jim Norris, owner of the Black Hawks, had offered the Leafs a cool one million dollars for the Big M, an offer born of Frank's 48-goal year and his subsequent negotiating difficulties even then. Stafford Smythe and Co. mulled the offer over for a few days before rebuffing Norris. Two Stanley Cups later Punch was offering $30,000. The Big M settled for $35,000, but the acrimony between him and Imlach that had been building for so many years was hardly softened by this process of "negotiation." By Christmas, even though Mahovlich was the team's leading scorer, Imlach was forcing him to practise twice daily. Seems he wasn't giving it his all in games.

The new year saw two major occurrences that shaped the destiny of the Leaf team as it headed toward the playoffs. First, they lost 10 games in a row, seven without the Big M who was injured, and plunged to fifth in the standings. Through it all, though, Imlach was supportive and generous to players whom he routinely mistreated when they played hard and won. "My guys are the best," was one of his favourite declarations of support that had always motivated the players to accomplish as a team what they never could have hoped to do as individuals. Second, although the Leafs ended their skid with two quick wins in mid-February, the stress of losing and doing double duty as both coach and general manager had proved exhausting for Imlach. Doctors advised him to rest, and on February 18 King Clancy took over behind the bench. That night, the Leafs beat the Bruins 5–3, their third win in a row, and the club was on a roll.

In 10 games under the King the team's won-lost-tied record was a superb 7–1–2. But more important, Clancy imbued the dressing room with such non-Punchian qualities as humour, joy, and fun. Players could not help but laugh with him (and sometimes at him!), and they instantly took to his carefree love of the game. As a result, when Imlach returned a month later, the players were on an emotional and professional high. Imlach in turn was more sedate and relaxed. Everyone was happy. Order had been restored and the playoffs were on everyone's mind.

The final standings for the 1966–67 season looked like this:

	GP	W	L	T	F	A	PTS
Chicago	70	41	17	12	264	170	94
Montreal	70	32	25	13	202	188	77
Toronto	70	32	27	11	204	211	75
New York	70	30	28	12	188	189	72
Detroit	70	27	39	4	212	241	58
Boston	70	17	43	10	182	253	44

In the first round of the playoffs, Toronto would play Chicago while Montreal met New York. Detroit and Boston failed to qualify. Prospects for a Cup did not look particularly good for the Leafs. Even by Original Six standards, this was an ageing, ancient team that didn't seem to have a snowball's chance in post-season hell of going anywhere. The goalies were anachronisms called Johnny Bower and Terry Sawchuk (42 and 37 years old respectively), and time had cut a large swathe through the core of their defence: Allan Stanley was 41, Red Kelly 39, Tim Horton 37, Bobby Baun 30. They weren't called the Over-the-Hill Gang for nothing.

How could these men hope to stop the likes of a first-place Chicago team that had been going great guns all season? The Black Hawks had five 20-goal scorers — Bobby Hull (52), Stan Mikita (35), Ken Wharram (31), Doug Mohns (25), and Phil Esposito (21) — when there were only 20 in the entire league that year. The Leafs had only two: Ron Ellis (22) and Jim Pappin (21). Five of the nine leading scorers in the league played for Chicago, and the team finished at the top of the standings for the first time since the club's founding in 1927, nine wins and 19 points ahead of Toronto. Stan Mikita became the first player to win the Art Ross, Hart, and Lady Byng Trophies in the same year, and the combo of Glenn Hall and Denis Dejordy won the Vezina. The Black Hawks placed an incredible four players — Mikita, Wharram, Hull, and Pierre Pilote — to the First All-Star team, and Glenn Hall to the Second; the Leafs had but Horton on the Second Team defence. Toronto actually allowed more goals than they scored, and their leading point-getter, Keon with 52, would have tied for sixth on the Black Hawk team. On paper, this was as mis- a match as you could possibly get.

But the Leafs had one psychological advantage that gave them at least a glimmer of hope — they had thrashed this same Chicago team 9–5 just a couple of weeks earlier in their last regular season meeting. The Leafs *knew* they could win. Besides, hockey's post-season had long ago proved its unpredictability. And that spring in 1967 was very special, indeed. To honour the country's Centennial, the Leafs altered the crest on their jersey for the first time in a quarter century:

the playoff sweater used a solid, 11-point Maple Leaf similar to the one on the new Canadian flag, replacing the 35-point crest that was introduced by Conn Smythe in 1942.

Imlach had always maintained that goaltending was 80% of the game. In the first round of the playoffs, he was given remarkable 100% performances by his ancient pair, particularly Sawchuk who played brilliantly in three 3–1 wins against Chicago. The other, a 4–2 win in Game 5 in the Stadium, was pivotal; Sawchuk replaced Bower at the start of the second and stoned the Hawks — 37 shots' worth — while the Leafs rallied. Chicago was gone in six.

For Chicago fans, the excitement of the regular season had given way to frustration with their stars, particularly the goal scorers. Hull, Mikita, and Wharram managed only eight goals in the six games, Mohns was held goalless, and the young Espo pointless. This spelled the end for the Hawks and set up a Canadian final with the Habs who had swept the New York Rangers in four games straight.

Ticket stub for the Cup-winning game in 1967

In the finals, goaltending would once again be the deciding factor. While the two teams had similar records, Montreal's team speed — Béliveau, Cournoyer, Richard, Ralph Backstrom, and Bobby Rousseau — was a good bet to leave Toronto's defence wheezing, and the first game indicated this would hold true for the series.

Sawchuk was pulled after letting in four goals over the first two periods and Montreal coasted to a 6–2 win. But Bower was incomparable in the next two games, shutting out the Habs 3–0 and then making 52 saves in a 3–2 win back at the Gardens. Sawchuk returned for Game 4, but again was weak in another 6–2 loss. In Game 5 at the Forum, the pivotal game, Montreal goalie Rogie Vachon let in two softies and the Leafs won 4–1. Then Sawchuk, atoning for his two weak performances and looking every bit the goalie who stymied Chicago, shone in the deciding game, particularly the first period when he stopped 17 shots.

Imlach seemed to know almost intuitively that 1967 would be his last chance for a Cup. With expansion, the league would irrevocably change and the power of the players was about to increase exponentially with the formation of Alan Eagleson's Players' Association, a union that ran contrary to Imlach's every way of doing business. For him, 1967 was the last year he could have assembled the team in his special manner.

Imlach's hiring was the result of an odd situation in the Leaf organization. In 1957 Conn Smythe "removed" Hap Day as General

Manager of the Leafs to make room for his son. But rather than hire Stafford alone to replace Day, he put together a committee to oversee the club's operations. Nicknamed the Silver Seven after the old Ottawa hockey club, it consisted of Stafford as chairman, Harold Ballard, John Bassett, and four wealthy businessmen: Jack Amell, vice-president of Robert Amell and Co. Ltd., a jewellery firm; William Hatch, vice-president of McLaren's Food Products; George Gardiner, president of Gardiner, Watson Ltd., a stockbroking firm; and George Mara, former Marlie and president of William Mara & Co., a wine importing business. The next year Stafford offered the job of General Manager to Billy Reay, but Reay elected to remain the Leafs' coach. He then offered George "Punch" Imlach the position of *Assistant* General Manager. The term "Assistant" was intended as a means of limiting Punch's power, but a more misleading title has never been assigned. Imlach had the gumption to challenge the owner's authority from the get-go. "First, I'll run things my way, Mr. Smythe," he declared. "If it doesn't work, we'll run it your way." Such a declaration was brazen coming from a man whose only professional experience was coaching the Quebec Aces in the Quebec senior league (1947–57) and one year with the Springfield Indians of the American Hockey League (1957–58).

Run it he did. His first move was to bring Johnny Bower into the nets. Bower was nicknamed the "China Wall" by his Cleveland teammates because of his age (35) and the length of his duty in the American Hockey League (1945–58). There was only one blemish on his otherwise unbroken minor league career: in 1953–54 he played with the Rangers, but the next year he was demoted to make way for the younger Lorne Worsley (a.k.a. the Gumper). When Bower first heard he was headed to Punch's Leafs, he protested that he couldn't possibly help the club. Twelve years and four Stanley Cups later, the great-great-grandfather of the poke check had proved himself wrong.

Punch's next move as GM was to fire Billy Reay and take over the coaching duties himself. The Leafs had finished dead last the year before, hadn't won the Cup since 1951, and were reeling from a 5–12–3 beginning to the current season. He originally took over on an interim basis, hoping to hire Alf Pike, coach of the Winnipeg Warriors of the Western (Pro) Hockey League. When they couldn't reach an agreement, Punch decided he was the man for the job (he had a 5–5–5 record in his first 15 games). Bert Olmstead, his great left winger who was acquired in the June '58 draft, acted as a player/assistant coach for a few months after.* At Christmas, the Leafs remained in last place, but Imlach staunchly supported his team by boasting that a playoff spot was inevitable (under Reay in

---

* The Leafs had first pick in the draft (used to select Olmstead) because of their last-place finish in the '57–'58 season.

'57–'58 and Howie Meeker in '56–'57 the team had missed the playoffs). By March 11, with five games to play and the Leafs still seven points behind the Rangers for the final playoff spot, Toronto needed a miracle to accomplish what Punch had predicted.

The Rangers had two games in hand, but promptly lost both, 5–3 to Chicago, 5–4 to Boston. New York and Toronto then played a home-and-home series. The Leafs swept: 5–0 at the Gardens, 6–5 in the Garden. Then, on the final night of the season, the Leafs beat Detroit 6–4 in Motor City and the Broadway Blueshirts lost 4–2 to Montreal at home. The Leafs were in, the Rangers out! Punch was King in the Land of Hockey. His prediction, his bravura, his personality, all propelled him to Saviourdom in Hogtown and right across Canada.

It was during that season and the next two that Punch began to assemble his Over-the-Hill Gang dynasty. First came Bower and Olmstead, then Allan Stanley, whom he acquired from Boston for Jim Morrison the day the '58–'59 season began. In February 1960 he made what is frequently regarded as the most successfully one-sided trade in team history, stealing Red Kelly from Detroit for Marc Réaume. Kelly would prove an instrumental force over the next seven years and four Cups; Réaume never scored another goal in the NHL.

Later that year Imlach traded Pat Hannigan and Johnny Wilson to New York for Eddie Shack, the clown prince of hockey, a checker and jokester who could give you 20 goals per and often did (with five different clubs, in fact). Also in 1960 Punch selected Larry Hillman from Boston at the annual draft meetings in June, and in 1962 he bought Kent Douglas from Eddie Shore's minor league chamber of horrors, the Springfield Indians. Douglas joined the Leafs that autumn and won the Calder trophy the following spring.

Imlach's next big coup was to claim Terry Sawchuk in 1964 after the Red Wings left him unprotected. Sawchuk, who had played 15 years with Detroit but was now considered too old, proved the perfect ingredient in Punch's Cup plans. And for a mere $20,000, even Imlach couldn't resist.

These additions supplemented perfectly the core of the team who had apprenticed with St. Mike's and the Marlies: Armstrong, Keon, Baun, Conacher, Ellis, Horton, Mahovlich, Pappin, and Pulford. All in all, an extraordinary 10 future Hall of Famers played on that '67 team, the heart of which came from Toronto's developmental teams and junior ranks.

Yet, just as Punch was a genius in acquiring the right players and producing the right mixture of skill and grit, age and youth, so too was he capable of shunning his players and creating an atmosphere of discontent if not out-and-out hatred for him. Most of the time, the players could do nothing but swallow his soul-sapping treatment. They had no choice.

A case in point was Mahovlich, who was misunderstood (ergo mistreated) by Imlach for much of his time in a Leaf uniform.

Mahovlich's holdout in 1962, which produced the million dollar offer from Chicago, was just the beginning of the unrest he felt until the day he was traded years later. In November 1964, he left the team, suffering from an "undisclosed ailment" which those in the know knew to be depression, stress, and nervousness — conditions created by Imlach's unyielding coaching methods.

STAR SPORTS PARADE

N THREE — PAGES 11 TO 32   TORONTO DAILY STAR SATURDAY, OCTOBER 6, 196?   REACH FOR A STAR — MOST PEOPLE DO

MILT DUNNELL Speaking on **SPORT**

$1,000,000 BY NORRIS...   ...HINGES ON SMYTHE

'Fantastic' Offer For The Big M

Frank Mahovlich suspended after turning down contract

Mahovlich, Bower Prove Again They're Leafs' One-Two Punch

Howe makes charge

Leaf fans blamed for Big M's illness

By KEN McKEE and RED BURNETT

Toronto Daily Star ☆ SPO

to enjoy hockey – and win

Big M manhandles Habs

SPORTS SCENE

Big M's Feud With Imlach Finally Over

THIS IS WHAT BUGS THE BIG

Harold Ballard says, "Someone should sock him so he gets mad or mean like Howe or Hull." But Frank is a most gentle player in a fierce sport
by JIM HUNT, Star Weekly sports editor

The night Frank Mahovlich came back

It might have been Grey Cup week in Ottawa
(see page 20), but for true followers of the great moments
of sport – the way they ought to occur – the
highlight was one very special moment in Toronto's Maple Leaf Gardens

by HARRY BRUCE

Fans turn emotional, Gardens' stock shares in decline after Mahovlich traded to Detroit Red Wings

Toronto Fans Protest Mahovlich Trade

Big M Has Figured Way to Beat Record

Simply a Matter of Playing Well in 8 of 11 Games

FRANK MAHOVLICH

BIG M WAS THE LAST TO HEAR

By JIM PROUDFOOT
Star sports writer

HOCKEY'S MISUNDERSTOOD HERO

Star Weekly writer Jim Hunt looks at the super-star who's often treated like a bush-league bum

WHAT MAKES MAHOVLICH TICK?

Big M Is A Big Mystery

Wins Calder But Frank Disappointed

'Very Bad' Finish Admits Mahovlich

By STAN HOUSTON

Argos Seek Protection From Pro Competition

Mahovlich:
Man In The News

'I was treated well'

Scored 296 goals

Leafs trade big, quiet kid from Timmins once valued at $1,000,000

By LOUIS CAUZ

Mahovlich was a quiet, sensitive man who needed assurance and support rather than discipline and alienation. He became frustrated, and finally emotionally wounded by Imlach's lack of sympathy and compassion. As a result, his goal production slid and the fans became hostile. During the 1960–61 season, when he was edging toward the

sacred 50-goal plateau, Mahovlich was praised for his smooth, effortless skill. By mid-1964 he was being pilloried for his complacent and lazy skating. The coach, the fans; either way, he couldn't win.

His contract dispute in 1966, and Imlach's continuing under-the-skin treatment, forced the Big M to leave again in November 1967, but this time the depression was more debilitating. Imlach was still the root of the problem, but the fans' vocal displeasure became unrelenting. On some nights Mahovlich would play great hockey, be named one of the three stars, and still get booed by Gardens fans as he took his celebratory skate to centre ice.

However, now there was even more pressure: he had declined to join Alan Eagleson's newly formed NHL Players' Association, and was receiving the cold shoulder from his teammates. One would have thought this refusal would have endeared him to Imlach — perhaps the NHLPA's greatest adversary — but the two were long past the point of no return for any reconciliation to occur.

In March 1968, Punch finally put the Big M out of his misery: Mahovlich, Pete Stemkowski, Garry Unger, and the rights to Carl Brewer were sent to Detroit for Paul Henderson, Norm Ullman, and Floyd Smith — an embarrassing deal that virtually eviscerated the core of future great teams. Irony of ironies, though, was the intense disapproval of the trade voiced by Leaf fans who clogged Gardens phone lines in the ensuing days. Evidently they loved to boo Mahovlich but knew that he was essential to the team's chances of winning.

Years earlier Hap Day had called Mahovlich "Moses"; days after the trade Punch was considered a Judas. Mahovlich went on to play with Montreal after the Red Wings, and in the six years following the deal had seasons of 49, 38, 31, 43, 38, and 31 goals. The connection between a player's inner happiness and his on-ice performance was not nearly as tenuous as Punch the inhuman coach had surmised.

The deal was made not just because Imlach considered Mahovlich a pain in the Big M but also because Punch needed Ullman to fill in for Jim Pappin. Pappin had walked out on the team because, yes, he couldn't get along with Imlach. During the 1963–64 season, Pappin had been called up from the minors to replace Ed Litzenberger on the Big M's line. At 24, he quickly proved he could play in the NHL. He helped Toronto win two Cups, became the first Leaf since Ted Kennedy in 1948 to lead the league in playoff scoring in 1967, and scored the Cup winner that spring as well (at 19:24 of the second period; Armstrong's empty-netter was the *insurance* goal). Still, Imlach bounced him between Rochester and the Gardens for years. Other players felt sorry for Pappin, who became known as Imlach's "whipping boy." In February 1968, Punch demoted him again, but this time Pappin refused to go. With the Leafs racing to make the playoffs, Punch couldn't afford to wait for Pappin to return from *his* walk, and he certainly wasn't about to capitulate to Pappin's "crazy"

demands to play. Thus the Mahovlich trade. Punch panicked, and the Leafs failed to make the post-season for the first time since he took over as coach a decade earlier. Two months later Pappin himself was traded to Chicago for Pierre Pilote. Pilote played 69 games in a Leaf uniform; Pappin went on to produce *seven* 30-goal seasons with Chicago.

During training camp in 1964, Billy Harris left the club — announced his retirement, in fact — because of Punch's negotiating tactics. Bob Pulford interceded and got Harris back in a Leaf uniform, but then found himself in the same situation days later. Pulford sat out an exhibition game because of his contract, and Imlach suspended him. This time King Clancy played arbitrator in a dispute which involved not millions, but hundreds of dollars. Three years later, Pulford became the first president of the NHLPA, a union committed to helping the plight of players who had been financially, and sometimes emotionally, mistreated by management for so many years. Imlach responded by removing the "A" from Pully's sweater. Like so many other great players from those Cup-winning teams, Pulford was mistreated and judged by qualities that had nothing to do with his on-ice performance. In September 1970, he, too, was traded. At least he outlasted Imlach.

Mike Walton also incurred the wrath of Imlach by joining the NHLPA and was kept unhappy during his many years with the Leafs (despite, or perhaps because of, being married to Conn Smythe's granddaughter). Walton left the team in February 1969, was coaxed back by the players, and left a second time in December 1970. He produced the testimony of a psychiatrist not only to corroborate his unhappiness and poor health but also to force the Leafs to trade him (which they did, to Philadelphia, a month later).

It was Carl Brewer, though, who did what other Leafs only threatened to do. He left and never came back. At least, not for a *really* long time. His premature retirement was the result of an incident at camp in 1965, the worst of a series of hellish camps which revolved as much around negotiating contracts as preparing for a run at the Stanley Cup. Imlach never negotiated at any other time of year; he felt a player who had secured a contract going into camp would be complacent and lazy. In 1965 there were many uncomplacent Leafs: Kelly, Keon, Baun, Pulford, and Horton were all very unhappy campers. All threatened to walk out, and one did — Baun.

Baun eventually returned to the club, and the other disgruntleds all signed new deals, but Brewer was on the wrong end of a small but meaningful incident. One day in the dressing room, he and Bower got into a fight, and when the dust had cleared Punch supported the China Wall. This was all Brewer needed. He favoured retirement at age 27 to even one more day under Imlach's tyranny, and didn't play another game in the NHL until Punch traded him to Detroit in the Big M deal.

The big problem was that the two sides — players and Punch — approached the negotiating table from very different perspectives. The players judged their worth according to their individual achievements. As well, they knew that Maple Leaf Gardens had started to generate enormous, previously unheard-of profits from advertisements, promotions, and endorsements. While the players were an integral reason for this income, they received a paltry $1,500 annually (Eagleson believed, for instance, that Mahovlich alone could have made $25,000 a year easily, such was his popularity and marketability in Toronto). Imlach, on the other hand, looked only at team performance, and at the start of the 1965–66 season the Leafs were coming off a first-round loss to Montreal in the playoffs the previous spring. To Punch, no player deserved a pay increase.

Wheeling and dealing in camp created stress for another reason. Until 1967, the All-Star game was played at the start of the year, but only those players under contract were eligible to play. It would have been embarrassing to Punch and the Leaf organization if a player missed the game for contract reasons, but the money the players collected from the game was an important part of their pension fund. So, it was mutually advantageous to work out contracts before the first game of the year.

As anyone with a little horse sense knows, the relation between management and team performance is inextricable. Good management produces intelligent decisions, a fertile environment, a winning team; bad management does just the opposite. Although Punch had his flaws, an even more significant event in the demise of the Leafs occurred in two stages, August 1966 and June 1967, when Leaf bosses Harold Ballard and Stafford Smythe sold their most important farm clubs — the Rochester Americans and the Victoria Maple Leafs — for cash. A measly $500,000 and $400,000.*

The Rochester sale was made to a civic group headed by an attorney, Robert W. Clarke, and included the contracts of 18 players. The Leafs made no formal announcement of the sale, but when asked to comment Clarke said that the Leafs could use the money in their building program!

One wonders what half a million dollars could do to help build a successful hockey team that had been around for 40 years, won 10 Stanley Cups, and had the largest pool of talent in the world from which to draw, that keeping a minor league, player-development farm team couldn't do. In fact, Conn Smythe had bought controlling interest in the Americans in 1959 from Montreal in an effort to provide a broader base for developing talent. The club, under GM and coach Joe Crozier, had won the Calder Cup just weeks earlier,

---

* Such greed right after the Leafs had pulled in $2 million for expansion fees from the six new teams.

Al Arbour in his Rochester Americans days.
HOCKEY HALL OF FAME

and it was a generally accepted belief that Rochester was good enough to compete as a seventh team in the NHL. Of those 18 players "sold," 10 went on to play at least 368 games each in the NHL.* The following year Stafford and Ballard moved the Victoria Maple Leafs to Phoenix, Arizona, where it became the Roadrunners under new ownership. Victoria had just won the Patrick Cup, as Western Hockey League champions, and it too had talent of the highest calibre; six of the 18 players appeared in at least 164 NHL games each, a significant figure given the league's inferiority to the AHL.** In other words, an irreplaceable development program was lost from the Leaf system.

These sales were even more nearsighted given that in 1961 St. Mike's had abandoned its hockey program. Under Father David Bauer, the Toronto high school had produced a significant number of NHLers, fulfilling an important role in player development for the Leafs. The Leafs' unofficial rule was that Protestants played for the Marlies and Catholics played for St. Mike's. The end of St. Mike's meant that players such as Gary Monahan and Pete Mahovlich left the school (i.e., the Leafs) to continue their development elsewhere. As a result, they wound up playing for Montreal and Detroit instead of Toronto. By 1967, Ballard and Stafford, if anything, needed to *add* teams to the Leafs' system. They threw away the future for a few inconsequential dollars and left Toronto with only the Tulsa Oilers in the Central Pro League as a minor league affiliate, a team just established in 1964 and weak on talent, depth, and experience. The Leafs now had virtually no minor league team left to apprentice their stars of tomorrow.

A little money was made in the short term, but a great deal of talent was lost in the long. With the sale of the farm clubs went the advantage the Leafs should have had during the post-expansion years. Instead, by 1969, their talent pool was no deeper than that of the Oakland Seals, L.A. Kings, or St. Louis Blues. Gone was half a century of natural order advantage and organizational genius.

When the 1968–69 season began, 14 of the 21 Leafs who played in the '67 Cup final had, for one reason or another, left the team. The Leafs were never to be the same again. Because he had no farm system left, Imlach no longer had a huge number of personnel options. His player threats and vicious contract negotiations became

---

* Pete Stemkowski (967 games), Al Arbour (626), Eddie Litzenberger (618), Mike Corrigan (594), Gary Smith (532), Darryl Edestrand (455), Bronco Horvath (434), Garry Ehman (429), Duane Rupp (374), and Larry Jeffrey (368), as well as Darryl Sly, Don Cherry, Dick Gamble, Stan Smrke, Terry Clancy, Les Duff, Red Armstrong, and Brian Conacher.

** Andy Hebenton (630 games), Mike Corrigan (594), John Henderson (405), Larry Keenan (234), Aut Erickson (227), and Fred Hucul (164), as well as Bill Shvetz, Frank Mario, Garry Holland, Gord Marchant, Steve Witiuk, Dave Parenteau, John Sleaver, Dick Lamoureux, Claude Labrosse, Bob Barlow, Mike Labadie, and Milan Marcetta.

counterproductive, and the players he hated could no longer be so easily replaced by others of equal talent.

While Punch's knack for making just the right trade at just the right time had never been questioned, his ability to make a stinker was by no means out of the question. Through one series of trades in 1964, Imlach cut the core out of his '60s champions. That February he traded Dick Duff, Bob Nevin, Rod Seiling, Arnie Brown, and Bill Collins to New York for Andy Bathgate and Don McKenney. A little more than a year later he traded Bathgate, Billy Harris, and Gary Janet to Detroit for Marcel Pronovost, Lowell MacDonald, Ed Joyal, Larry Jeffrey, and Aut Erickson. The upshot of the two trades worked out to look like this:

IN	OUT
Pronovost	Joyal
MacDonald	Duff
McKenney	Nevin
Erickson	Seiling
Jeffrey	Harris
Joyal	Bathgate
	Brown
	Collins
	Janet

McKenney proved ineffective and played part-time in Detroit the next year. Erickson, though his name is on the Leafs' '67 Cup, never played even *one* regular season game with the Leafs. Jeffrey scored 12 goals over two seasons before fizzling away in New York; Joyal had two assists before being lost to L.A. in the expansion draft; MacDonald never played for the team; and Pronovost scored eight goals in five on-and-off seasons with Toronto.

As for the former Leafs, Nevin played 13 years with the Rangers, becoming captain; Duff played nine years, four with Cup-winning Montreal teams; Seiling played 978 games after the trade, establishing himself as the archetypal stay-at-home defenceman that any successful team needs to win.

Although the real value of the trades was shrouded by success — the Leafs won the Cup in '64 and then '67 — they can be identified as the beginning of the end for a dynasty, many of whose other players seriously thought the Leafs should have won *every* Cup in the '60s, so rich in talent was the team when the decade began. However, the same mind that made these poor trades also acquired Kelly, Bower, and Sawchuk, and won four Stanley Cups. These days, that doesn't sound half bad. Imlach was, in every sense, the Alpha and Omega of Leaf glory, the man who brought greatness to the city's hockey team, and the man who took it away.

With Stafford and Ballard running the business end of things, the club began to deteriorate. Yet the decline was either too subtle for them to recognize or too monetarily insignificant for them to care about. The "money first" attitude of these men was induced by their feeling of invincibility. Because this was *the* Toronto Maple Leafs, they felt they could do anything and the team would continue to win. They were wrong.

The appalling, sickening nearsightedness was just beginning.

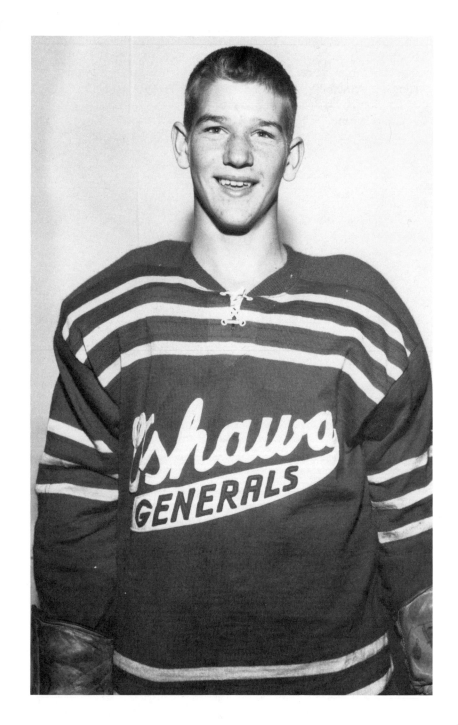

Bobby Orr.
HOCKEY HALL OF FAME

II

Expansion:
The New NHL

The celebratory spring of 1967 became the fall — the expansion, the amateur draft, the Players' Association — the Modern Era. The Leafs lost an incredible 15 players from their system in the expansion draft, including six from the Cup-winning team: Baun, Douglas, and Erickson to Oakland, Sawchuk to Los Angeles, Jeffrey to the Rangers, and Marcetta to Minnesota.* Also gone were Shack (traded to the Bruins for Murray Oliver), Kelly (who retired to coach the Kings), and Stanley (who retired). With the loss or decline of the ageing players from the glory team of the season before, the absence of farm teams, and fairer competition among now 12 teams for young players, the hopes for defending their Cup championship had all but vanished.

Under Imlach, the club was still living in the past. By mid-May of 1967, two weeks after the Leafs had won the Cup, each of the Original Six teams had to submit a list of protected players for the upcoming expansion draft (a special draft held *prior to* the later amateur draft). Imlach operated in exactly the same way he always had: his way.

The Leafs' list looked as follows:

Bower, Horton, Hillman, Pronovost, Keon, Conacher,
Mahovlich, Pulford, Stemkowski, Pappin, Walton, and Ellis.

Baun had been used sparingly the previous spring in the finals and expected to be left unprotected, his previously desired "experience" now interpreted undesirably as "age." Ditto for Sawchuk. But the Chief? The team captain, the number 10 who had been with the Leafs for 16 years and four Stanley Cups? Why wasn't he protected? Imlach manipulated Armstrong's loyalty for tactical purposes; the Chief had told all expansion teams he would retire if taken, so no one took him. But after two rounds of selections Imlach put him back on the list, as a refill, without caring for the insult Armstrong suffered by the

---

* From their Tulsa farm team they lost Bill Flett, Ed Joyal, and Lowell MacDonald to Los Angeles, and Gary Veneruzzo to St. Louis; from Victoria they lost Gary Smith and Mike Laughton to Oakland, Brit Selby to Philadelphia, Fred Hucul and Larry Keenan to St. Louis.

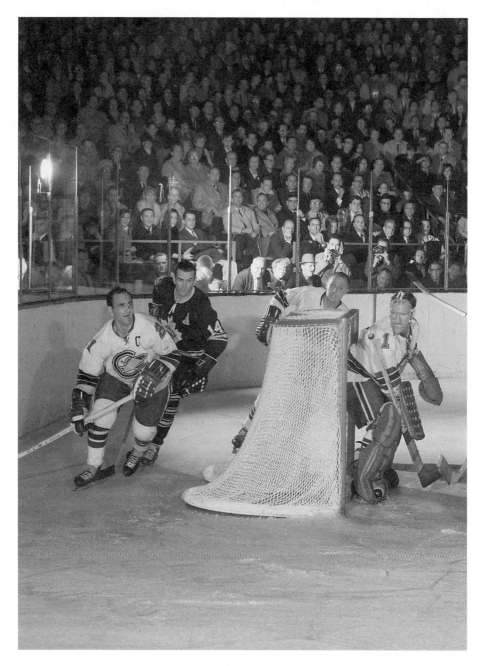

GRAPHIC ARTISTS / HOCKEY HALL OF FAME

strategy. It took much talking and persuading to get him back into a Leaf uniform, but of course Imlach knew that Armstrong's love of hockey and loyalty to the Leafs would endure even the outrage and humiliation the team captain felt.

Imlach treated Leonard Kelly with similar disdain. He had promised Red he wouldn't be protected, so that Los Angeles could draft him and make him their first coach. But Imlach went ahead and protected him anyway, making the normally genial Kelly furious. It wasn't until a few days later, and a minor trade, that Kelly's wish was "respected."

The league's new format was simple. The East Division comprised the Original Six, the West the new clubs: Philadelphia Flyers, Los Angeles Kings, St. Louis Blues, Minnesota North Stars, Pittsburgh Penguins, and Oakland Seals. This meant that the finals would feature one Original team and one new team, a concept that sounded fair enough but one that produced a series of lopsided Cup wins for the established clubs in the East. Unfortunately, the Leafs finished fifth in the East and missed the playoffs in '67–'68. The first expansion season proved every bit as ignominious as the '67 win was spectacular. While the ensuing years were a boon for the other established teams (Boston and Montreal won the next six Cups), the Leafs iced further and further expansion-quality teams. The toll of Ballard's influence was starting to take.

The end of the Imlach era came on the Leafs' final game of the '68–'69 season. They made it into the playoffs by a seven-point cushion over Detroit and faced Boston in the first round, only to suffer the worst defeat in team history. These were the classic Big Bad Bruins of Orr, Esposito, Hodge, Bucyk, Westfall, and Sanderson, talent virtually impossible to overcome. The team was *destined* to win the Cup — when and how often were the only unknowns. The first two games in Boston were humiliating whitewashes (10–0 and 7–0), and back home the scores, while closer (4–3 and 3–2), still spelled abject elimination. Immediately after the fourth and final game Stafford dismissed Punch, ending a relationship that began when the two played on the Donnell and Mudge team that won the Toronto Mercantile League Championship in 1941. In his place Smythe hired Tulsa Oilers farm coach John McLellan. Punch was given his next year's salary — $38,000 — as severance and thank-you pay, but the Leafs had lost their pride, the fans their future.

Gone was the icon and "antique" of the '60s, the man who refused to adapt to change and was left behind to shake his head at the stupidity of modernism. The NHLPA gave the players a stronger voice and more clout in how the players and the league worked together. Imlach refused to adapt. He lost his touch. His feel for the game disappeared, and he became an ineffective leader behind the bench. He traded the heart and soul of the team (Mahovlich and Pappin) simply to alleviate clashes in personality and to make patchwork repairs to team chemistry which was forever imbalanced by his very

treatment of these players. In return, he got little on-ice skill. His coaching and managing philosophy was the polar opposite of all that expansion stood for. The bottom line: the team began to lose.

When he was hired by the Buffalo Sabres in 1970, Imlach maintained his character and personality. He drafted well for the expansion team and got them to the finals in 1975 before losing to Philadelphia. This was a typical Imlach team: he extracted the most from his players on ice at the expense of player anger, resentment, and discontent off ice. He aggravated the Knox owners, and over time players began to hate him. Finally in 1979, a core of the team threatened to quit if Punch were not replaced. He were.

In 1967, NHL sponsorship of junior teams ended, so that by 1969 all graduating players from Canadian junior hockey leagues were available to be drafted by all teams. The ramifications of this were enormous, yet while Toronto and Montreal were affected more than the other teams, the results were strikingly dissimilar.

NHL sponsorship meant that the NHL club "owned" the players it had under contract, including those on all minor and junior teams. In the Ontario Hockey League, for instance, New York owned the Guelph Biltmore-Madhatters, Boston owned the Barrie Flyers and then the Oshawa Generals, Detroit the Hamilton Red Wings, Chicago the St. Catharines Black Hawks. Montreal controlled all of Quebec and had the special privilege of being allowed to draft the first two French players each year (an advantage that ended with their drafting Réjean Houle and Marc Tardif in 1969). For the Leafs, the teams were the Marlies and St. Mike's, not to mention a myriad of minor league affiliates right across the country. This meant that all players on the Marlies or any other Leaf-owned club would play for the Leafs and only the Leafs if they made it to the NHL; they were under contract by virtue of the team they played for. They could be traded, of course, or sent to the minors, but the Leafs controlled the players' destiny.

For fans, the system was marvellous because watching the Marlies or St. Mike's meant you were watching young Leafs. Before the mid-'70s, the Marlies were as big a draw as the Leafs, and the Memorial Cup as important as the Stanley Cup. Doubleheaders on Saturday would always see the Marlie boys sell out in the afternoon (16,382) before the Leaf men hit the ice in the evening. But when the family ties were severed, and the draft prevented the Leafs from "owning" all Marlies, fans became less fanatical. Who wanted to see a junior score 50 with the Marlies only to be drafted by Pittsburgh or Los Angeles? It didn't seem fair. Saturday afternoon attendance dropped sharply.

In 1963, the first Amateur Draft was held in Montreal, but only players 18 and older who were not sponsored or affiliated with one of the six parent clubs were eligible. Not surprisingly, only a few players were taken because most who had talent were already under

contract. Before the end of sponsorship in 1967, getting someone to play for the Leafs was as easy as those old sports movies made it seem: a rough, brusque man in a flea-bitten suit is sitting in some dingy, freezing arena in northern Ontario and sees some 15, 16, 17-year-old phenom outplay the whole other team single-handedly. After the game, he visits the dressing room and asks to speak to the player. Some small-town grocery clerk child with pock marks reddened by sweat, a shiner under one eye, and a little blood on an otherwise colourless undershirt appears. The suit introduces himself as a scout for the Toronto Maple Leafs. The kid's jaw drops. The suit says, "I'd like you to play for the Marlies next year. Whaddya say?" "Sure, mister." "Good. Sign here. Camp opens in September."

Tom "Windy" O'Neill.

It was a cinch. Ontario produced — and still does — more professional players than any other country or territory in the world. Any kid's dream was to play at Maple Leaf Gardens, so signing players was like taking candy from a baby. But after 1967, the only thing the scout could do was take the kid's name, address, and phone number, and hope he was available when it was the Leafs' turn in

the draft. Even then the team had to negotiate a contract with the player's agent in order to sign him. The player couldn't pick his team, but neither could the team always pick its player.

This was expansion, the first step toward parity by way of spreading talent more evenly and fairly. If the Leafs were to win championships in the future with the same regularity as they had in the past, adjustments would have to be made. But adjustments require thought, and thought intelligence, and these were commodities in very short supply at Church and Carlton in 1969. In Montreal, farm teams were being *added*, the scouting staff *increased*. In Toronto, the more things stayed the same, the more things changed for the worse. In 1967 and 1968 the Leafs drafted just two players: Bob Kelly (16th in '67) and Brad Selwood (10th in '68). The following year they selected Ernie Moser (9th overall), Doug Brindley (20th), Larry McIntyre (31st), Frank Hughes (43rd), Brian Spencer (55th), and Bob Neufeld (67th). Only Spencer played any sort of role with the Leafs who instead could have drafted Bobby Clarke (17th by the Flyers), Ivan Boldirev (11th by Boston), Jim Rutherford (10th by Detroit), or Butch Goring (51st by the Kings). The missed opportunity of Clarke is an embarrassment even today, long after his Hall of Fame career has ended. Before the draft every conscious person from here to eternity knew Clarke would be a great player. But Stafford and his scouts told GM Jim Gregory in no uncertain terms *not* to draft Clarke because he had diabetes!

This despite the fact that 45 years earlier Banting and Best had discovered insulin, and Ballard himself was diabetic. The Leafs chose Moser instead, who went on to play zero games in a long non-career at Maple Leaf Gardens.

While the Leafs' organizational descent was just beginning, the successful introduction of a players' union became a fait accompli on June 6, 1967, when Alan Eagleson formally announced the inception of the NHLPA and his appointment as Executive Director thereto. No more would players negotiate their own contracts, squabble over a few hundred dollars on a three-year deal, or be abused and humiliated by autocratic coaches, general managers, and owners. This was the Year of the Player, the year the Boy became Man, the year the NHL evolved into a player-dominated society where remuneration started to match services and contributions rendered. The addition of six teams, all in the United States, meant an enormous increase in exposure to the 250 million people called Americans. In simple money terms this translated to television revenues, endorsements, and advertisements — greater popularity, greater wealth. All of a sudden the players' talent was more important than the name of the scout or coach or club. Players began to recognize it was *they* who were the attractions, *they* who made the league run.

This newfound knowledge was obviously disconcerting to the millionaire owners whose penchant toward egomaniacal behaviour

had been tolerated by the powerless players for so long. Now the players wanted their contracts to reflect their own importance. In Eagleson they had someone to help them achieve this reasonable, long-awaited goal.

More than anything else, the players had been encouraged to trust and respect Eagleson on the strength of one contract, one negotiation, one player of the Modern Era who personified skill, fame, marketability, guts, glory, pain, victory: Bobby Orr.

In 1964, as a member of the Ontario legislature,* Eagleson returned to the stomping ground of his youth, a Scottish-sounding place called MacTier, Ontario, some 35 kilometres southeast of Parry Sound if you take Highway 69. The Eagle presented a trophy to a local baseball league, but the meeting he had later in the evening with an old teammate in that same league from many years before would prove to be of far greater significance. Doug Orr introduced himself, reminded Eagleson of their ancient, tenuous connection, and introduced his son Bobby by way of a further how-dee-do. He asked the lawyer to look after Bobby if the teenager made it to the big leagues. Eagle promised, and Bobby Orr became the first player to use a lawyer to negotiate a contract in the NHL.

Orr was first scouted by the Bruins' Baldy Cotton, and later Wren Blair, and was paid in the neighbourhood of $1,000 to play for Oshawa in the OHA. He joined the Generals at age 14, making the Bruins the owner of his NHL rights. He would play with Boston or not at all in the NHL. Eagleson didn't much like Orr's "options," especially given his client's clear superiority on skates to the rest of mankind. So Eagleson tried to balance the scales. In the summer of 1966 he represented Orr in talks with Boston general manager Hap Emms. Emms, unfamiliar with this sort of negotiation, offered Eagle a $10,000-a-year contract for Orr, reminding this Adam of player-agents that Orr really didn't have much choice. Take the ten grand or don't play in the NHL.

Eagle told Emms, the Eve of agent-negotiators, that his Bruins hadn't made the playoffs in seven years, that Orr was a guaranteed bringer of the Stanley Cup, and that his client would be more than happy to remain an amateur and play with Canada's national team while the Bruins endured another season of losing while the Garden fans booed the Orr-less team into oblivion. Emms agreed to Eagle's "offer" of $40,000, making Orr, an 18-year-old, crew-cutted, small-town child, not only the richest rookie ever signed but also one of the highest-paid players in the league.

That same fall Carl Brewer was looking for a little legal help. He called Eagle. Since walking out on Imlach's Leafs the year before, Brewer had been trying to get reinstated as an amateur, but league

---

* The previous election he lost the York West riding to Red Kelly by 41,000–26,000 votes.

president Clarence Campbell scoffed at the idea time and again. However, one phone call threatening legal action by Eagleson turned Campbell's scoffing to quiet acquiescence. Brewer was an amateur. Clearly Eagleson knew what he was doing, and he quickly had the players listening to his every word. He started an investment group in Toronto with Pulford, Baun, Billy Harris, and Brewer, called the Blue and White, that stemmed from the players' need to protect their money. The rest is history.

Eagleson's perceived injustice of a system of drafting and paying involved him with players more every day. His success in dealing with the NHL had so far outstripped the only other serious attempt to unionize that he was seen as a godsend to most NHLers. Back in '57 four players — Ted Lindsay, captain of Detroit, Tod Sloan and Jim Thomson of Toronto, and Doug Harvey of Montreal — tried to organize the players and improve benefits in four areas: the pension fund, minimum rookie salary, moving expenses for traded players, and meal money. For the previous 13 years the players' playoff revenues hadn't increased a cent, even though owners' revenues and profits had risen consistently. The result of their attempt was that all but Harvey, the brilliant Habs defenceman, were traded to the then hapless Black Hawks, the worst team in the league.* The mission was aborted, the association lost momentum. As Conn quite bluntly confessed at the time: "As far as I'm concerned, that [Sloan's part in the attempt to unionize] was the reason for getting rid of him."

The day after the NHLPA announced its existence, with 110 of 120 players agreeing to pay an annual membership fee of $150, the respect (which for the owners meant money) the players had been looking for arrived in the form of three Eagleson-arranged agreements. Players would now be paid $100–$150 for exhibition games (previously these were "charity gigs"); their per diem road expenses increased from $10 to $15; and the minimum salary rose in principle from $7,500 to $10,000. Not bad for a first day on the job.

The Orr-Eagleson relationship symbolized all the new 12-team NHL stood for. Orr's contracts were used as the measuring stick by which all other players could negotiate, and as a result salaries almost quadrupled (from less than $15,000 to $55,000) between 1967 and 1975. After 1967, most players had an agent perform the dirty task of money talk. Two years after Orr's historic 1966 signing, Bobby Hull, the Golden Jet, arranged a $100,000-a-year contract, a sum inconceivable without the precedent-setting Bobby Orr deal. In 1971, Eagleson made Orr hockey's first millionaire, negotiating a five-year deal for a cool mil. By 1972, Eagleson alone had 200 player-clients. Contracts would never be the same again.

On ice everything changed with the maturity of Number Four. Orr played *his* game *his* way, and everyone else had to adapt or be left

---

* Lindsay was the first to go; Detroit hasn't won a Cup since.

behind. The big question now was, how do you shadow a defence-man? What do you do to stop him? Everywhere he went, sellout crowds followed, some to marvel in awe, others, as in Toronto, to boo with envy. His effect on the game as a sport and an attraction took the league out of the '60s and into the '70s, from the black-and-white of Armstrong and Richard to the colour of Number Four, Bobby Orr. With his flash and good looks, unsurpassed skill, quirky habits, and quiet Canadian humility, he *was* the era of expansion.

Orr moved as effortlessly as the Big M, but twice as quickly. He eschewed tape on his stick save two or three strands, and you'd look at it and kind of scrinch your brow and turn your head, perplexed, and then he'd shoot and you somehow understood. When you heard he never wore socks inside those skates your feet would kind of hurt by the very idea, but you'd try it yourself only to feel awkward and cold and somehow you just didn't know *how* to skate without socks because really only one person did, could — Orr. You'd watch him play two, three, four, five shifts in a row, not only keeping up with the play but *leading* it, and it took you a long time to realize he could catch his wind *while playing*. You could try to strip him of the puck, but one thing fans didn't see clearly that opponents did was just how strong, how *physically* superior he was to other players. He was as tough as nails, rough as anyone, but you'd never believe it because he was so enormously skilled and so classily smooth.

You would see him skate circles around everyone and say to yourself, "Why doesn't someone check him?" "Why do they let him do that?" or "*I* could have deked that defenceman," and then playing shinny with friends you'd be checked whenever you made the same Orr move. Because of his knee problems, every time he fell to the ice you gasped and closed your eyes and prayed he'd be up by the time you opened them. You'd rub your knees and shake your head with sadness and wonder why he, of all people, was given super-human talent but all-too human joints. You thought of famous goals you'd seen and all the great players you knew but your mind always went to Orr flying through the air after converting Sanderson's pass. You felt shivers down your spine, and at night in the safety of dream you scored goals like that yourself. And if you were a Leaf fan you cringed and cried and sighed and shook your head at what might have been had the blue and white signed him. You can just hear Paul Morris announce: "Toronto goal scored by Number Four, Bobby Orr. Unassisted. Time 4:04."

And so it was for a generation of fans.

In November 1961, Conn Smythe had discussed the possibility of selling his shares in Maple Leaf Gardens (i.e., his ownership of the Leafs) to his son Stafford. Stafford had become increasingly unhappy under his father's patriarchal rule, and felt that at 40 he was old enough to take over the club from Conn, now 66. Rather than create filial unrest, Conn agreed to sell all his shares, thereby

relinquishing control of the Gardens to his son on condition that "nothing substantial would be changed around the Gardens . . . that the honesty and class that I tried to bring to the place would continue."

Conn, who was always forward-looking, saw a smooth deal with Stafford not only as healthy in the short-term but also as a hopeful sign that Stafford's eldest son Tom would one day inherit the club. A third Smythe generation at the Gardens. Such admirable intentions, however, were left in the hands of the unappreciative. In the days following their agreement, Stafford negotiated with Ballard and Bassett to split the shares three ways, a decision that enraged Conn and threatened the completion of the deal. Later in life Conn would say of Ballard: "I've known him most of my life as a good giver, a good friend, but I would not give him a job at ten cents a week. His way of doing things is not mine." But Conn relented, and on November 23, 1961, the deal for 45,000 shares at $40 each was consummated. Stafford now owned 60% of voting rights. Ballard became executive vice-president in charge of the Gardens and Bassett became chair of the company's Board of Directors. A vital clause in the pre-nuptial agreement to their three-way business marriage gave the remaining parties an option to buy the shares of a party who dies, a clause that would become the single most important factor in the demise of the club.

Ace Bailey's blades.

Under Ballard, the managing of the Maple Leaf organization took a swift and all-encompassing nosedive. Anyone who wanted to use the Gardens could do so, as long as the fee was anted. "Cash ahead of class," Conn called it. Circuses, concerts, entertainers, conventions all began invading the great hockey palace that had rarely

hosted anything but a Leaf event since Conn built the place in 1931. Advertisements were placed everywhere in the Gardens (on walls, escalators, under seats), and merchandising expanded. Whatever made money or profit was all Ballard was interested in.

Typical was the scheduling of the March 29, 1966, Cassius Clay–Ernie Terrell fight. One of the growing number of non-hockey events in the Gardens, it symbolized the new credo of greed. Clay — Muhammad Ali — was a Vietnam draft dodger who could not find anywhere to fight. No arena, club, stadium, or hall would rent to an unpatriotic criminal. Conn was enraged that the Gardens, *the* bastion of tradition and honour in Canada, would be so sullied by courting — in essence *supporting* — a draft dodger. So was Terrell; he pulled out at the last minute and was replaced by local boy George Chuvalo, who took a beating but never fell, and became the first man to go 15 rounds with Ali.

Ballard didn't care about the backlash he received for hosting the fight. To him money was money. Major Conn Smythe begged to differ: "The Gardens was founded by men — sportsmen — who fought for their country. It is no place for those who want to evade conscription in their own country. The Gardens was built for many things, but not for picking up things that no one else wants." He resigned from the board and sold his few remaining private shares, thus severing all ties with an organization he had established 40 years earlier. Ballard was not noticeably shaken by the decision.

Leaf fans of today have Ballard and Stafford to thank for the Gardens' infamously small seats. Between 1962 and 1969 they increased capacity from a comfortable 12,737 to a squished 16,700 by simply putting seats everywhere and making them smaller. The diminution of the seats inflamed the ire of Conn, whose oft-repeated aphorism went something like this: "They're too high-priced for the thin and too small for the fat folks who can afford them." Except Ballard, of course, who ensconced his hugeness in his own private bunker.

During these renovations, a picture of Queen Elizabeth was removed from the Gardens' rafters to make room for more seats. In response to the criticism raised by many hockey fans and monarchists, Ballard merely shot back: "If people want to see a picture of the Queen, they can go to an art gallery. What the hell, she doesn't pay me." Conn, a teetotaller, also had to endure the creation of the Hot Stove Club in 1964, the immensely popular licensed restaurant (read "cash cow") Ballard opened by gutting the interior of the southeast corner of the building.* Ballard took the name from a radio talk show, the Hot Stove League, featured between periods of Leaf games. It started in 1936 with Court Benson, Bobby Hewitson,

---

* For years he spoke defiantly into television cameras or interviewers' microphones and promised that liquor would never be sold at the Gardens! It was there the whole time, but only the monied had access to it.

Elmer Ferguson, and Wes McKnight, and was later hosted by Baldy
Cotton, Jack Dennett, and Syl Apps. They had eight seats in the
Reds, and during intermissions would hustle over to the CBC's Jarvis
Street studios just north of Carlton to do the radio program. The
broadcast was sponsored by Imperial Oil, which at the time was
selling a gasoline called Three Stars. Thus came the Hot Stove
invention of the game's three stars, a tradition that is as much a part
of today's games as it was then. The show moved to television in the
early '50s, using a studio set consisting of a pot-bellied stove and

HOCKEY HALL OF FAME

grocery-store counter. Ballard's steal of the name was clever, and
licensing it even more clever, though it was in keeping with neither
Conn's Gardens nor the Hot Stove League tradition. It was pure
Haroldry.

In October 1964, Stafford and Ballard opened a bank account in
the name of S.H. Marlie ("S" for Stafford, "H" for Harold). Over
the next five years they siphoned hundreds of thousands of dollars
from Gardens' and Marlies' coffers into this new account. The
money was used to finance major construction to their private

houses and cottages (on Lake Joseph and at Thunder Beach, Georgian Bay) and even to claim minor personal expenses on their tax returns.

For instance, Ballard bought his boy Bill a beautiful bicycle that cost $440.83. In the S.H. Marlie books the purchase was referred to as "144 CCM hockey sticks." Later, $16,500 worth of renovations to Ballard's Etobicoke home at 6 Montgomery Road was querulously confused at tax time with "alterations south end, installation red seats, directors' room, concessions." And still later, $120,000 of plans for Stafford's new home at 15 Ashley Park Drive somehow got mistaken for "progress south end alterations, pre-cast installation red seats, directors' room, concessions, re-arranging north end seats." In Canada and other civilized democracies this behaviour is known as fraud. They were caught. In October 1968, the RCMP confiscated various books and documents from the Gardens, and the Department of National Revenue began an investigation into the bookkeeping practices of the two men.

In June 1969, John Bassett had Ballard and Stafford removed from the Board of Directors on the sound basis that their fraudulent activities were not good for the company. George Mara was made the new president of the Gardens and S and H were furious at what they considered the betrayal by Bassett of their joint and equal partnership. At a Board meeting in December 1970, though, the two excommunicatees called in their chips with the other members. With the number of friends they had, they were easily voted back to office. Mara never even moved his papers into the president's office.

Facts were facts, and Stafford and Ballard knew they were in trouble. On July 9, 1969, the rest of the country knew, too. The *Toronto Star* headline that day read:

STAFF SMYTHE, HAROLD BALLARD CHARGED
AS INCOME TAX EVADERS

The *Globe* ran a similar line:

TWO DIRECTORS OF MAPLE LEAF GARDENS ARE
CHARGED WITH TAX EVASION

Class at the Gardens? Forget it.

The ensuing investigation by the Attorney General's Office of the business activities of the Gardens was thorough and protracted. Finally on June 17, 1971, Stafford and Ballard were formally charged. For tax evasion: C. Stafford Smythe $278,920, Harold E. Ballard $134,685. For theft and fraud: both men for a total of $146,000 in cash and securities. The two were released on $50,000 bail and the trial was set for October 25.

Bassett was a businessman, plain and simple, and he didn't like what he was seeing. By far the quietest of the three partners, his

investment was nonetheless substantial. He owned the *Telegram* and Baton Broadcasting ("Ba" for Bassett and "-ton" for John David Eaton, his friend and partner) and had a solid reputation in the community that he didn't want sullied by his association with criminals. On September 1, 1971, he again tried to gain control of the Gardens at a Board of Directors meeting, but Stafford and Ballard still had too much support. Bassett, like Conn before him, got out. He sold his shares to the two crooks for $5,886,600 and with the money bought 99% of the Toronto Argonauts football club.

And then there were two.

Stafford was a Smythe, and that counted for a great deal. He felt mortified by the charges, not only for himself, *least of all* himself, but for his father with whom he had been so close and who had trusted him with the ownership. He didn't want to be considered a jailbird, or to see the name and honour of his family publicly dragged through mud in the process. Staff was always one who liked to tipple, and his legal difficulties only exacerbated this tendency. His health deteriorated rapidly. Just a few days before he was to stand trial, he succumbed to stomach cancer and died October 13.

Stafford had avoided the disgrace of prison and so restored some dignity to the name of Smythe. Conn knew his son had done wrong and should be punished, but also felt that Stafford had been very badly treated and subjected to duress from both the media and the law far exceeding the severity of the crime. Stafford was buried in the small village of Gregory, in Muskoka, and on his tombstone is engraved:

> Here lies Conn Stafford Smythe, Lieut. RCNVR 1940–44. He was dearly loved by his wife, children and many friends. He was persecuted to death by his enemies. Now he sleeps peacefully in the quiet north country that loved him for the person he really was.
> Born Toronto March 15, 1921.
> Died October 13, 1971.

Ballard was deeply shaken by the loss of his friend, but entirely untouched by the legal proceedings he now had to face alone. Being charged with a crime of character held little significance for him save for the prospect of losing his liberty. To the public and the media he resembled nothing so much as a punch-drunk clown and seemed more proud than humiliated by the trial. He bragged and boasted before, during, and after, and tried to mock both his crime and the justice system.

His gallows humour may have been due to his successful and somewhat malicious takeover of Maple Leaf Gardens in February 1972. As the original 1961 agreement between the three men stipulated, the death of one of the three would allow the other(s) to buy the shares of the deceased. Bassett was no longer part of the ownership, so Ballard — as executor of Smythe's estate — had only

to sell the shares to himself, through his own company, HEB Ltd., at fair market value and the Gardens would be his. The only way he was able to do this was through his friend Don Giffin. Giffin, who had helped produce the cash for the Bassett buyout through a loan from the Toronto-Dominion Bank, now arranged for Ballard to receive a loan of $7.4 million. When the dust had settled, Ballard owned 513,832 of 735,580 shares (or 69.8%) of Maple Leaf Gardens stock.

And then there was one.

Ballard was now in full control of the Gardens, but not of his own immediate future. On August 15, 1972, he got his comeuppance — he was found guilty on 47 of 49 charges of fraud. Judge Harry Deyman's remarks were simple and frank: "I find it completely incredible that a businessman of Mr. Ballard's acumen could have goods and services of such a variety and cost furnished to him to his knowledge without expecting to pay for them. I am driven to the inescapable conclusion that in the particulars set out against Ballard, he did have knowledge and in fact instigated most of them and I must find him guilty." Ballard, ever the Harold that he was, maintained moral and legal innocence outside the courtroom: "I don't feel badly because I still don't feel I did anything wrong."

He was scheduled to be sentenced on September 7. However, as he was involved with the historic Canada–Russia Summit Series — he had given over the Gardens for Team Canada's training camp — he sought to have the date put off so he could travel to Russia for the final four games. He inveigled Alan Eagleson to appeal the date and the Eagle, in a highly irregular legal gesture, phoned Judge Deyman at his home in Peterborough to ask for a postponement. Deyman was furious. He allowed the delay, but said he would add a year to the term for good measure!

And so it came to pass. On October 20, 1972, after Paul Henderson's miracle-winning goal in Moscow, Ballard was sentenced to three concurrent three-year terms. He was trundled off to Millhaven and left the running of the Gardens to his law-graduate son Bill, who became the titular vice-president. Whether Bill rode to work on his illegally acquired bike isn't known.

Just one year later, on October 19, 1973, Ballard was back on the streets. The Gardens was his. He was free. He was 69 years old. He would live 17 more years. He would ruin the enjoyment of the game, of being a Leaf supporter, of loving the Gardens, for an entire generation of Canadian hockey fans.

MAPLE LEAFS

BERNIE
PARENT

TORONTO
MAPLE
LEAFS

GOALIE

HOCKEY HALL OF FAME

42

III

Ballard Takes Over

All hope abandon, ye who enter here.
— Dante, *The Inferno*, Canto III, line 9

Throughout the '60s Ballard was essentially in charge of the Gardens, but nothing he did had much direct bearing on the actual hockey team and its performance. The sale of the farm clubs was stupidity personified, but a few years would pass before the repercussions from the sale were felt. When he turned a section of the Reds to Golds and increased the price of tickets, he was merely extracting more dollars from well-heeled hockey-loving fans who grudgingly paid the extra stipend. When he put advertisements under the seats and in the hallways and anywhere else he could find a place, he was "generating revenue" but not tampering with the players on the ice below. While he upset Conn Smythe by renting the Gardens for other events, he did bring in millions of dollars in income. Why shouldn't Bob Hope or Frank Sinatra play the Gardens? If the building were dark, as it was all summer, why not use it, put the Ol' Lady to work, as it were?

The problem was that Ballard always went too far. When he booked the Beatles in 1965, he sold tickets for *two* shows, unbeknown to their manager Brian Epstein, who had made arrangements for only one. Ballard told Epstein that if the Beatles refused to play the second concert the fans would rip the Fab Four to pieces. HEB Ltd. got his second show and his added revenue, but through means deceptive, vicious, and ungentlemanly (for him, a handshake did not seal a deal, it meant a trip to the washroom to get the taint of honesty off his mitts). Even then he delayed the start of the two shows by more than an hour each, turning on the heat until the Gardens was sweltering, and making a royal killing on concessions. That many fans fainted and had to be taken out was of no concern to him.

MLG shareholders could hardly complain about Ballard. Regardless of what they thought of him personally, he generated profits like never before. In 1961, before he became a partner, shares traded at $26.50. By 1965, they were going for $114.75 and four years later were split five for one with dividends increasing tenfold over the Conn era.

All this time, though, Ballard's mobility had always been kept in check by co-owners Bassett and Stafford. He couldn't really do much *directly* about the hockey players who came and went, about

coaching and general managing decisions, about those moves and decisions that produced Stanley Cups. He was operating very much in the shadows of the Smythe myth, and he knew it. The rules of the game changed in 1972, however, when he bought the late Stafford's shares. Bassett had already been taken out in an ugly power play that created a hatred that lasted until the day Ballard dropped dead. Whenever Ballard had a chance to shaft Bassett, he took it. One such chance came in 1973 when Bassett rented the Gardens for his Toronto Toros of the new World Hockey Association. The contract between the Gardens and the Toros (i.e., Ballard and Bassett) called for a flat rental fee of $15,000 per game, but there was no stipulation about using television lights. Bassett assumed this was part of the contract. Nope. For this extra service Ballard gleefully extracted an additional $5,000 per game.* His vindictiveness went even further. He had Bassett's head removed from *all* Leaf photographs, including the '67 Cup champions team picture, replacing it with the head of his eldest son, Bill.

After 1972, HEB was in complete control of Maple Leaf Gardens. He alone had the keys to the front door, and his first order of business was to pull the welcome mat inside. He didn't have to answer to anyone. He could do as he damn well pleased and to hell with those who got in his way or objected. There was just one small problem: Ballard didn't know a thing about hockey. Sure, he knew what offside and icing and tripping were, but player development, team performance, tradition, trading, assessing talent? Forget it. His experience at the playing level consisted of one fiasco in 1933 when he coached the first Canadian team ever to lose at the world championships, 2–1 to a Boston team. He should have quit the game then and there.

In 1969 his wife Dorothy died, and when Stafford died two years later he lost his closest friend. All he had left in the world were the Leafs. He had an apartment built inside the Gardens and gave up his Etobicoke home. Soon his personality began to take control of the club. His ego had to be fed, his ravenous appetite for media attention sated. The great discovery Ballard made during his trial and incarceration was that whoever owned the Leafs was forever being sought after, forever telephoned, photographed, quoted, listened to, envied, respected. He gloried in the attention and, skilful manipulator of the media that he was, created more and more interest in himself. He pried the Leafs off the sports pages and got himself onto them in their stead. *He* became the dominant player, the one to whom all respect and credit and attention should be paid, not Keon or Ullman or Ellis. He became involved in all aspects of the hockey team. He took part in all of the decision-making processes; *he* became the reason for the decision and usurped

---

* After three years the Toros packed up and moved to Birmingham to continue in the WHA as the Bulls.

the decision itself in importance. He was not only sole owner, he was also GM, coach, trainer, PR man. His egomaniacal fantasies grew and grew and, like his never-ending quest for more and more money, were never satisfied. And all this time he would never have known talent in a hockey player if it had smashed him in the nose and ripped his yellow hair out of his head strand by strand.

Nothing more clearly indicated the beginning of the Ballard Era (the beginning of the end) than the way the Leafs lost goaltender Bernie Parent. In February 1971, GM Jim Gregory made a stunning deal: Bruce Gamble, Mike Walton, and the Leafs' first-round pick in the 1971 draft (who turned out to be Pierre Plante) for Bernie Parent and Philadelphia's second-round pick (Rick Kehoe). It was a masterful trade on Gregory's part. Gamble had not been the franchise-Bower replacement he was expected to be in 1968, and Walton was clinically depressed after suffering from Punchitis for a number of years. Parent and partner Doug Favell were proven number-one goalies in the city of brotherly love, and Philadelphia thought they could afford to trade one. Parent was coming to a Leaf team that had the great Jacques Plante. Although Plante was the first goalie to use the face mask regularly, and the first to really master the skill of handling the puck (a skill expected of all goalies now), he was 42 in 1971 and at the end of his career. Both he and Parent were cast from the same mould (stand up square, play the angle), so it seemed perfect for the young Parent to learn from, and then inherit the throne of, the ageing Plante.

The '71–'72 season was the only full one Parent played with the Leafs, a team that had much promise but little experience on the blueline. Brad Selwood was in his second year, Jim McKenny and Brian Glennie their third, Rick Ley and Mike Pelyk their fourth. Only Baun, in his sixteenth year, could be called a veteran (and in his case, maybe too veteran). In goal, the pairing of Parent and Plante worked well, finishing sixth overall in goals against:

	G	MINS	GA	SO	AVG	W	L	T
Parent	47	2715	116	3	2.56	17	18	9
Plante	34	1965	86	2	2.62	16	13	5

The Leafs finished fourth in the East and were eviscerated by the eventual Cup-winning Bruins 4–1 in the first round of the playoffs. They were shut out twice by Gerry Cheevers and scored just ten goals in the series. But as any keen hockey observer knows, you build a team from the goal out, so the Leafs' future looked very good despite the .500 season and early playoff exit.

At virtually the same time in early 1972 that Ballard was busy buying Stafford's shares, a new league was in the process of offering NHLers lucrative contracts to abandon the tradition of the NHL and

venture to the brave new World Hockey Association. The NHL considered the WHA a pirate league, and Ballard scoffed at anyone who took it seriously: "They might not start the season. They haven't even got a schedule yet. Some of the teams don't even have buildings." So when a silly-sounding team called the Miami Screaming Eagles dangled a long-term, $700,000 contract in its talons for Parent to snatch, Ballard laughed long and hard while the underpaid goaler scrunched his brow and listened intently to the offer.

Ballard's refusal to acknowledge the competition reflected a total lack of respect for Parent. He was clearly one of the top goalies in the league but was earning a miserable $25,000 with the Leafs. Ballard treated Parent's agent, Howard Casper, with disdain, and figured all too casually he was using the WHA as leverage to negotiate a lucrative contract with the Leafs. "We're not worrying about them," Ballard said. "If Parent doesn't show up at training camp, we'll find some answer to the problem. If he became sick and couldn't play, it would be the same thing."

That summer, the nomadic Miami franchise became the Philadelphia Blazers. Parent became very sick (Ballard's analogy), and signed with the Blazers for the '72–'73 season. Meanwhile, Ballard's goaltending "answer" seemed embarrassingly inadequate. Plante, now 43, played 32 games during the season, Ron Low 42, and Gord McRae 11. The result was 13th in the 16-team league in goals against. The offence finished 10th, and the team sixth of eight in the East with a record of 27–41–10, good enough *not* to make the playoffs in Ballard's first year as sole proprietor.

The '73–'74 season was even more frustrating, though the team finished with a solid 35–27–16 record. The Leafs had five goalies on their training camp roster: Low, McRae, Eddie Johnston, Dunc Wilson, and Grant Cole. Parent wanted to return to the NHL after his year with the Blazers, but understandably refused to join Ballard's Leafs. Toronto had little choice but to trade him, which GM Jim Gregory did, back to the Flyers. The Leafs got Favell and Philadelphia's first-round draft choice (Bob Neely, as it turned out).

Favell played very well that year for the Leafs; Parent was a miracle in Philadelphia. He won the Vezina with a goals-against average of 1.89, played 73 of 78 games, had 12 shutouts, led the Flyers to the first Stanley Cup win by an expansion club, and won the Conn Smythe trophy. The next year? A 2.03 average, 68 games, 12 shutouts, Vezina winner, Cup champ, Conn Smythe winner. Not bad for a guy Ballard thought he could replace as easily as any injured player. But to Ballard he didn't lose two Stanley Cups when he let Parent go; he saved $25,000–$50,000 a season!

The creation of the WHA was of paramount importance to the development of the NHL for two reasons. First, the NHL's "reserve clause" was struck down. This clause was as antediluvian as the Original Six was glorious. It was a putatively binding contract that lasted the duration of a player's career. If he signed with one club,

he could not play professionally with any other club anywhere, anytime, *ever*. Alan Eagleson thought such a clause was invalid. To be bound for all time on the basis of one three- or four-year contract seemed unjust. He conjectured that after a contract had expired, the player had certain mobility. Not total mobility which would imply total free agency, and doesn't even exist today, but at least *some* freedom. When he suggested that his player-clients sign with generous WHA clubs in 1972, he was advising them to violate the reserve clause. But were they breaching their contracts? In its first year the WHA signed many NHLers — through Eagleson, other agents, and independently — in effect challenging the clause. The NHL took its rival to court and lost. The reserve clause was struck down. Players could legally leave the NHL if they so desired.

Second, the players' salaries increased as significantly now as they had five years earlier, after the creation of the new NHLPA. Because the WHA was more pro-active and bid-hungry, the end of the reserve clause signalled the beginning of much higher salaries in the NHL. WHA owners were prepared to offer players rich contracts and create sensational publicity by luring NHLers their way. This would, in turn, produce good hockey teams and draw good crowds. Many players who had little or no interest in playing in the WHA used these high offers to gauge their worth in negotiations with their NHL team. Others happily left and earned more money in one WHA contract than they had earned in a decade in the NHL.

Because of these two factors, and the loathing most players felt for Ballard's stinginess, the Leaf organization lost an incredible 14 players to the WHA that first summer of 1972: Jim Dorey, Rick Ley, and Brad Selwood to the New England Whalers; Steve King, Gavin Kirk, Guy Trottier, and Rick Cunningham to the Ottawa Nationals; Doug Brindley to the Cleveland Crusaders; Jim Harrison to the Alberta Oilers; Bob Liddington and Jan Popiel to the Chicago Cougars; Bob MacMillan to the Minnesota Fighting Saints; Ken Desjardine to the Quebec Nordiques; and Bernie Parent to the Philadelphia Blazers. In the ensuing years the Leafs also lost Keon, Henderson, Pelyk, Blaine Stoughton, Dave Dunn, Lyle Moffat, and others, a sign not of underestimating the WHA but simply of ill-will toward players wanting to be well paid and a poor managerial strategy for assembling a winning team.

Further proof of the Leafs' decline can be seen by looking at the roster of Team Canada for the Summit Series in September 1972:

Phil Esposito (Boston)	Don Awrey (Boston)
Wayne Cashman (Boston)	Gilbert Perreault (Buffalo)
Tony Esposito (Chicago)	Bobby Hull (Chicago)
Pat Stapleton (Chicago)	Bill White (Chicago)
Stan Mikita (Chicago)	Mickey Redmond (Detroit)
Garry Bergman (Detroit)	Red Berenson (Detroit)

Bill Goldsworthy (Minnesota)	J.P. Parise (Minnesota)
Yvan Cournoyer (Montreal)	Frank Mahovlich (Montreal)
Ken Dryden (Montreal)	Guy Lapointe (Montreal)
Serge Savard (Montreal)	Pete Mahovlich (Montreal)
Brad Park (New York)	Rod Seiling (New York)
Jean Ratelle (New York)	Rod Gilbert (New York)
Vic Hadfield (New York)	Bobby Clarke (Philadelphia)
Ron Ellis (Toronto)	Paul Henderson (Toronto)

This was Canada's greatest team of the time (sans the knee-injured Orr), yet on a roster of 28 NHLers the Leafs had but *two* players, Henderson and Ellis. Minnesota, a franchise only five years old, also had two. This is only the half of it. The other half is in the Team Canada players who *ought to* have been Leafs. The Big M, traded by Imlach in 1968; his brother Pete, who played for St. Mike's before their program ceased and was not pursued by the Leafs thereafter; Seiling, traded in '64 in the Bathgate deal; Parise, who was bought by the Leafs in 1967 only to be sold three months later; and Clarke, whom the Leafs had a chance to draft in 1969.

Just as it takes a few years to build a winning team, so it also takes a few to ruin one. Nineteen seventy-three was still a pretty good year. Jim Gregory was permitted to draft Lanny McDonald 4th overall and Ian Turnbull 15th, and these selections promised to gel nicely with Darryl Sittler and Errol Thompson (8th and 22nd in 1970), and George Ferguson and Pat Boutette (11th and 139th in '72) as the nucleus of a fine young, though Parent-less, club. A few months earlier, head scout Gerry McNamara — a goaler for the Leafs' Rochester farm club in the '50s and a seven-game veteran of the Leafs in the '60s — was despatched to Sweden, at the time hockey's

Ticket stub for Game 8 of the Summit Series,
September 28, 1972, Moscow.
GARY SMITH / HOCKEY HALL OF FAME

North Pole, to follow the Barrie Flyers on a tour of the country and to suss out local talent, particularly Curt Larsson, a goalie for Sodertajle. He was also advised to look at another team, Brynas, because they reputedly had tough, Canadian-style players. The night Brynas played the Flyers, the Flyers tried to outmuscle the Swedes. In one altercation, a 22-year-old local boy named Borje Salming decked the referee and was tossed out. Another, 24-year-old Inge Hammarstrom, scored four goals. That was all McNamara needed. After the game he started making arrangements to get the pair in Toronto jerseys. This was in the days when there were few hard rules about drafting Europeans and hearkened back to the pre-1967 days when a scout could simply offer a contract to a player. It was a comparatively simple process: sell the players on the idea of the NHL, and negotiate a transfer fee (about $60,000) with Brynas. No draft, no delay — signing the old-fashioned way.

Getting Salming and Hammarstrom to join the blue and white was a cutting-edge move. The Leafs became the first team to scout European hockey clubs and had the inside track to what was to become one of the most lucrative non-Canadian regions for NHL-calibre skills. But Ballard was not convinced by the Salming-Hammarstrom finds. He was neither impressed nor convinced by what Sweden had to offer and refused to put up the money to establish a scouting base in Europe. While Salming became a first-rate player, a loyal friend of Ballard, and a devoted Leaf, Ballard publicly humiliated the more timorous Inge by uttering the now immortal insult: "He could go into the corner with six eggs in his pocket and not break any of them."

The following year the Leafs drafted another Swede — Per-Arne Alexandersson, who never played in the NHL — and then gave up; they didn't draft another for 15 years.* During that same time (1974–88) the rest of the league drafted a total of 142 Swedes. While he may have been more right than wrong about Hammarstrom, Ballard should have realized that one trip by one scout produced a dominant NHLer and that surely more talent could be found with a little more effort. What he didn't realize was that Salming was a bit of a lucky find. Scouting by nature is a plodding, arduous task. It takes time, expertise, luck, and much travelling to "discover" franchise-making talent. However, one success story was quite enough for H.B.

The process of maintaining superiority in an organization is ongoing. Just as a team needs star players in their prime, it must also have experience at one end and good drafting for future young talent at the other. While the Leafs of Sittler, McDonald, Salming, and Turnbull were developing into a true force, the drafting and trading

---

* Roger Elvenas from Rogle (153rd in 1988), who played not one minute in the NHL.

needed to plan for the future were suspect at best, as the Leafs' picks from 1975 to 1979 attest.

These years were crucial for strengthening a team that was becoming perilously close to challenging for the Stanley Cup. However, these five years produced only three real prospects, Jarvis, Carlyle, and Boschman, each of whom was traded before having a chance to peak with the Leafs.

1975	1976
6 – Don Ashby	30 – Randy Carlyle
24 – Doug Jarvis	48 – Alain Belanger
42 – Bruce Boudreau	52 – Gary McFayden
78 – Ted Long	66 – Tim Williams
96 – Kevin Campbell	84 – Greg Hotham
114 – Mario Rouillard	102 – Dan Dkjakalovic
132 – Ron Wilson	
149 – Paul Evans	
165 – Jean Latendresse	
166 – Paul Crowley	
179 – Dan D'Alvise	
180 – Jack Laine	
188 – Ken Holland	

1977	1978
11 – John Anderson	21 – Joel Quenneville
12 – Trevor Johansen	48 – Mark Kirton
24 – Bob Gladney	65 – Bob Parent
29 – Rocky Saganiuk	81 – Jordy Douglas
65 – Dan Eastman	92 – Mel Hewitt
83 – John Wilson	98 – Normand Lefebvre
101 – Roy Sommer	115 – John Scammell
119 – Lynn Jorgenson	132 – Kevin Reinhart
	149 – Mike Waghorne
	166 – Laurie Cuvelier

1979	
9 – Laurie Boschman	
51 – Normand Aubin	
72 – Vincent Tremblay	
93 – Frank Nigro	
114 – Bill McCreary	

In the summer of '75 Jim Gregory traded Doug Jarvis, the team's number-one draft pick, to Montreal for Greg Hubick. Gregory felt Jarvis, a centre, would be redundant given that the Leafs had Sittler, Ferguson, Stan Weir, Boutette, and their young 1974 number one pick, Jack Valiquette. Hubick, a left-winger, was thought to be capable of filling a weakness on this side, but it never worked out that way. He played 72 games with the Leafs and five more with Vancouver years later. That was all she wrote. Jarvis went on to play a record 964 straight games. He played on four Stanley Cup teams, won Selke and Masterton Trophies, and became respected as the best defensive forward in the game.

Another disaster occurred when Randy Carlyle and George Ferguson were traded to Pittsburgh for Dave Burrows on June 14, 1978. Burrows sustained a serious knee injury just a few games into the '78–'79 season and played poorly for two seasons before being shipped back to Pittsburgh with Paul Gardner for Kim Davis (career total: 36 NHL games) and Paul Marshall (95 games). In other words, the Leafs gave Carlyle away. He developed into an excellent and consistent offensive defenceman who played 17 seasons and 1,055 games in the NHL, and won the Norris Trophy in 1981.

To make matters worse, with each trade Gregory orchestrated he included his own high draft choices. He traded the Leafs' first pick in the '76 draft, third in '77, first and second in '78, second in '79, first and third in '80, and fourth and sixth in '81. In the mid-'70s, when the Leafs were so close to success, management was unable to make those small moves needed to put the team in the uppermost of echelons. By the time the '80s arrived, the in-prime veteran players had no new quality talent to play with, tutor, and develop. The team arrived at a dead end.

These draft gaffes look even worse when juxtaposed to a list of players the Leafs *didn't* pick those same years. In 1977, they had two consecutive selections, numbers 11 and 12 overall, yet passed on Mike Bossy (15th, New York Islanders), John Tonelli (33rd, Islanders), and Rod Langway (36th, Montreal) in favour of John Anderson and Trevor Johansen. Bossy was a scorer in junior, peewee, road hockey, and in the womb. He was as sure a super- as ever a star existed. But he had one flaw in the eyes of Ballard: he wanted to be paid well. Well, Ballard's idea of "well" clearly didn't jive well with Bossy's, and Ballard told Gregory to avoid Bossy, who went on to score 573 goals and win four Stanley Cups with the more generous Islanders in New York. In 1979, the Leafs had one decent pick — Boschman (9th) — whom they gave up on after a couple of years — and passed on Paul Reinhart (12th, Atlanta), Brian Propp (14th, Philadelphia), Brad McCrimmon (15th, Boston), Duane Sutter (17th, Islanders), Michel Goulet (20th, Quebec), Kevin Lowe (21st, Edmonton), Dale Hunter (41st, Quebec), and Neal Broten (42nd, Minnesota). It's utterly heartrending to think of what might have been.

Not all the blame should fall at Gregory's puppeted feet. His actions were dictated by Ballard's unpredictable, senseless directives and by a depleted scouting staff unable to assess the available worldwide talent because of Ballard's stinginess. In many cases, the Leafs simply didn't know firsthand whether a player was good or not. They relied heavily on the league's scouting reports rather than sending their own scouts to see players. The superstars, the obvious talent, were too rich for Ballard's blood, and besides, Gardens stock kept going up and up, and wasn't that what this was all about anyway?

Part of Ballard's reluctance to spend was justified in his mind by the fact the Leafs were still winning often enough to pass as a decent hockey team. Their young players were becoming experienced and developing into dominant NHL stars, and each draft up to 1975 produced a little more promise. In 1973, he hired Red Kelly as coach to replace the ailing John McLellan who had resigned because of a duodenal ulcer. Kelly had coached two years in L.A. and the last four in Pittsburgh, and was an articulate, calm man who brought his Detroit and Toronto Stanley Cup values — eight of them, to be exact — to a team that was improving daily.

Kelly was from the old school, but not the Imlach school. He was kind, often too kind, and believed the pressures of the game from fans, media, and management were great enough for the players to deal with without the coach's contribution. In successive playoffs he tried to direct the players' attention from this pressure, first with Pyramid Power, then positive ions.

Pyramids had long been considered a mystical source of power, so Kelly had them placed throughout the Leafs' locker room and under the players' bench rinkside. Everyone around the team became preoccupied with the coach who mistook his wife for a hat, and the players did in fact feel more relaxed. For the same reasons he tried positive ions the next year, but while his intentions were good these weren't the ways to motivate a team to play up to its potential, especially when the opposition was as formidable as that which the Leafs faced in the playoffs.

Under Kelly the team failed to reach a higher level of play, even though his first of four years was much more productive than McLellan's last of four:

McLellan's record:

1969–70	29–34–13	222	242	71	6th of 6 in East
1970–71	37–33–8	248	211	82	4th of 7 in East
1971–72	33–31–14	209	208	80	4th of 7 in East
1972–73	27–41–10	247	279	64	6th of 8 in East

Kelly's record:

1973–74	35–27–16	274	230	86	4th of 8 in East
1974–75	31–33–16	280	309	78	3rd of 4 in Adams
1975–76	34–31–15	294	276	83	3rd of 4 in Adams
1976–77	33–32–15	301	285	81	3rd of 4 in Adams

By 1976, the Leafs had the nucleus of a Cup winner. Sittler, McDonald, and Thompson formed one of the strongest, most potent lines in the league, while the defence had the perfect mixture of puck carriers (Salming, McKenny, Ian Turnbull) and shot-blocking, stay-at-home men (Brian Glennie, Claire Alexander, Bob Neely). Mike Palmateer was a quirky, flickety goalie, and up front they had toughness in Tiger Williams, Pat Boutette, and George Ferguson. But while the players matured and their regular season point total remained at a consistently high level, their performance in the playoffs was aggravatingly stagnant. In 1974, they were blown away by four strong games from the still mighty Bruins, and the next year were similarly whitewashed by Parent and the Flyers. In 1976, they came perilously close to upsetting the same Flyer team, but Pyramid Power lost 7–3 to Kate Smith's "God Bless America" at the Spectrum in the deciding, unlucky seventh game.

In 1977, the Leafs finished the season with virtually the same record as the year before, an indication that they were levelling off. For the third year in a row they faced the Flyers, but the test was to finally demonstrate an improvement in the playoffs. The first two games gave every indication this would occur: they won 3–2 and 4–1 at the Spectrum, and headed home for Games 3 and 4. With the right killer instinct, they could sweep the Broad Street Bullies at the Gardens. Instead, Philly won the pair in Toronto's backyard, both heartbreakers in overtime, 4–3 and 6–5, to even the series. They regained home-ice advantage, and ripped the momentum out of the Leafs' bellies and hope out of the fans' hearts. They then did what the Leafs didn't, or couldn't, do — they went for the jugular. The Flyers won 2–0 at home and finished Toronto off right in the Gardens 4–3. After establishing a stranglehold, the Leafs lost four games in a row and their third successive playoff series to Philadelphia. They were a consistently good team, but being stalled in "good" and unable to gear up to "great" became a frustration insoluble to Kelly and unacceptable to the Leafs.

In the summer of 1975, Dave Keon signed a three-year, $400,000 contract with the Minnesota Fighting Saints of the WHA. He was looking for a no-trade, no-cut, $135,000-a-year pact with Toronto, figuring that after 15 years, 1,000 games, and four Cups the team captain's contract should reflect a commensurate monetary respect from management that his reputation had among the players. Ballard

GRAIG ABEL

disagreed and, in one of his most despicable, Haroldian acts, let him go. Keon was one of many who "flew out of the cuckoo's nest," in the words of writer Trent Frayne.

As a result of Ballard's odious behaviour, the captain's jersey became available. There was only one man for the job — Darryl Sittler. Entering his sixth year with the team, he had been respected as a man of distinction and talent ever since taking over the heralded number 27 of Frank Mahovlich in 1970. He wore the Leaf crest on his arm, his heart, his forehead, and wherever else loyalty is commonly and uncommonly worn. He was following in the noble footsteps of Day, Conacher, Horner, Apps, Davidson, Kennedy, Smith, Thomson, Armstrong, and of course Keon. The weight of obligation contained in that "C" was offset easily by the pride Sittler brought to the wearing of it. He was a gentleman whose integrity helped shape the character of the team he represented.

All optimism about the Leafs was predicated by Sittler's very presence. He was a winner. That he would one day sip champagne from the Stanley Cup seemed inevitable. He had developed command around the league and his style on ice was inimitable. His choppy strides, his erect body cutting through centre, both hands always on the stick, will forever be remembered, as will his quirky pursed lips and furrowed brow, and his habit of jamming his left elbow pad into place before spinning into the faceoff circle. His unselfish playmaking, his warm friendship with Lanny McDonald, his strength, his ability to perform gracefully under pressure all endeared him to fans as both a superb hockey player and an ambassador for the game. As captain, he shone.

His reputation was greatly enhanced by one remarkable year — 1976. Common wisdom holds that good things come in threes. For Sittler, 1976 was uncommon good.

1. **February 7, 1976,** was, at around dinnertime, just like any other day. Sittler arrived at the Gardens in a tan suit and tie at around 6 p.m. The Leafs were playing Boston that night and it wasn't going to be easy. Boston was in first place in the Adams Division with a superb record of 32–10–9 for 73 points. Buffalo with 66 points was in second, and the .500 Leafs at 21–20–11 were in third with 53 points. It was a typical Toronto winter day. Since it was a Saturday, that meant *Hockey Night in Canada.* By 11:00 p.m. the greatest achievement of all time by one player in one game was being added to the record books, for Darryl Sittler had scored six goals and four assists as the Leafs beat the Bruins 11–4, the first time a player had registered ten points in a single NHL game. For a night, Sittler ruled supreme.

    Dave Reece was the Bruins' goalie, a rookie call-up who never played another minute in the NHL, but the rest of the Boston lineup was nothing to shake a black-taped stick at: Ratelle, Bucyk, Cashman, Schmautz, Hodge, Park, O'Reilly. Orr was injured, Grapes the coach. This was no patsy expansion lineup.

Ratelle scored his 350th in the first period, and Bucyk got an assist in the second to move him into second place on the all-time scoring list. But Sittler stole the show. Ten points in one game! Perfection. He finished the year with exactly 100 points, one-tenth of which came on just one unbelievable night in February at Maple Leaf Gardens.

2. **April 22** was an important night at the Gardens even before the game began. The playoffs were in full swing, and for the Leafs the golf course beckoned. They were in tough against Philadelphia, the Flyers, the Broad Street Bullies. Down three games to two, this was a do-or-die game. Sittler arrived at the rink around six; he was wearing a tan suit and tie. The team won 8–5 to force a seventh game; he scored an incredible *five* goals, tying an NHL playoff record set by Newsy Lalonde in 1919 and equalled only by Maurice Richard in 1944.*

3. **Wednesday, September 15**. The Forum in Montreal. Sittler arrived at the rink wearing his lucky tan tie that clashed with his stylish Team Canada blazer. Roger Doucet roared the Canadian and Czech anthems before 18,040 hysterical fans. Canada wore the home white, the Czechs red, Sittler his familiar 27. This was Game 2 in the best-of-three Canada Cup finals. Two nights earlier the Canadians had shelled the daunted Czechs 6–0. No contest. But this night was more dramatic. Scotty Bowman was behind the bench, changing his lines like a race car driver does gears. Holecek started in net for the Czechs, but after two quick goals by Gil Perreault and Espo, he was replaced by Dzurilla. The Czechs tied the game with goals by Novy in the second and Pouzar early in the third. But then Bobby Clarke, the tiny toothless Flyer with a heart as big as the Great Lakes, scored with just over 12 minutes left to give Team Canada a 3–2 lead. In the misty, overjoyed opinion of the fans, victory was assured.

But the night had only just begun. Two late Czech goals from Augusta and Marian Stastny turned joy to seeming trauma. With four minutes to go, the Czechs were up 4–3. Game 3 seemed inevitable. But Bowman put out the Flyer line of Barber and Leach to bookend Clarke, and sure enough at 17:48 they tied the score, Barber converting a rebound off his own shot. 4–4. Overtime.

There is nothing in sports more dramatic, more exciting, more cathartic, than sudden-death overtime. Baseball has this laconic thing called extra innings. If one team gets a run in the top of the 12th, the other gets a crack at getting it back. In basketball and soccer, a whole extra period is played regardless of what happens during it. In hockey, there is no second chance. One goal ends the game.

---

* The record was tied again in 1989 by Mario Lemieux.

Sudden death wrenches the heart. It is not called "sudden victory" for it is the fear of losing — the death — that gives as much to the emotional impact as the thrill of winning. You can envision a great goal to win, but you fear, almost anticipate, the possibility of losing. The fear of a bad bounce or misplayed puck, a crazy deflection or a small mental lapse, all wreak havoc on a player's concentration. No one ever dreams of scoring a fluke goal; most have nightmares of giving one up. In the dressing room the players are told not to do anything foolish, not to take chances, not to stay on too long, not to panic, not to go in too deep or ice the puck or chance a penalty. Accentuate the negative.

Team Canada got to their dressing room knowing overtime would be their greatest challenge as a team, but they had to get rid of any lazy feeling that there was still another game. After all, they didn't *have* to win. There was always the third game. Assistant coach Don Cherry hurried down from his perch high atop the Forum to the Canadian dressing room. He told the team that he spotted a weakness in Droozilla's (Cherry's Czech/English pronunciation) style: the Czech goalie had a penchant for moving out of his net too quickly and too far when cutting down the angles. If you can, Cherry suggested, fake a shot and go wide.

By the midway point of the overtime, the game had nearly been decided half a dozen times, but both goalies had made big saves. In overtime a big save is half luck, half ability not to think. The Forum was in awe, the tension every bit as thick as Game 7 of a Stanley Cup final. All of Canada knew their team was the better, but that didn't mean they'd win this game. Results were what counted, not boasts. Enjoying the overtime was impossible except in retrospect, after the outcome had been decided. At the time, it was excruciating.

Bowman changed gears one more time, one last time, sending out the Hall of Fame trio of Marcel Dionne, Lanny McDonald, and Darryl Sittler. Lanny got the puck in the Canada zone and flipped it quickly to Dionne outside the blueline. Dionne then hit Sittler in full flight down the left boards. He flew by the last defenceman, had him beat, and had the amazing calm and presence of mind to remember Cherry's advice. He wound up at the top of the circle, and looked up; Dzurilla was already coming out, way out, too far out; Sittler then drew the puck outside. A few feet later, Dzurilla twisting, trying to recover from the surprise, Sittler had an empty net. As the puck went in, Dzurilla now sprawling, Sittler flung his arms high as he backed into the end boards. The fans behind him had already leapt from their seats, the Canadian bench was emptying. Darryl Sittler, captain of the Toronto Maple Leafs, had won the Canada Cup with a spectacular goal in overtime!

Lanny McDonald.
HOCKEY HALL OF FAME

IV

Close, but . . .

Red Kelly took the Leafs to a respectable level that surpassed anything done by the other post-'67 Cup coaches. But by 1977, Kelly had peaked. For perhaps the first time, Ballard made an intelligent hockey decision, which he executed in a typically hideous fashion. He "de-hired" Kelly. He didn't fire him; he simply refused to renew Kelly's contract, fearing, he said, that Kelly might "aggravate a back injury he had suffered earlier in his career and which had flared up during the latest season." On June 29, 1977, he hired Roger Neilson as coach, a workaholic who had coached the Peterborough Petes of the Ontario Hockey League for a decade before moving to the Leafs–Black Hawks Central Hockey League affiliate in Dallas the past year.

Neilson was a young afroed intellectual innovator who relied upon research and video analysis to prepare his team for specific opponents and craft a season-long strategy. He hired an assistant, Ron Smith, and a statistician, Al Dunford. He was as "new-fashioned" as Kelly was "old." Tiger Williams described perfectly how the two coaches differed in approach: "He [Neilson] wanted me to check and scuffle and fight, and he would give me a lot of ice time. . . . Red Kelly's device was to talk about carriers of water and choppers of wood."

The media took to the dry-lipped, lip-smacking Neilson, facetiously at first, and dubbed him "Captain Video." His methods, which were considered quirky but experimental in 1977, have not only endured but have changed every aspect of a coach's job. Today, video analysis and preparation are a part of every team's operation, and while a Neilson team has never won the Cup, he has always been a popular choice for teams in need of a new coach.

Captain Video's practices were interesting, productive, and fun. He exuded determination, intelligence, and professionalism in everything he did. He kept a raft of statistics (number of hits, scoring chances, faceoff percentages, success of particular matchups) that again were as uncommon then as they are common now. He established a weight program for each player, during and off-season, and set up a weight room in the dressing room. He initiated ideas such as setting up wingers on their off side on the power play (i.e., a right-hand shot playing the left wing), and "playing the pick" (i.e., running a little "legal interference"). As Borje Salming said,

Roger Neilson.

"Neilson brought competence to the job, rather than old newspaper clippings."

Neilson was just what the Leafs needed. Kelly was a nice man, but didn't know how to treat young players of the '70s. Neilson knew exactly how, and his presence was like a breath of fresh air around the Gardens. The team had the talent to do something big in the playoffs, it just needed guidance to know *how* to do that something. The future was *now*.

The players that Neilson inherited were enormously popular in Toronto, thanks to their on-ice success and their personality and charm off it. Sittler personified leadership; he was responsible and well-liked, and was active in community and charity work. McDonald was loved for his devotion to the Special Olympics, and his moustache was always an amusing topic of conversation. His television commercial with Brian Glennie for Swanson TV dinners was wildly popular; it ended with the leonine Lanny growling "Meeeoowwww" into the camera, and many a subway chat or party joke revolved around this playful growl. Salming was nicknamed "the King." He was the strong, skilled, romantic foreigner, whose perfect body and graceful skating were admired by all. Turnbull owned a successful restaurant called Grapes, and Palmateer was the cocky, curly-haired, cute conversationalist, as quick with a joke as his glove hand. After a two-year hiatus, Ron Ellis was back, wearing the unique number 6 that Ace Bailey had allowed.* Like Sittler, he was a gentleman, but from the good old days of '60s glory. He brought experience and Stanley Cup respect to a team that had only seen the trophy in the display case at the Hockey Hall of Fame.

And then there was "Tiger," the modern-day Eddie Shack. A scrapper but not a brawler, a checker who could score a bit, a mean guy with a great personality, a guy whose nose had been broken so many times he looked more ancient Greek than modern Saskatchewan. He'd punch his way through a brick wall to help his team. He dropped his gloves more than anyone else in the history of the game, but was never dirty or cheap. He put up his dukes, plain and simple. He made the words "done like dinner" a symbol of his humour, competitive desire, and charisma. He was the Leafs' character, the motivator.

---

* Ace Bailey's career ended after a vicious check by Boston's Eddie Shore on December 12, 1933. Out of respect, no one wore Bailey's number 6 afterwards, until Ellis, who was much admired by Ace and who received permission to wear the number.

Tiger Williams crashes the net.
HOCKEY HALL OF FAME

With this roster, the '77–'78 season went well. The Neilson Leafs finished a strong sixth overall with a record of 41–29–10 for 92 points. Sittler was third in league scoring with a team record 117 points, behind only Guy Lafleur (132) and Bryan Trottier (123). The only other time the Leafs had won 40 games was way back in '50–'51 with Turk Broda in the nets and Max Bentley, Ted Kennedy, and Tod Sloan leading the attack. That team won the Cup. Now was the time for this team to test their mettle in the playoffs. "By the spring of 1978," Tiger recalled, "we were so close we could taste the Stanley Cup."

In the first round of the playoffs, the best two of three, the Leafs easily beat Marcel Dionne and his Los Angeles-never-make-the-playoffs-Kings, 7–3 and 4–0, setting up a showdown with the soon-to-be-powerful New York Islanders. The Leafs were not expected to win, but Neilson prepared a game plan that his players executed to perfection. Even though they lost the first two games on the Island 4–1 and 3–2, the team felt confident of its chances. The second game had gone into overtime, and on the flight home the boys in blue longed for home ice. They knew they could play with the Islanders; now it was time to beat them.

Win they did, but the price was high. They lost Salming in Game 3 when he caught Lorne Henning's stick in the eye. Those who remember seeing the play at the blueline, Salming lying in agony with his hands to his eye, the blood on the ice gruesome testimony to the severity of the injury, can't help but squint and cringe at that horrible, though wholly accidental, incident. To read his own description of it is almost impossible: "When the point of his blade stabbed my eye, I felt as if my eye was going to come out the back of my head. My nose was broken and I was bleeding into my sinuses." Down two games to the Islanders, without Salming to lead a comeback, the Leafs seemed headed for elimination.

But something miraculous happened after Salming was taken off the ice. Ian Turnbull took over. In the next four-and-a-half games he played the best hockey of his career and looked every bit the Salming Borje was. The Leafs won that third game 2–0, allowing New York only 19 shots, and the next 3–1 in a rough contest that saw goaler Palmateer ejected for fighting. Indeed, the fight was back for the whole Leaf team, and the series even 2–2. The Leafs lost another overtime on the Island in Game 5, this one 2–1, and again came back to the Gardens needing a win to avoid elimination. Midway through the game, Jerry Butler levelled Mike Bossy, the Islanders' star scorer. He lay motionless on the frozen water and was removed on a stretcher. That was the turning point, the defining moment in the game. Toronto won 5–2, forcing a seventh game back in New York.

This game too went into overtime, but the result was different. Four minutes into the OT, Turnbull threw a waist-high pass to Lanny at the Islander blueline. McDonald, a broken bone in his wrist and a cage on his helmet to protect a broken beak, knocked the pass down and beat Chico Resch cleanly with a wobbly wrist shot. The Leafs had eliminated New York (Neilson had beaten counterpart Al Arbour) and were on their way to the semifinals against Montreal! It was their best showing in 11 years, and it couldn't have happened to a more tightly knit Leaf team.

But the worst nightmare for a Leaf fan came true in the semis. Toronto lost to Montreal. Only a non-Leaf fan would say Montreal was in the middle of a four-Cup dynasty and was simply the superior team. A true-blue Leaf fan would say that was nonsense, would point to the absence of Salming, would point to the most overrated player in the history of the game — Ken Dryden — as merely a luckster who had a great defence in front of him, yet who let in 19 goals in his four games during the Summit Series '72 and who almost lost it for us (fortunately Henderson, the Leaf King, saved our country's pride). A Leaf fan would call Larry Robinson the player with the most lucky goals from the point; would ridicule Serge Savard's spinarama as a child's copy of Orr's magnificent intuition; would call Lafleur a blind passer who didn't know what to do with the puck much of the time; coach Bowman a crybaby yapper with his chin always arrogantly in the air, a non-coach who could have been replaced by air and the team still would have won (his record since leaving Montreal in 1979 confirms as much). A Leaf fan would vilify the referees for giving the "Forum break" to Montreal every game; the Forum fans for crying endlessly if their players fell to the ice and jeering if the nearest opponent didn't get a penalty; blame Dick Irvin, the intolerably biased Montreal/CBC broadcaster, whose pro-Montreal calls were as repulsive as the guys in Buffalo everyone always parodied.

Montreal was the worst, the most over-rated, the luckiest, the most privileged. They were the arch-enemy, the pirate, the villain. Their fans were loathsome, the players grossly over-rated, their building without aura despite its history.

Montreal beat Neilson's Leafs 5–3, 3–2, 6–1, and 2–0.

The decent performance of the previous spring was buried under the oppressive dirt of tyrant Ballard's rule. In the off-season, Neilson wanted to trade Turnbull. The Bull was not Captain Video's kind of player. He was considered a lazy floater by his teammates, who liked him well enough off-ice but felt he didn't give his all in the games. Turnbull liked late nights and didn't embrace the Neilson work ethic. More important, he was coming off an extraordinary playoffs during which he played well above his ability and proved a genuine force in the place of Salming. His market value would never be higher. The Leafs could have traded him for a bona fide first stringer, someone who might have helped push the team into the finals the following spring.

But Ballard liked Turnbull. He *loved* him. He said frankly he wouldn't trade Turnbull for God. Al Dunford, the statistician whom Ballard loathed and called the "cruise director," quipped, "How about God and a fourth-round draft choice?" Ballard was not amused.* Turnbull was eventually traded, but not until November 11, 1981. In return, the Leafs got John Gibson and Billy Harris. In other words, slightly less than nothing.

Meanwhile, Ballard had a chance to acquit himself for his Swedish reticence of '73 when two WHA stars, Ulf Nilsson and Anders Hedberg, were looking to join the NHL. Toronto was their city of preference, but the price would have to be right. Ballard didn't pursue them and merely scoffed when told of their salary expectations. This at a time when the Leafs were serious Cup contenders and probably only two or three players away from making the finals. Not that these were necessarily the two, but signing them would have been better than standing pat. Hedberg and Nilsson were not about to go to a team that treated them poorly *before* they got there, so they signed with the Rangers. The next spring New York was playing in the finals against Montreal.

To Ballard, Neilson simply thought too much, tried too hard, coached in a way with which he was thoroughly unfamiliar, and, therefore, didn't like. By February 1979, midway through Neilson's second season, Toronto hit the skids for a while, losing games they should have won. On Thursday, March 1, the Leafs visited Montreal, and before the game Ballard told Neilson that if the club lost that night he'd be fired. They lost 2–1, and true to his word Ballard fired him moments after the final siren by telling journalist and friend Dick Beddoes of the decision. Beddoes ran to the television studio to broadcast the news over the airwaves. Class at the Gardens? Forget it.

---

* One time, after a road loss, Ballard saw Dunford get on the team bus carrying videos and reams of statistical information. He spat out: "The game's over for Chrissake. What are you going to learn from those goddamn things now?" Harold Ballard, General Manager, Toronto Maple Leafs, circa 1978.

There was only one problem with the firing: Ballard couldn't find a replacement. He called Eddie Johnston, coach of the joint Toronto–Chicago AHL farm team now in New Brunswick. Johnston rejected the offer, saying he was under contract to the Hawks. He then tried John McLellan and Gerry McNamara. Both said no. Ballard was furious!

After the Montreal game and the firing, the team was in a state of shock. Neilson himself had delivered the news to the players in the dressing room, and that night and the next morning many of them got together to see what they could do. Even though the team had not been playing well, they loved Neilson and firmly believed in his system. They also felt good about their chances in the playoffs and worried that it was too late in the season to adapt to a new coach, a new style, a new method. Sittler, as captain, visited Ballard and voiced the team's concerns, detailing the reasons for such an impractical dismissal and asking that Neilson be reinstated. Without any other option, Ballard grudgingly relented. But while he realized bringing Neilson back would be the sensible thing to do, he also had to save face and not look like the fool that he was in this charade. So Ballard conceived a plan to reveal that the firing was just a hoax, a trick, a prank. For the game Saturday night against Philadelphia, he wanted Neilson to wait until the anthems were over and then appear behind the Leaf bench with a bag over his head. Then he would remove the bag and the fans would see it was Roger and cheer. Harold would have played a fun game, and the players would have their old coach back.

That's what the owner of the Toronto Maple Leafs hockey club wanted to do.

Neilson, firmly rooted in the real world of planet Earth, rejected the bag idea, but he did return to a standing ovation. The Leafs showed their appreciation for Neilson by beating the Flyers 4–3 that night and winning the next five in a row. They finished eleven points lighter than the season before with a record of 34–33–13 and again started strongly in the playoffs, beating Atlanta 2–1 in the Omni and 7–4 at the Gardens. The next round they played the Enemy again, the Club d'hockey Canadiens.

The first two games were at the Forum, and Montreal won both, the first 5–2 before the traditional non-sellout apathetic playoff crowd, and the second 5–1. Game 3 at the Gardens went into double overtime and was won in typical Montreal fashion when Cam Connor, on his first shift of the game, scored a fluke goal at 5:25. The goal led to Mike Palmateer's now famous quip: "That's one thing I can't do — stop a guy who doesn't know what he's doing."

Game 4 was a spectacular hockey game. Montreal was up 4–0 by the midway point, but the Leafs rallied to tie with just over six minutes to play. Another overtime followed. At 2:38 of the extra period, referee Bob Myers penalized Tiger Williams for an innocuous high-stick on Larry Robinson. This was just the "Montreal break"

the Habs were looking for, and on the ensuing power play Robinson scored to eliminate the Leafs.*

The elimination was all Ballard needed. He fired Neilson for good.

During Neilson's two years, two critical trades were made that hurt Toronto's chances to improve. First, Randy Carlyle and George Ferguson were traded to Pittsburgh for Dave Burrows, a move initiated by Neilson after Carlyle had violated curfew one night. While it was important to establish discipline, Neilson went a little too far, especially considering what the Leafs got out of Burrows. Neilson too often expected the players' every breath to be hockey, as his was, and he had little sympathy for those who wanted a break now and then. Violating curfew merited some form of punishment, but trading an important part of the team's future for one minor, irresponsible evening was itself irresponsible.

Second, on March 13, 1978, Jim Gregory traded Errol Thompson along with the Leafs' 1st- and 2nd-round draft picks in 1978 and their 1st in 1980 to Detroit for Dan Maloney and a 2nd-round pick in '80.** Neilson and Gregory felt that the team needed more toughness up front, a questionable assessment at best. In Thompson, Toronto had a great scorer, a speedy left-winger, and a perfect linemate for Sittler and McDonald. In Maloney, they got a grinder and a leader, but not much talent. To trade one-for-one to get Maloney would have been bad enough, but including three high draft choices went a long way to contributing to the demise of the team.

The season's-end bloodletting did not end with the dismissal of Neilson. Ballard also fired GM Gregory, who had been with the Leafs since 1959 (before that he had worked at Conn Smythe's gravel pit). Earlier in the year, just days before Christmas 1978, Ballard cut the salary of chief scout Bob Davidson by two-thirds, in effect forcing the 66-year-old to quit. Davidson began his Leaf life in 1934. He played 12 years with the Leafs, two as captain, coached the Marlies for a year, and was the team's chief scout for forever (27 years, to be exact). Forty-five years with Toronto and forced to leave just before Christmas! Ballard a "class" act? Only if you take off the first two letters.

Almost immediately, Gregory became Director of the NHL's Central Scouting Bureau. His first move was to hire Davidson. All's well that ends well, so long as it wasn't at Maple Harold Gardens.

---

* The '78–'79 playoffs had a total of 11 overtime games. In all those games, one penalty, that to Williams, was called.

** Detroit used these draft picks to select Brent Peterson (1st round in '78) and Al Jensen (2nd round in '78), and Mike Blaisdell (1st in '80). The Leafs got Craig Muni in the 2nd round in 1980.

HOCKEY HALL OF FAME

V

Imlach Returns

"And then came Punch and Friends. Life, as we had known it with the Toronto Maple Leafs, came to an end."
— Darryl Sittler

The second coming of Punch Imlach was torrential madness, a downpour of insanity and unrestricted bedlam unmatched even in the '80s. It was destructive, hellish, and insufferable. It was the most tumultuous two years under Ballard or anyone else in the history of the franchise. What actually occurred on the ice was by far the least important, and to many the least interesting, aspect of the hockey club.

Ballard had big plans after he fired Neilson. He was going to go after the best available coach and GM come hell or high water. He sounded convincing, but then Ballard always talked a good game and then hell or high water always arrived. His shortlist consisted of Scotty Bowman and Don Cherry, admirable men both according to their achievements and reputation. However, Bowman would agree to come to Toronto only as GM, and he wanted the power to hire the coach and run the whole hockey organization. Acceding to such a stipulation would have rendered Ballard's presence redundant, and this was far more important a consideration than the success and welfare of the hockey team. Bowman instead went to Buffalo, where his every wish was granted. His first order of business was to hire Neilson as coach, a royal slap in the face that left clear finger marks on Ballard's left cheek for a long time after. Cherry wanted to come to Toronto, he *really, really* wanted to come, but Ballard dithered away the opportunity, hemming and hawing while Colorado wooed Grapes, his dog Blue, wife Rose, and collars high to the Rockies. The day after Grapes accepted the American offer, Ballard made his pitch.

So Harold craned his neck back, way way way back, to a time that "was," not "is," to a place that looked the same but wasn't, to a hero who had used up his glory a score of seasons ago. He called George Imlach, the very Punch who had brought four Cups to Toronto in the '60s but who had been canned by the Sabres December 4, 1978, after eight years of acrimony between himself, the owners, and the players. Imlach agreed to return under one condition: he wanted complete control of all hockey operations (everyone seemed to want this). Unlike Bowman, Punch got his way, and on July 4, 1979, he

began his relentless march into the past as the Leafs' new/old General Manager. He promptly hired Floyd Smith as coach and Dick Duff as assistant, and it became clearer and clearer with the passage of each day they were as much coaches as puppets are flesh and blood.

The retrieval of Imlach from hockey's archives was foolish and ill-timed, coming as it did after two excellent seasons with a sophisticated, modern-day coach named Neilson. Such were the edicts laid down by coach Imlach (er, check that — GM Imlach), such was the atmosphere he strove to establish, that the start of training camp plunged the players into a time warp, making them feel they were competing for jobs with Syl Apps, Terry Sawchuk, and George Armstrong. He instituted a jacket-and-tie dress code that had to be adhered to at *all* times. If you were a player living in, say, Scarborough, and wanted a bottle of milk from the corner store on a Saturday morning, you wore a jacket and tie to get it or you stayed home and drank water. (Although this seemed an easy rule to circumvent, with Punch you felt like he'd be the guy in the corner store just waiting to catch you.) He took the telephone out of the dressing room so players had to make all calls through the switchboard. He removed the gym equipment and dismantled the weight room, saying, "You don't need that stuff; we didn't have it when we won the Cup in '67." Punch, you see, came from a time when players would report to camp a little heavy and skate their way into shape. His was also a time when bread was a quarter a loaf, Pearson prime minister, and Eglinton the last stop north on the subway. He scheduled practices at peak rush hours in the morning and afternoon. That way the players would have to drive to and from the Gardens in traffic, thus appreciating all the more — to follow Punch's logic — their privileged social position. Then the ping-pong table was taken out of the change room. On road trips players would *not* have regular roommates because this tried-and-true travel ritual apparently encouraged cliques. During intermissions of games, Leafs would *not* be available for interviews. On non-game nights curfew was 10:30.

On the surface, the resulting tension appeared to derive simply from two different points of view. The GM wanted to establish discipline, a concept undeniably essential to the conduct and integrity of players representing the Toronto Maple Leafs hockey club and also important for developing a disciplined effort on the ice. This is exactly what Neilson had done, differently and successfully, and with the players' blessings. The players, though, believed Imlach's moves were not so much about discipline as simply power. Imlach established rules because he *could*, because they were *his*, and *he* was the boss. These rules weren't intended to help the team with hockey games, but to establish the difference between those who gave orders and those who obeyed them. The master/slave school for hockey.

Neilson had focused on each player as an individual. He was interested only in getting the most out of them, and he made each

player feel important, motivating him to strive to do better, to work for the betterment of himself and the team. That meant strategy, practise, diet, weight training, social habits, everything.

Imlach, however, made *himself* the focus. Players worked for Imlach. He was the boss, the heart of the team. The players were merely hired by the club, just like the secretaries, ticket sellers, and maintenance men. To this end, Imlach concocted a rule that he typed on a sheet of paper and expected all the players to sign. It read: "Anyone who does anything that is contrary to good hockey discipline may be fined or suspended." This nebulous law could be applied to anything Punch wished. It was subject to interpretation and was as open-ended as the Macdonald–Cartier Freeway. The players refused to sign, citing NHLPA guidelines. By so doing they struck a nerve with Punch. The war was on. Imlach, the great Eagle-hater, was immersed in a Leaf team that had 14 Eagleson-represented players, foremost among whom were McDonald (team representative) and Sittler (league vice-president). They were not about  to be bullied into signing something that had little to do with team discipline, spirit, or morale, let alone winning hockey games.

"Showdown in the NHL." Those words, spoken each week by Dick Irvin, were magic to any kid's ears on a Saturday night on the CBC in the late '70s. "Showdown" was an intermission feature that pitted the league's top players against each other in various skills competitions: shooting accuracy, passing, penalty shots, three-on-three games. It was so much fun to watch, so novel. The players clearly enjoyed themselves, yet tried their best. The camaraderie you saw with what you thought were players from enemy teams left you in awe. How could they be so friendly on "Showdown," yet so competitive during games? The skills displayed at such high speeds during games were slowed down, so you could see that that amazing shot really was accurate, that speed was not deceptive but real, those passes brutally quick and hard and right on the mark. The segment was an ingenious way to fill those quarter-hour rests the players needed between periods.

Imlach hated it. But then again he hated the '76 Canada Cup. He said such nonsense non-club events put the team's star players needlessly at risk.* At camp in 1979, he challenged Sittler and Palmateer on this point. Both had been invited to compete in "Showdown," but Imlach told them not to participate. Of course,

---

* In fact, Borje Salming had broken his finger at a previous "Showdown" taping.

he knew he couldn't actually tell them not to go because "Showdown" was approved by both the NHL and the NHLPA. It was simply a petty, personal dislike all his own. He told Sittler that as team captain he had an obligation to be loyal to his team first. To risk injury for fun and money was selfish.

Sittler was captain. To Punch, that meant he was the connection between management and players, but his allegiance was to *management*. Sittler, however, saw himself as captain of the *team*. He was the leader of the *players* and VP of the NHLPA. His loyalty was to his teammates, and his job was to clarify and represent the team's feelings when management came calling. To him, representing the team at "Showdown" was a prestigious — in a fun sort of way — responsibility. He was one of the league's All-Stars.

Imlach had successfully talked Danny Gare and Gil Perreault out of taking part in "Showdown" for Buffalo a couple of years earlier.* But Sittler was adamant, and he had the league and the union's backing. Ballard and Imlach actually issued a court injunction to Sittler and Palmateer to prevent them from participating in "Showdown," but the motion was summarily dismissed and the two took part. League President John Zeigler then fined Ballard $10,000 for interfering.

Ballard played his trump card. He refused to allow "Showdown" to be shown from all games broadcast out of the Gardens. Because advertisers wanted to buy commercial time only for the lucrative southern Ontario market, "Showdown" disappeared and CSN, the production company, went bankrupt, the unfortunate victim of a Ballard power play. For the millions of viewers, intermissions reverted to the drab old format. For the fat cat in his bunker, it was a sweet victory.

Before the Leafs had played even a single game under Imlach, one thing became clear: Sittler was the target. He was the bull's-eye at which Imlach was forever aiming his managerial arrow. But while Imlach had the captain lined up, he had three problems to overcome. First, Sittler was captain for good reason; he was immensely liked by the players and recognized as a premier player in the league. Second, he was as popular a Leaf in Toronto and coast-to-coast as any who had ever worn the blue and white. Third, he had a no-trade clause in his contract. Needless to say, Punch could handle the first two problems; the third was not so soluble.

In November, Imlach put both Sittler and McDonald on recallable waivers, a bush-league move that served to let all other general managers know quickly and not quietly that he was ready to trade *anybody*, including his stars. It was a cheap and malicious prank

---

* Imlach's logic was also much the same as what he used to remove Jim Schoenfeld, whom he hated, as captain. Imlach suggested Schoenfeld resign his leadership because the team's incoming coach, Marcel Pronovost, should have free reign to decide who the players' leader would be.

intended to aggravate and insult the two players. As such, it worked, but how it could help the team win games was beyond comprehension.

The saga continued. In December, Sittler raised the ire of Ballard by publicly embarrassing him at a press conference. Ballard stood before microphones and strobe lights to announce that the Leafs would play a game against the Canadian Olympic team in February with all proceeds going to Ronald McDonald House. The problem was that Ballard hadn't consulted the players. The game was to be played just before the All-Star Game, a hectic time in the league schedule. For those Leafs who would play in the Annual Festival of Talent it meant playing four games in five nights, a cruel stretch at the best of times.

The players asked for a trade-off; they would play the Olympic game if Ballard would schedule a game with the Russians the next year. Ballard scoffed at the mere suggestion and went ahead with the charity announcement without resolving the players' concerns. During the press conference — *Ballard's* press conference — Sittler told reporters the Leafs would not play the game. Ballard was livid. He felt betrayed by the team, Sittler in particular. The war was in full swing.

A few days later, Christmas Eve, 1979, the decimation began in earnest. Imlach sent Pat Boutette to Hartford for Bob Stephenson. Stephenson disappeared almost before he got to the Gardens, while Boutette had a number of fine statistical years with the Whalers and Penguins. But the real reason for the trade lay in Boutette's popularity with the players — particularly Sittler. His loss was measured not on the scoresheet but in the team chemistry, the imbalance of which was felt immediately.

Three days later all hell broke loose. Imlach gave away Lanny McDonald and Joel Quenneville to Colorado for Wilf Paiement and Pat Hickey, a move predicated entirely on malice. Since Imlach couldn't trade Sittler, he was intent on doing the next worst thing — trading the captain's best friends. The uproar was immediate. Fans protested and thrust placards in the air outside the Gardens that night:

BAD PUNCH SPOILS A PARTY

KICK PUNCH'S FANNY FOR TRADING LANNY

TRADE PUNCH BEFORE HE DESTROYS THE LEAFS

LANNY PLEASE COME BACK AND KICK OUT KOJAK

Newspaper headlines were equally volatile: GRUMBLING AT GARDENS OVER MCDONALD, announced the *Globe*; the *Sunday Sun* flashed simply the words A SHOCKER!; the *Star* had STORM HITS LEAF LOCKER ROOM AFTER MCDONALD TOLD OF TRADE, and LANNY'S QUICK EXIT SHOCKS THE FANS: 'STUPID, DUMB, CRAZY' IS REACTION TO BALLARD'S LATEST 'ALMIGHTY BUCK' DEAL.

Moments before the game that night, Sittler resigned as captain of the team, ripping the "C" off his jersey in protest of both the trade and the way he had been treated since Imlach's arrival (Tiger Williams became interim captain). Afterwards, Sittler provided the following press release to explain his action:

> I have tried to handle my duties as captain in an honest and fair manner. I took player complaints to management, and discussed management ideas with players.
>
> At the start of this season I was personally sued by my own hockey team management. I was told it was nothing personal. I explained my position to Mr. Imlach and Mr. Ballard at this time. I told them that I felt a captain's role was to work with players and management, not just with management.

SITTLER GOES AWOL

Sittler's stock hits new high

Like Big M, Leafs' Rookie Sittler Wears No. 27 In Bid To Win Stardom

Punch ruining us, Leafs say

Darryl Sittler rewrites record book

Sittler denied an invitation to Leaf camp

Taking dive: Defenceman Ian Turnbull of Leafs trips over goalie Murray Bannerman of Black Hawks during first period of game last night in Chicago. Leafs' captain Darryl Sittler got plenty of ice time and sparked his club to 6-3 victory with three goals as Toronto snapped four-game losing streak.

Darryl Sittler's old form puts Leafs back on rails

Sittler, Palmateer to defy Leafs' Showdown ban

Mr. Ballard and Mr. Imlach made some negative comments about me and my teammates some weeks ago and I met them to discuss it. I was told I was being too sensitive.

I have had little or no contact with Mr. Imlach and it is clear to me that he and I have different ideas about player and management communication.

I have recently been told that management has prevented me from appearing on *Hockey Night in Canada* telecasts. I am spending more and more time on player/management problems, and I don't feel I am accomplishing enough for my teammates.

The war between Mr. Eagleson and Mr. Imlach should not overshadow the most important matter — the Toronto Maple Leafs.

I am totally loyal to the Toronto Maple Leafs. I don't want to let my teammates down. But I have to be honest with myself. I will continue to fight for players' rights, but not as captain of the team.

All I want to do is give all my energy and all my ability to my team as a player.

Imlach could not possibly have predicted the public backlash over the trade and ensuing resignation. Although he never wanted Sittler to be captain in the first place, he certainly didn't want him *not* to be captain in this way. In an effort to stem the tide of violent negative publicity, he tried to get Sittler to go on a vacation with his family for a few days. Sittler saw the move for the ruse it was (get Sittler out of town, calm the natives, restore order, win the fans over by painting Sittler as the culprit . . .) and refused.

Two weeks later a group of players was at Delaney's, a popular neighbourhood bar, enjoying a round after practice. Dave Hutchison was called to the phone and was told by Imlach at the other end that he'd been given a one-way cab chit to YYZ. He was off to Chicago in exchange for Pat Ribble. Nothing for something. Again. He went back to the table and the players began playing darts using a picture of Imlach's face as the target. Sittler later wrote: "It was a circus, a soap opera. . . . Would this season from hell ever end?"

By this time, everyone and his dog could see Imlach was out of control, a malfunctioning martinet running amok. Even Ballard was beginning to tire of his new powerlessness and Punch's headline-grabbing, power-motivated antics (this was Hal's job, after all). In February 1980, Imlach made his only acceptable trade of the 16 he concocted in two years: Tiger Williams and Jerry Butler to Vancouver for Rick Vaive and Bill Derlago. Of course Vaive would go on to great things in the vacuum called the '80s, but after the trade Sittler looked utterly vulnerable. Gone were his best friends McDonald, Williams, Boutette, and Hutchison. The team he once captained was no longer recognizable. It had no spirit, no passion, no character, no fire.

Everything about Sittler had an eerie similarity to Frank Mahovlich's situation in the mid-'60s. Both men wore number 27, a possibly trivial fact to most people but not necessarily so to the very superstitious Imlach. Was it a coincidence that in his eight years in Buffalo no regular player wore 27, but his favourite "lucky" number 11 was worn by his (and the franchise's) first-ever draft choice, Gil Perreault? In his glory days he gave the number 11 to rookie Ron Ellis in 1964 and the following year gave it to his new rookie Brit Selby for good luck (Ellis almost won the Calder Trophy; Selby did). Sittler and Mahovlich were both the most popular figures in the city during their years. They were excellent team players and well-liked. Strangely, the night of the 1980 All-Star game in Detroit, Wings owner Bruce Norris offered to pay Sittler $1 million if the Leafs could get him to agree to a trade, much as Bruce's father Jim had offered in Chicago for the Big M 18 years earlier. Furthermore, by

this time, Sittler was in a state of clinical depression and his doctor suggested he take some time off. Sittler refused, but couldn't avoid a smile at the irony of the similarity of his emotional state to Mahovlich's.

In another attempt to structure the team his way and resuscitate the 1960s, Punch enlisted the services of three washed-up defencemen — Darryl Maggs, Larry Carrière, and Carl Brewer — to get that all-important "experience" on the blueline, just like he did in 1967. The moves were both a failure and an embarrassment, a further indication that Punch simply didn't have "it," that magical hockey sense that makes all uncertainties good, all possibly's definitely's, all chances sure things.

On Friday, March 14, Floyd Smith was driving to St. Catharines to attend a friend's birthday party when he got into a serious accident in which two people were killed. Smith sustained a fractured knee cap and Dick Duff had to take over puppet duties behind the bench. He lost the only two games he coached, 8–4 to the Rangers and 5–1 to the Flames (the Atlanta version). Imlach then brought in Joe Crozier, a man he had known for years, first as a coach in the Leaf farm system in the '50s and '60s, then in Buffalo as the man who replaced him after he suffered a heart attack, and finally as the Leafs' current minor league coach in Moncton. Another Imlach ally, Crozier would make sure the club continued to spiral downward. As with his predecessors, Joe's every move was plotted carefully by Imlach. His first game as coach was significant, not because the team beat the Jets 9–1 but because Sittler scored a goal with the team *two* men short, the only time a Leaf has ever done this and just about the only memorable on-ice event during Crow's time behind the bench.

As with all mistakes, it takes a while for them to realize their full impact. Considering how much the team changed under Imlach, the Leafs' record for '79–'80 was only six points worse than the year before. They even won one more game:

		W–L–T	GF	GA	PTS
(Gregory/Neilson)	1978–79	34–33–13	267	252	81
(Imlach/Smith, Duff, Crozier)	1979–80	35–40–5	304	327	75

The team finished 11th overall (of 21 teams) but dead last in goals against, using the rare five-goalie system of Palmateer, Paul Harrison, Jiri Crha, Vincent Tremblay, and Curt Ridley. An even bigger part of the problem was that the Leafs used 10 defencemen during the course of the year: Maggs, Brewer, Carrière, Salming, Turnbull, Dave Burrows, Greg Hotham, Richard Mulhern, Dave Farrish, and Bob Stephenson. No rhythm or partner development could possibly

be established with so many comings and goings. The result was defensive-zone chaos.

On the bright side, the many Sittler trade rumours that had been growing more and more numerous abated during his great finish. Over the last half of the year he was second in scoring only to Wayne Gretzky, making his value to the team indisputable once again.

The team finished third of four teams in the Adams Division and their first-round opponent in the playoffs was the Minnesota North Stars. For the opening game, Punch thought he'd go back to the good ol' days for a little strategy by starting five defencemen. The players looked dumbstruck when told of the plan. Burrows played left wing, Salming right, Carrière centre. Minnesota managed to recover from this opening-faceoff Trojan horse play by winning 6–3. The Stars followed up with a 7–2 win the next night and shook hands in the Gardens after a 4–3 result 48 hours later to sweep the best of five 3–0. So much for the '60s playing the '80s. Everything old is old again.

That summer was further proof that Imlach was out of control. It started when he and Ballard declared Sittler a "cancer" to the team. In the training camp media guide for the upcoming year (September 1980), Sittler's name was not even on the roster, implying none too subtly that he'd be traded by then. Imlach was also upset by Palmateer's contract negotiations and was leery of the goalie's wonky knees. He felt the young Czech Jiri Crha had acquitted himself well enough part-time the previous season and could do Palmy's job for much less money (even though he couldn't handle the puck to save his life and if he ever straightened up he'd knock the goal off its moorings, so close to the goal line did he play the angles). Rather than work out a deal, Imlach traded Palmateer and a 3rd-round pick in June (Torrie Robertson) to Washington for Tim Coulis, Robert Picard, and the Caps' 2nd-rounder in '80 (Bob McGill). Crha went on to play one whole season with the team, coughing up more than four goals a game, before clearing waivers and signing with Bayreuth in Germany, the Wagnerian hockey capital of Europe and on a skill par with shinny hockey at Moss Park Arena in downtown Toronto.

Imlach was equally testy about the demands Borje Salming was making that summer, about 400,000 of them per year. He travelled to Sweden with the express purpose of signing Salming, but offered a much smaller figure in light of what Imlach thought was a too common Salming practice of falling on the ice and being on for too many goals against. He returned to Toronto without Salming's signature, and Ballard was furious that his favourite hockey son had not had the hem of his contract kissed.

On August 26, Imlach suffered a heart attack. He was in the hospital and out of the Leaf picture, and Ballard could not have been happier. He quickly assumed the mantle of GM as if it were second nature, signing Salming to a brand spanking new five-year contract for $325,000 a year, and then making up with Sittler who agreed to accept the role of captain once again. Crozier was appointed coach

full-time, although not, as things turned out, for a long-time.

Training camp was relatively calm without Imlach, and the season began in sublime peace. But the players detested Crozier, who was cut from Imlach's cloth, and by January 1981 they were playing themselves out of a playoff spot. Imlach was back in charge and suggested ditching Crozier for either Doug Carpenter (the New Brunswick farm team coach) or Mike Nykoluk (recently fired as an assistant by the Flyers). Ballard agreed, but even while Imlach was interviewing and assessing the suitability of the two men, Harold declared to the media that Crozier's job was safe for the season. As he explained to a livid Punch: "You know me. I had to say something to them so I told them the exact opposite of what we're doing." It was up to Imlach, after an horrific 8–2 home loss that very night to the Jets, to fire Crozier.

At about this same time, Punch was performing another classic Imlach manoeuvre by getting rid of Ron Ellis, the only player left from Punch's '67 team. One of the classiest players ever to skate in the NHL, Ellis cleared waivers and was told by Punch either to report to the farm club or retire. Meanwhile, Nykoluk, at Ballard's insistence, replaced Crozier. Nykoluk resembled nothing so much as an innocuous silent movie villain, always bumbling, always caught in the final scene. He had the temerity to use Ellis for three games; Imlach reacted by tearing the nameplate from Ellis' locker, leaving him behind on the next road trip, and releasing him outright a few days later. A proud and honourable man, Ellis had played 1,034 games in the NHL, all in a Leaf uniform, yet was forced to retire under insulting conditions.

The team made the playoffs on the final night of the year by beating Quebec 4–2 at the Colisée, giving them 71 points, one more than Washington. A week later, after being shelled 9–2, 5–1, and 6–2 by the soon-to-be dynastic Islanders, the season was over, the destruction complete. Eliminated by Toronto three years earlier, the Islanders were moving in the opposite direction to the Leafs. Even Sittler, ever the optimist during this time of overt pessimism, conceded that he "had lost faith in the ability of the Toronto Maple Leafs hockey team to compete."

So, too, had Ballard. The return of Imlach had not been a phoenix rising but rather a mummy taken out of its sarcophagus and propped up behind the Leaf bench. To make matters worse, Ballard had given Punch a three-year contract, which meant there was, technically, one more year of hell to endure. But the problem solved itself when, in September 1981, just before the start of the season, Imlach suffered his second heart attack within a year. This one was more serious and Imlach required a life-saving triple bypass to survive. Ballard never went to see him in the hospital, and, too much the coward to fire him, took the opportunity to "de-hire" him as he had Red Kelly. A few weeks later, on radio station CFRB, host Bill Stephenson questioned Ballard about his methods after Ballard had casually commented

that Punch had "made up his mind not to come back" as General Manager.

> STEPHENSON: It's been my understanding that Punch wanted to come back and you said, no, he could not come back.

> BALLARD: Oh, that is true in one sense . . . but he's had three heart attacks, new plumbing put in his heart. How can a guy come back and be General Manager?

After he was released from hospital, Imlach went to the Gardens assuming he'd resume his GM duties, only to see his parking spot gone. The Second Coming of Punch Imlach was over.

Imlach destroyed the better part of a decade's worth of Jim Gregory's work. While Gregory made some weak deals, he also built up an organization decimated by expansion, the WHA, and Ballard himself, to produce a club with a great nucleus of players: McDonald, Sittler, Williams, Salming, Turnbull, Palmateer. A simple comparison of two rosters, the first showing the team before Punch took over, the second the 1981 roster that Punch created, indicates the carnage left from the Two Years' War:

Spring 1979	*Fall 1981*
John Anderson	John Anderson
Pat Boutette	Normand Aubin
Jerry Butler	Jim Benning
Dave Burrows	Fred Boimistruck
Ron Ellis	Laurie Boschman
Paul Gardner	Jiri Crha
Paul Harrison	Bill Derlago
Pierre Hamel	Stewart Gavin
Dave Hutchison	Bob Manno
Jimmy Jones	Pat Hickey
Dan Maloney	Mike Kaszycki
Lanny McDonald	Michel Larocque
Walt McKechnie	Dan Maloney
Garry Monahan	Bob McGill
Mike Palmateer	Craig Muni
Joel Quenneville	Wilf Paiement
Rocky Saganiuk	Bob Parent
Borje Salming	Barry Melrose
Darryl Sittler	René Robert
Lorne Stamler	Rocky Saganiuk
Ian Turnbull	Borje Salming
Dave Williams	Darryl Sittler
Ron Wilson	Vincent Tremblay
	Ian Turnbull
	Rick Vaive
	Gary Yaremchuk
	Terry Martin

The loss of talent and chemistry in just two years was the work of a reckless, power-hungry man who thought least of all about on-ice performance, who traded irresponsibly and never got near full value for what he traded away. Although Imlach did establish a CHL franchise in Cincinnati, his drafting proved as impotent as his managing was arcane:

1980	1981
25 – Craig Muni	6 – Jim Benning
26 – Bob McGill	24 – Gary Yaremchuk
43 – Fred Boimistruck	55 – Ernie Godden
74 – Stewart Gavin	90 – Normand LeFrançois
95 – Hugh Larkin	102– Barry Brigley
116 – Ron Dennis	132 – Andrew Wright
137 – Russ Adam	153 – Richard Turmel
158 – Fred Perlini	174 – Greg Barber
179 – Darwin McCutcheon	195 – Marc Magnan
200 – Paul Higgins	

In 1980 Imlach chose Muni 25th overall, but gave a pass on Jarri Kurri (69th, Edmonton), Steve Larmer (120th, Chicago), Bernie Nicholls (73rd, L.A.), Craig Ludwig (61st, Montreal), and Don Beaupré (38th, Minnesota). In 1981 the Leafs chose 6th and could have selected Grant Fuhr (8th Edmonton), Al MacInnis (15th Calgary), Chris Chelios (40th Montreal), Mike Vernon (56th Calgary), James Patrick (9th Rangers), John Vanbiesbrouck (72nd Rangers), or Steve Smith (111th Edmonton). But Imlach *loved* Jim Benning: "He's a very smart offensive hockey player and frankly, if he develops as he should, he might be the best defenceman Toronto has ever come up with." Benning averaged fewer than six goals and 33 points over a nine-year career with the Leafs and Vancouver. Frankly, he was *not* the best defenceman the Leafs ever came up with.

Typical of Imlach's out-of-touchness with the reality of '80s hockey was the time he talked trade with Pittsburgh in November 1980. He agreed to part with Dave Burrows and Paul Gardner and was given a list of five Penguins by GM Baz Bastien from which to choose two to complete the deal. He consulted with Gord Stellick, "Assistant to Leaf Hockey Club" according to the Toronto media guide and whose work was in a capacity nowhere near important enough to merit consultation. Imlach then referred to the Pittsburgh media guide to decide on Kim Davis and Paul Marshall, who together played a total of 25 games with the Leafs and managed six points.

On another occasion during practice, Imlach had "lanes" painted on the ice for the wingers. These lanes went from one red line to the other, were about ten feet from the sideboards, and indicated the

area wingers had to stay in. This was a drill Toronto was practising while the Edmonton Oilers were whirling and circling and free-wheeling around Punch's linear '60s approach, leaving the Leafs dizzy from skill overdose.

Much later Imlach said of Ballard: "He was far from being the world's greatest at picking hockey players himself, or keeping good ones he had, yet he always had the final say." Almost always. For two years Punch had the final say. He left behind him a team that had a record of 20–44–16 in 1981–82 with the players he acquired through trades and drafts, and those 56 points did not even get the Leafs into the playoffs. They ended up dead last again in goals against, third last in points behind every WHA and expansion team except Colorado — teams that were not even in existence when Punch coached the Cup-winning Leafs in the '60s.

The Fourth Act was ended.

Exit Punch Imlach. Enter Harold Ballard and Attendants.

VI

Deliver Us from Evil:
The Death of Ballard

Harold Ballard was not just a person; he was a jurisdiction, a world, a place you entered on his terms, with his permission. He issued the passports and he could deport you any time he wished. You abided by his decrees, adhered to his laws, lived always in the shadow of his sun. He was whimsical and totalitarian, and often decided whether or not he liked you based on the strangest, pettiest things. This "like" was your birth certificate, the thing that decided your fate and employability in Ballardville. Without it, you were forced into exile.

GRAIG ABEL

With Imlach's passport freshly revoked, Ballard was back in control for the '81–'82 season, one which produced a revolting 20 wins over seven months and 80 games. In December, after going without a general manager for the better part of half a year, Ballard hired Gerry McNamara to fill the void. The move could not have been worse. McNamara quickly established his desire to coddle Ballard's

ego rather than build a solid hockey team. He recognized that cheapness was the finest attribute a Leaf GM could possess and went about demonstrating that attribute with all his energy.

He participated only once in the annual October waiver draft (taking Jeff Brubaker in 1984) because it featured older players with often large contracts. Skill was not a consideration. Other teams saw the draft as an opportunity to pick up a valuable role player or two. In 1982, for instance, New Jersey claimed Carol Vadnais and Dave Hutchison. In '83 the Whalers took Mike Zuke, Mike Crombeen, and Bob Crawford. The next year, Pittsburgh scooped up Wayne Babych; the Oilers got Billy Carroll and Terry Martin (from the Leafs), and Hartford Wally Weir and Dave Lumley. In 1986, Buffalo got Clark Gillies and Wilf Paiement; Los Angeles acquired Bob Bourne. Talent was available — it just had to be sought out.

McNamara considered scouting the bane of his duties. Even though the Leafs had the smallest scouting staff in the NHL, he disliked actually going to games to assess talent. As a result, the Leafs were the joke of the league and had to rely heavily upon the Central Bureau's scouting reports to decide the skill, calibre, and NHL potential of players. McNamara's drafting reflected his unpardonable laziness and virtual ignorance of promising juniors.

His relationship with the media was a public relations disaster and merely exacerbated an already strained situation (a losing hockey club). While the media sensationalized everything McNamara did or said, he didn't help his own cause. The occasional intelligent transaction, for example, would surely have silenced his critics, but in fact, the trades he made were woeful. He also had a knack for saying the wrong thing at the wrong time, appearing more a parody of a GM than the real thing. To take him seriously was very difficult.

To compound his problems, McNamara was in the midst of highly unusual legal action. On June 21, 1980, while driving on Elmhurst Road near his home in Etobicoke, he was sideswiped by another car. He suffered a fractured skull and claimed that because his "brain got bruised in the accident" he could no longer work to the fullest of his ability! Other symptoms he suffered from included speech impediment, recurring fatigue, and neck pains. He filed a $1,050,000 lawsuit, which raised obvious questions about his ability to manage the Leafs. Surely Ballard could have found a more suitable candidate, one who could have expanded the scouting staff or performed the double duty of scout and GM simultaneously. As the Leafs continued to lose and McNamara became more and more belligerent with reporters, his brain litigation became an easy target, a metaphor for his ineptitude as GM. On November 23, 1984, he won $110,000 in an out-of-court settlement, but he was forever ridiculed for having proven he was brain-damaged.

By December 1981, Darryl Sittler was once again concerned about his future with the team. It was two years since McDonald had been traded, but the situation hadn't changed much. Imlach was gone but

the owner wasn't, and one incident in particular renewed Sittler's antipathy toward Ballard. Ballard started to malign rookie centre Laurie Boschman, who had rediscovered the values of Christianity during the first part of the year. Ballard publicly admonished Boschman, saying the religion thing was interfering with his play and a demotion to the minors was inevitable. Sittler was dumbfounded by the insensitivity of remarks which obviously hurt Boschman deeply.

Furthermore, for the first time Sittler saw money as a real issue that needed to be addressed. Pat Hickey and Wilf Paiement, the two Rockies who came to Toronto in the McDonald trade, were each making more than $200,000, and Ballard had just given Salming a five-year deal at $325,000. Sittler, in his 12th year as a Leaf and seventh as captain, was making $175,000 and wanted a new contract that reflected his relative importance to the team and indicated a show of support from the owner. Neither was forthcoming. (Déjà vu? See Keon.) Instead, Ballard suggested it was time Sittler move on, and the captain resignedly agreed. Sittler gave two names — Philadelphia and Minnesota — as places he'd be willing to go.

Two weeks passed. Nothing happened. Then Sittler added Buffalo and the Islanders to his list. Still nothing. After making a few calls himself, he discovered that McNamara was asking the moon for the captain. While Sittler could understand the Leafs' reluctance to "give" him away, he knew at this rate he'd never be traded. On January 5, 1982, he left the team, citing doctor's orders as a result of stress and exhaustion. (Déjà vu? See the Big M.) After much greatness and heartache, he had breathed his last as a Toronto Maple Leaf.

The very next day, Ballard announced that Rick Vaive, at the ripe young age of 22, would become the 14th captain of the Leafs, a move purposefully made to insult Sittler, saying, in effect that his leadership skills were immediately replaceable. That Vaive was inexperienced didn't matter to Ballard. What mattered was that he slap Sittler in the face fast and hard (four years later, Vaive stayed out late one night, slept in the next morning and missed practice, and was stripped of his captaincy).

Two weeks after Sittler's walkout, McNamara made a deal with Keith Allen in Philadelphia: Sittler for Rich Costello, a 2nd-round pick in '82, and future considerations. It was one of the worst trades ever made by the Leafs. Costello scored two goals in 12 games over two years before being bought out. The draft choice turned out to be Peter Ihnacak, who lasted a little more than seven seasons and scored 102 goals in a very modest career, while the future considerations was Ken Strong, a left-winger who played 15 games over three seasons (two goals, four points, six penalty minutes) before disappearing. In Sittler the Leafs gave up what the team once stood for — pride, character, class. In return, they got filler.

The drafting of Ihnacak was no accident. In 1982, McNamara thought Czechoslovakia was the undiscovered hotbed of the '80s

that Sweden had been in the '70s. Incredibly, he was right, only he didn't have any scouts there to determine who was worth drafting. In the same year he also selected Vladimir Ruzicka (73rd overall), Eduard Uvira (87th), and Peter's brother Miroslav Ihnacak (171st), but the master plan never produced a Salming/Hammarstrom ending. The Leafs spent $850,000 to get Miroslav out of Czechoslovakia and into Toronto's blue and white, even though McNamara had never seen him play, never seen him skate, never seen a picture of him skating, never seen him hold a hockey stick or even pack an equipment bag. Leaf fans didn't, either. Miroslav scored eight goals before being released outright in 1988. The Czechs-ercise was concluded. Everybody went home.

McNamara appeared to understand little about handling player movement. Time after time young players were forced to join the Leafs before they had developed, and when they didn't show immediate talent, they were traded. By then, the youngster was a veteran of four or five years and was able to make a solid contribution to his

Steve Thomas as a New York Islander.
DOUG MACLELLAN / HOCKEY HALL OF FAME

new team. The Leafs, in a sense, became a farm team for the rest of the league.

McNamara's first-round draft choice in 1982 was Gary Nylund (3rd overall), a big, tough, defenceman who sustained two serious knee injuries in successive seasons after joining the Leafs. But by 1986 he was turning a corner, developing into just the kind of blue-liner he was thought to have been. When he wanted a new contract with a reasonable pay increase, McNamara balked and Bob Pulford paid $140,000 to sign Nylund to a Chicago contract. The Nylund acquisition meant Chicago owed the Leafs compensation of equal player value. The Hawks offered Jerome Dupont and Ken Yaremchuk, while the Leafs asked for Ed Olczyk, obviously far too much. The arbitrator had no trouble awarding the two lesser players to the Leafs, players whose combined contracts were substantially more than what it would have cost to re-sign Nylund, a far superior player to the pair Toronto inherited.

In 1984, the Leafs made a smart move by signing Steve Thomas, a Marlie graduate who was not selected at all in the '84 entry draft. He scored 42 goals with Toronto's farm club in St. Catharines (the Saints) and was named the AHL's rookie of the year. The following September he was invited to the big camp and made the team. He had 20 goals and 57 points in 65 games with the Leafs and led the team in playoff scoring with 14 points in 10 games. He was proving that as the level of play increased, so did his performance. At 22, he was a bona fide NHL star-in-the-making. Unfortunately, he asked for a raise — from $80,000 to $125,000. McNamara offered $95,000. Thomas decided to play out his option and scored 35 times in his final year with the Leafs, a vast improvement over the year before and even further proof of his value. An agreement still could have been reached, but instead McNamara traded Thomas, Vaive, and Bob McGill to Chicago for Olczyk and Al Secord. A bomb by any other name would sound so loud.

McNamara also allowed Lee Norwood and Basil McRae to depart as free agents, but the worst case of all was Craig Muni, who left the Leafs through even more inept means. McNamara reached into his bag of skunks and offered Muni a one-year termination contract in 1985, meaning that after a year he was a free agent without compensation. The move violated the first rule of the *GM's Hockey Handbook* published by Simpleton Press: if you don't want a player, make sure you get *something* for him, even if you just trade him for future considerations or a low draft pick. McNamara let a perfectly able-bodied 24-year-old just leave. Somehow, Glen Sather found a small full-time spot for Muni on the Edmonton blueline and after helping the Oilers win the Stanley Cup in 1987, 1988, and 1990, Muni no longer looked quite so terminationable.

How Muni remained in Edmonton is an interesting example of how a *real* GM works. After signing Muni on August 18, 1986, Sather found he didn't have room to protect him in the upcoming waiver

draft. So, he made a three-way deal with Buffalo and Pittsburgh in which Scotty Bowman in Buffalo received future considerations and Eddie Johnston in Pittsburgh used Muni as future considerations from another trade he had made with Sather the year before.

The '80s were, ostensibly, a time of likes and dislikes at the Gardens. To Ballard, talent and skill were merely incidental qualities that had little to do with whether someone remained employed. His Big Like, of course, was King Clancy. They first met in 1932 (Ballard) or 1921 (Clancy) depending on whom you believed, a long enough time ago when memories were being made, not recollected. Their friendship became brotherly in the early '70s when Ballard's best friends, his wife Dorothy and associate Stafford Smythe, died at the same time as King's wife, Rae, died of cancer. Ballard affectionately called King "Mike," and their car licence plates were "MLG 001" and "MLG 002."

The reason Nykoluk, and not Carpenter, replaced Crozier in 1982 was that Ballard *liked* the former and didn't know the latter. But Nykoluk's approach was ineffective. His most famous utterance — "I just hate that word, motivation" — came to symbolize his weakness as a leader for his players and his lack of managerial power in the front office. He was Jell-o. At one point, Nykoluk asked Ballard for a second assistant coach to pair with Dan Maloney, but he made the mistake of suggesting Gary Aldcorn, the director of programming for Hockey Canada and a friend of Nykoluk's. Ballard hated Aldcorn. Then Jim Morrison, a Bruin scout, was mooted. Ballard disliked him, too. It was then discovered that Doug McKay, a 28-year-old coaching in Cortina, Italy, was available and prepared to work for a pittance. He was hired. Ballard figured it was as easy to make a Rolls-Royce using Volkswagen parts as Rolls-Royce parts.

By 1984, Ballard had had enough of his most recent Kleenex-coach and threw Nykoluk out. He picked up a new, bigger, man-size tissue named Dan Maloney who, like McKay, had little experience, and who had the same assistant-coach problems as his predecessor. Maloney wanted Walt McKechnie, but McNamara hated him and refused to hire him. Instead, Maloney got John Brophy, the Grey Ghost, whose hair was as white and pure as street-quality cocaine. Under the inexperienced tutelage of Maloney, the Leafs made their worst-ever appearance in the NHL, a 20–52–8 year that had them 61 points behind the league champion Edmonton Oilers.

Maloney and Brophy didn't like each other, so Brophy went down early the next year to coach the Saints in St. Kitts while farm coach Claire Alexander reluctantly moved beside Maloney in the Gardens. However, Brophy had made an impression on Ballard, who saw in the gruff, fierce tiger a sort of idyllic mirror-image. Ballard liked a man's man, the Hemingway type, a big, bold, brash, vulgar guy. Ballard liked a loud man who was not only not embarrassed by the decibel of his voice but proud of it. And Brophy was fearless. As a career minor leaguer, he had the reputation as a son-of-a-bitch in a

league so tough that players' children were sons-of-bitches. He liked to watch Oliver Stone's *Platoon* over and over. He'd been shot at in the minors by a deranged fan from another club — not with a stick and puck but with a gun and bullets. He'd take nothing from no one and liked players who scowled menacingly and wanted to win so badly they'd beat fans up to prove it. So when Maloney embarrassed the city again with a 25–48–7 record in '85–'86, Ballard "de-hired" him (i.e., refused to give Maloney a new contract) and brought in a man he *liked*, a man who *meant business*. John Brophy.

The short happy life of John Brophy as coach was disastrous. While he was tough as nails as a player in the Eastern League, and a hard-nosed coach in the Southern League, winning was different in the NHL. Wins in minor pro hockey were often borne of war-like chaos and manic desperation. A win in the CHL was nasty, desperate, painful, ugly. There was no time to develop talent, to gain experience, to work on a game plan or strategy. Each game was like going through a brick wall. In the NHL, winning required innovation, technique, talent, process. It was a rhythm. The smoother the surface, the easier it was to win. In the smallness of the minors, the surfaces were all hard. Winning in the NHL was more subtle, more refined. Brophy was the hard surface, the brick wall, the desperate. He was a winner much of his life, but there wasn't anything NHL about the way he did it.

However, by this time bad was looking pretty good, so when the Broph got the team to win 32 games and lose only 42 in the '86–'87 season it looked as though things were better, or at least, getting better, or at least, not getting worse. But the following season began poorly in the likes/dislikes department when Brophy made a derogatory remark to Ballard about Borje Salming, Ballard's Big Like No. 2, suggesting Salming be traded. With more than a grain of truth, Brophy argued that Salming had become good at losing, good at fighting the good fight but always losing it, at trying hard but losing, good at losing at any cost, looking good in a losing cause, losing because it was as tough to do over a decade as winning was, losing 'til the cows came home (but they never would because they were lost). Salming also fell down too often while he swept the slot with his stick, played half a dozen years too many and took 1,292 penalty minutes in a career without major penalties, leaving the team short-handed night after night. Brophy, however, didn't know how much Ballard adored Borje. For example, Ballard had arranged for Salming to win the Charlie Conacher award for community service in 1982. Salming was at times an exceptional hockey player, but in 16 years didn't so much as lick a stamp for the Cancer Society or any other charitable organization. Ballard liked Salming, and would do anything he liked for a friend.

On Monday, February 8, 1988, the front page of the *Sun* featured a picture of the certifiably brain-damaged McNamara with his dog Puck and an insert of Ballard. The headline ran MCNAMARA FIRED.

By this time, he had compiled the fifth worst GM record in the history of the game, and the worst among non-expansion incompetents:

		W–L–T	PCT.
1. Ray Miron Colorado	1976–81	73–187–60	.321
2. Max McNab Washington/New Jersey	1975–81/1983–87	224–513–109	.329
3. Jack Gordon Minnesota/Vancouver	1974–78/1985–87	130–269–59	.348
4. Larry Regan Los Angeles	1967–73	119–228–55	.364
5. Gerry McNamara Toronto	1981–88	166–302–65	.373

The anus horribilis continued his reign by replacing McNamara with Gord Stellick, a 30-year-old with a blue-Leaf heart of gold and no experience, who became the youngest General Manager in the history of the NHL. Stellick's job was without hidden burden or responsibility: "My options," he later wrote, "were simple: heed Ballard's bidding or quit." So as not to upset Stellick, Ballard let him keep the office he had had, and in a manner befitting the times turned McNamara's office into a walk-in clothes closet for himself and his companion. Stellick became most infamous for trading Russ Courtnall to Montreal for John Kordic, a trade not nearly as bad as was made out (Courtnall was not nearly as good as he thought he was), but a bad deal all the same.

MILES NADAL / HOCKEY HALL OF FAME

Shortly after Stellick's hiring, the '88–'89 season began to fall apart. After a third successive strong start under Brophy, the Leafs put together a string of lost evenings that was ensuring another 40 loss season. So Ballard told Brophy to take a month off (read "you're de-hired"). By this time Ballard must have had double pneumonia he was using so many Kleenex-coaches. Now he brought in the Chief, George Armstrong, who publicly announced he'd finish off

the year as coach out of loyalty, *not* desire. Just the man to have behind the bench for the last 47 games of the year.

The spring of 1989 also marked the end of the Marlies in Maple Leaf Gardens and Toronto, the victims of dwindling attendance and unprofitability. Established in 1926 by Frank Selke, this was the most successful team in Canadian junior hockey history, winning an unprecedented seven Memorial Cups.* More than 200 Marlies went on to play in the NHL, but the music stopped March 17 when they beat the Kingston Knights 9–4 in their final home game before just 1,318 fans. They were eliminated from the playoffs a week later four games to two by Cornwall and moved down the Queen Elizabeth Way to continue in Hamilton as the pitiful Dukes before re-establishing themselves as the Guelph Storm for the '91–'92 season. Thus fell another giant of Toronto's hockey tradition.

The mid-'80s were almost wholly without excitement. Rick Vaive became the first Leaf to score 50 goals in a year, and did it three successive times (54 in '82, 51 in '83, and 52 in '84), and Gary Leeman turned the trick in 1989–90 with 51. But there was no team benefit in these accomplishments, only personal and record-book memories. The numbers somehow made little difference when the team was playing so hopelessly and showed almost no regular season or playoff promise.

But in 1985 Wendel Clark grabbed the city by the scruff of its collective neck and pulled the fans out of their seats, voices roaring, hands clapping, eyes popping. The number one pick overall in that year's entry draft, he was a tiger shrimp from Saskatchewan who became renowned for his tough play. His personality came to personify the Leafs and his style was emblematic of the frustrations Leaf fans had fostered for years. He was a reckless, take-no-prisoners rock of a man who could have more impact on the team with one hit or fight than any Leeman or Vaive hat trick. He hit brutally, fiercely, and cleanly. He skated like most people ran: arms clenched at 90 degrees, close to his side, pushing forward with the menace and recklessness of a man hell-bent on winning. He could also fight, but it wasn't goonery; it seemed to announce that, if nothing else, *his* Leafs weren't going down easily. Maybe the team would lose, but the opponents would be lining up to see their trainer after the game.

Midway through his rookie year Clark had been in more than a dozen fights and instilled in opposition defencemen an apprehension, if not downright fear, of chasing the puck behind their own net. More than one player had found himself semi-comatose after only the slightest mishandling of the puck there, and Clark's hunting abilities along the boards and in open ice quickly brought him and his team big-league respect. His charisma, his honesty, his McDonald-growl moustache all drove the fans mad-happy with

---

* 1929, '55, '56, '64, '67, '73, '75.

GRAIG ABEL

excitement and eagerness for the next home game. There was nothing slick about his play. His wrist shot was dangerous (he didn't deke) and he skated *through* an opponent as often as around him. He charged the front of the net, scrapped for his mates, and was relentless in finishing the check. He seemed to grow a foot taller when he stepped on the ice, and his quiet determination exemplified his no-nonsense commitment to improving the fortunes of the team. He was runner-up for the Calder Trophy to Calgary's Gary Suter, a reflection itself of the Ballard influence. Because he played in Toronto, the hockey and media capital of the country, Clark should have won the award running away, but such was the hideous reputation of the franchise under Ballard that a Westerner won by a comfortable margin (230–165), capturing 35 of 60 first-place votes.

Unfortunately, the reality of Clark's size and style caught up with him. After a strong camp in August 1987 for the Canada Cup (he was one of the final cuts), Clark began to experience serious back pains which cost him 159 games over the next three years. His injury — time-consuming, frustrating, seemingly without cure — led him to seek help with a specialist in Chicago, an acupuncturist in Barrie, a British specialist in London, and a doctor at the Mayo Clinic in Minneapolis.

Unlike other '80s general managers at the Gardens, Gord Stellick knew an important player when one smacked him in the face, and no one smacked harder than Clark. When the time came to negotiate a new contract, Clark's agent Don Meehan was looking for a big raise for his star client. Stellick wanted to keep Clark, but he didn't want to look like a fool in the process and throw a pile of money away on an injury-prone player with just three years' experience. So Stellick talked to Cliff Fletcher in Calgary who suggested a contract similar to the one he had just devised for Suter: an honest base salary with generous performance clauses to augment it. Clark would be very well paid if he were healthy enough to play and the Leafs covered their financial tooshies if he weren't. For a change, Toronto kept their franchise player in the franchise.

The war cry of the '80s was always the same: teams come into Maple Leaf Gardens to play their best hockey of the season because so many of the players are from the Toronto area and want to play well before their friends and family. This was a lame excuse and spoke volumes for the character of the players on the Leafs at the time. After all, just as many Leafs were from the Toronto area but couldn't seem to play well before *their* family and friends (the thought of doing so 40 times a year seemed unfair given the opposition only had to do it two or three times). The problem was that the fans still came to the game, but the players had become comfortable trying "pretty" hard, playing, say, 30 or 40 minutes of solid hockey and doing their damnedest to make a game of it, without developing the killer instinct needed to actually win. All of the Leafs' finest players of the '80s lacked what it takes to take individual skill

and talent and use it to better the team. Vaive, Derlago, Leeman, Fergus, Anderson, Salming all had marvellous ability but never pushed themselves to excel as team players and, more important, never motivated those around them to play up to or beyond their capability. As individuals, they could go home and sleep well after a "good" defeat, but as team players they lacked the unselfish determination to contribute the hard way, by taking an extra hit, blocking a shot, backchecking, sacrificing life and limb to win.

In the '80s there was no one around to straighten out the players, the coach, or the GM. The rotting began at the top with the termite Ballard. Even years later, some of the "lowlights" from this decade are appalling to read:

Buffalo wins 14–4 at the Aud, March 19, 1981
Buffalo wins 8–2 at the Aud, January 15, 1982
Minnesota wins 9–2 at the Gardens, January 25, 1982
Islanders win 10–1 on Long Island, March 4, 1982
Winnipeg wins 10–2 at the Gardens, March 13, 1982
Winnipeg wins 7–0 in Winnipeg, March 20, 1982
Washington wins 11–2 in Washington, December 11, 1982
Detroit wins 9–2 at Joe Louis, December 23, 1983
Washington wins 8–0 at the Gardens, January 28, 1984
Philadelphia wins 7–0 at the Spectrum, February 5, 1984
Hartford wins 8–2 at the Gardens, February 18, 1984
Quebec wins 12–3 at the Gardens, October 20, 1984
Los Angeles wins 7–0 at the Great Western Forum, November 3, 1984
Minnesota wins 7–1 in Minnesota, November 21, 1984
Edmonton wins 7–1 at the Gardens, November 27, 1984
Buffalo wins 6–0 at the Aud, December 26, 1984
Edmonton wins 9–4 at the Gardens, February 19, 1985
Detroit wins 9–3 at the Gardens, March 30, 1985
Edmonton wins 7–1 at Northlands Coliseum, November 3, 1985
Pittsburgh wins 7–1 in Pittsburgh, November 27, 1985
Islanders win 9–2 at Long Island, January 28, 1986
Quebec wins 7–1 at the Gardens, October 22, 1986
Pittsburgh wins 8–3 in Pittsburgh, December 12, 1986
Edmonton wins 9–2 at Northlands Coliseum, February 18, 1987
Calgary wins 7–2 in Saddledome, February 20, 1987
Washington wins 10–2 in Washington, March 13, 1987
Montreal wins 9–4 at the Forum, March 21, 1987
Calgary wins 11–3 at the Gardens, January 25, 1988
Winnipeg wins 10–1 at the Gardens, March 5, 1988
Calgary wins 7–1 at the Saddledome, March 24, 1988
Edmonton wins 8–2 at the Gardens, December 14, 1988
Winnipeg wins 10–2 at the Gardens, March 18, 1988
Edmonton wins 9–1 at Northlands Coliseum, November 19, 1988
Los Angeles wins 9–3 at Great Western Forum, December 1, 1988
Detroit wins 8–1 at Joe Louis, January 27, 1989

Buffalo wins 7–1 at the Gardens, October 11, 1989
Rangers win 8–2 at the Gardens, March 14, 1990
Calgary wins 10–2 at the Saddledome, February 22, 1990

And those are just the final scores. On two occasions the Leafs gave up *two* shorthanded goals *on the same power play*. On January 26, 1987, the Leafs were leading the Flames 5–0 with just 14 minutes left in the game. Steve Bozek, Joey Mullen, Jim Peplinski, Joel Otto, and Mullen again scored to tie it up, and then at 1:30 of overtime Colin Patterson scored to give Calgary a 6–5 win. On April 10, 1988, Brent Ashton scored at 5:08 of the third to give Detroit an 8–0 lead over the Leafs in Game 4 of their playoff series at the Gardens — perhaps the single lowest point in the history of the franchise. Fans littered the ice with everything from popcorn boxes to jerseys as has never been seen before or since and the headline in the *Star* the next day said it all: HAPLESS LEAFS EMBARRASSED BY WINGS: FANS SHOWER GARDENS' ICE WITH DEBRIS AS DETROIT ROMPS INTO 3–1 series lead. In 1985, after yet another loss, an usher threw his jacket and tie on the ice in disgust and quit. The Leafs' record book is full of "worsts," mostly from games played in the Black Hole that was the '80s.

The team's performance also paralleled Ballard's declining health. Always active and energetic, he now had to spend an ever-increasing amount of his time in hospitals and wheelchairs, and as the media reported his various fluctuations of pulse and breath the stock market reflected a commensurate optimism. The price of Gardens shares rose.

One of Ballard's greatest skills as owner was in convincing most of the people all of the time that he was a rich man who owned the Leafs outright. He wasn't and he didn't. In 1944, he had established his own company called HEB Limited. In December 1966 the company's structure changed significantly when he divided its shares equally among his offspring, Mary Elizabeth, Bill, and Harold Jr. Of the 103 shares, each received 34, and Dorothy, Ballard's wife, got the extra one (which Harold inherited upon her death in 1969). The three children paid a nominal $10 a share, but *control* of HEBL was to be Ballard's until his death. When he solidified his position in 1972 by buying Stafford's shares, the ownership pie looked as follows:

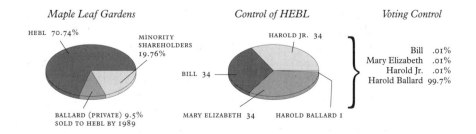

By 1980, soaring debt and increased interest payments that were outstripping MLG dividends put Ballard in a precarious situation. Despite an average return on capital of 95.21%, the second-best corporate performance in all of Canada, the Gardens was not making Ballard enough money to allow him to pay his debts. Ballard himself was earning just $300,000 annually as the President and CEO of MLG Ltd., and his interest payments were always rising.

To maintain his ownership, he struck a deal with Molson Breweries, owners of the Montreal Canadiens. The beer people agreed to pay Ballard's interest for 10 years, until October 31, 1990. In return, Molson was given a nontransferable first option to buy 19.99% of Gardens stock within 30 days of October 31, 1990, for $10,000, as well as right of first refusal on the remaining 50.75% of stock Ballard owned. In short, Molson's put itself in a position to own the Leafs by the end of the following decade, and saw the interest payments merely as supporting their own company-to-be. If a conflict of interest were ever ruled by the NHL, Molson's was prepared at the time to sell the Habs because Toronto's market was, is, and always will be more lucrative than Montreal's.

By the mid-'80s Ballard's detestation of his children was palpable, and his relationship with Yolanda MacMillan served only to harden familial hostilities. Yolanda, like Ballard, was a convicted felon who forged a will and served time in the Prison for Women at Kingston Penitentiary from December 18, 1981, to April 8, 1982, and again from April to June 1989. The closer she got to Ballard, the more the children grew suspicious of her motives. Mary Elizabeth called her a reptile and successfully had her access to Ballard severely restricted during his dying days. Bill apparently punched her in what she called a "vicious attack." But through it all Ballard kept Yolanda with him, increasingly out of loneliness and nursemaid necessity. In the fall of 1987 his eyes were opened to Yolanda's possible ulterior motives to her devotion to him. Michael Gobuty, a former part-owner of the Winnipeg Jets during its WHA days, became very good friends with Ballard in 1984, and his wife Adrian befriended Yolanda. The two men got along like father and son, despite their differences, and Ballard often helped extricate Gobuty from financial strife. In 1987, he guaranteed a loan for Gobuty of $2.5 million to pay off a Lloyd's debt, but Gobuty turned around and tried to buy out Ballard and take control of the Gardens. When the lenders — the National Bank — reclaimed $2,115,000 of the loan, Gobuty couldn't come up with the funds. The bank took him and Ballard to court and in their report to the Ontario Court of Justice wrote: "It is quite apparent that despite their friendship Ballard had no faith at all in Gobuty as a businessman, and none in his business judgement, at least in regard to hockey matters, and that the idea of Gobuty being involved in a major league hockey purchase, at least by way of acquisition of the Toronto Maple Leafs, was for Ballard little more than a joke." During the hearings it was also learned that Gobuty had written a

cheque to Yolanda for $75,000. Yolanda claimed she got the money from the sale of her jewellery, but the more likely truth was that she and Gobuty were trying to engage in a friendly, without-him-knowing takeover of the Gardens. On February 15, 1993, Gobuty was ordered by the Court to pay the National Bank $3,435,393.19 (including interest).

Only in 1987 did Ballard realize how fragile his control of the Gardens really was and sought to remedy his vulnerability. He wanted first to buy Harold Jr.'s shares, but his son Bill had already offered mini-Harry a nominal $10 for first option, an offer Junior couldn't refuse because of his financial dependence on Bill. In other words, Bill was also looking to solidify *his* position because once the Big Harold died, control would be up for grabs. Harold Junior agreed verbally to Bill's offer, but someone who breaks and enters his own father's house as Harry Jr. had done isn't likely to be trusted. The apple, as they say, never falls far from the tree.

At the same time, Harold discovered that Molson's, covering all bases, was also trying to buy the shares of the sons. Ballard infuriated Bill by finally convincing Harold Jr. to sell him his 34 shares for $21,050,000, a slightly more formal business arrangement than a sawbuck and an I.O.U. Ballard borrowed $25 million from the TD to pay off his son. Then in January 1989, Mary Elizabeth sold her shares to Ballard for $15.5 million, a deal made possible because of another Molson's loan. The more Ballard owned, the more they could take over in 1990. By June 1989, the structure of the ownership pie had changed significantly, and as the October 31, 1990, deadline approached and Ballard's health got worse, the drama became increasingly complex.

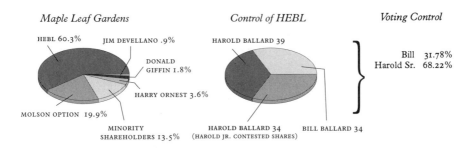

Yolanda, who could throw a punch as well as take one, was neither down nor out. She had changed her legal name to Ballard and was hoping to marry the old man before he breathed his last. On January 2, 1990, they were all set to tie the knot while vacationing in the Cayman Islands, until Ballard received a letter from his lawyer

Rosanne Rocchi in T.O. stating that "if you marry, your will will be revoked. Should you die before returning to Toronto, your children will receive two-thirds of your estate. They will end up controlling the Leafs or fighting for control of the Leafs. This is something you never wanted." Yolanda, as widow, would have received the other third. Bachelorhood never looked so good, and a discontent Ballard bowed out of the winter wedding.

While Ballard was solidifying his strength corporately, he was losing it corporeally. A sufferer of diabetes, he nonetheless routinely binged on chocolates, resulting in blackouts. In 1986, he needed prostate surgery and two years later a quintuple bypass operation. Later he developed kidney problems. On November 10, 1986, after 56 years in the Leaf organization, his great friend Francis Michael "King" Clancy died after a gall bladder operation.

On February 14, 1990, Ballard was declared *non compos mentis* by the Ontario courts, and therefore incapable of managing his affairs. Fewer than two months later, on April 11, 1990, he died at the age of 86. The cause of death was officially listed as "kidney and heart failure." His casket was placed in the Directors' Lounge in the Gardens for the sad and curious to take one final look. He was buried beside his wife Dorothy in Park Lawn Cemetery in Etobicoke five days later.

Ballard was, like everyone else, a human being. No one is without fault, no one beyond criticism of character, taste, ability, or judgement. It would be unfair to rail against his colourful language, personal habits, foibles, or anything else particular to a man's private life. But as a public figure and curator of a national institution, he was an unequivocal failure. The litany of hockey and managerial sins he committed continued unabated for almost 20 years, and by the time the soil was being turned in Park Lawn he left a ruined franchise that had but one thing to be thankful for — his death.

The team's statistics attesting to his incompetence are staggering, insulting, embarrassing, angering, wrenching, devastating, humiliating. In the first 46 years of the Leafs before Ballard took over (1927–73), the team had only 10 coaches: Conn Smythe, Art Duncan, Dick Irvin, Hap Day, Joe Primeau, King Clancy, Howie Meeker, Billy Reay, Punch Imlach, and John McLellan. From 1973 to 1990 there were nine: Red Kelly, Roger Neilson, Floyd Smith, Joe Crozier, Mike Nykoluk, Dan Maloney, John Brophy, George Armstrong, and Doug Carpenter. Between 1927 and 1979 (52 years) there were only four General Managers: Smythe, Day, Imlach, and Gregory. From 1979 to 1990 (11 years) also four: Imlach, McNamara, Stellick, Smith. In 1962 the Leafs had six minor league affiliates: Rochester Americans (AHL), Marlies (Jr. A), Neil McNeil (Jr. A up to midget), Winnipeg Monarchs (Jr. A, Manitoba), Melville Millionaires (Jr. A, Saskatchewan), Shawinigan Cataracts (Jr. A, Quebec). By 1990 they had one: the Newmarket Saints. Between 1921 and 1972 the Leafs used only 21 goalies; from 1972 to 1990 they tried 25:

Ceremony at Maple Leaf Gardens to raise
the Leafs' 1948 Stanley Cup banner.
Ballard pitched them all when he took over.
HOCKEY HALL OF FAME

The first 52 years	*The next 19 years*
John Ross Roach	Jacques Plante
Lorne Chabot	Gord McRae
George Hainsworth	Ron Low
Turk Broda	Doug Favell
Paul Bibeault	Dunc Wilson
Ben Grant	Ed Johnston
Frank McCool	Pierre Hamel
Gordie Bell	Wayne Thomas
Baz Bastien	Mike Palmateer
Al Rollins	Paul Harrison
Harry Lumley	Jiri Crha
Ed Chadwick	Curt Ridley
Johnny Bower	Vincent Tremblay
Don Simmons	Jim Rutherford
Terry Sawchuk	Michel Larocque
Bruce Gamble	Bob Parent
Marv Edwards	Rick St. Croix
Gerry McNamara	Alan Bester
Jacques Plante	Ken Wregget
Bernie Parent	Bruce Dowie
Murray McLachlan	Tim Bernhardt
	Don Edwards
	Jeff Reese
	Mark LaForest
	Peter Ing

In the decade 1981–91 the Leafs had a composite record of 261–450–89, 2,854 goals for and 3,521 against, and their point totals for those years were expansionesque: 56, 68, 61, 48, 57, 70, 52, 62, 80, 57. Their overall positions in the 21-team league reflected those hideous performances: 19th, 14th, 18th, 21st, 19th, 16th, 20th, 19th, 12th, 20th. They missed the playoffs five of 10 years and never won more than one round in any year they did qualify. It was enough to make your teeth curl.

Ballard removed and threw out plaques with the names of all the former Leaf players that had been installed in the dressing room as mementoes of appreciation and inspiration for current players; he took down a sign with the team motto on it that had produced 11 without-Harold Stanley Cups (DEFEAT DOES NOT REST LIGHTLY ON THEIR SHOULDERS); he reduced Foster Hewitt's historic gondola to kindling and put it out in the trash. He drove Leaf fans to other teams, hockey fans to other sports. The team became the butt of jokes, perhaps the most damning from former coach Roger Neilson: "Playing the Leafs is like eating Chinese food. Ten minutes later you want to play them again." His hatred for the Russians was only too

well-known, yet when he died he owned an 1898 5-Ruble Gold coin and an 1899 10-Ruble Gold coin.

Leaf fans went to games primarily to mock, to protest, to howl insults at the players, coaches, owner, to cheer the opposition with sarcastic enthusiasm. The sick atmosphere at the Gardens could not possibly have produced a healthy hockey team. Ballard's death precipitated a perestroika. Everyone and everything from Ballard- ville — the players, the fans, the employees, the Gardens itself — all became free. Once again, the future held the possibility of happiness, the pleasure of promise, the joy of anticipation, the prospect of winning. When Ballard died, the sun came out.

Time humbles the meek and mighty both.

Part Two

8⅝	Maclean Hunter	.25	$9⅛		9⅛	− ⅛	h10039	
15	Madeleine Mines o		$6¼	⅜	6¼		11632	
15	Magna Intl A f		355	34?	350	+ 5	264742	
10	Magna Intl B		$6¼	8½	7¼		nt	
5⅜	Maher Inc p A	80	$6	6	6		100	
10	Majestic Contract		455	450	450	− 5	1510	
10	Majestic Elctrnc		240	240	240	− 15	100	
10½	Malette f	50	$10¼	11	10¼		nt	
24½	Manitoba Prop p A	2.313	$24½	24½	24½		40200	
10	Mannville Oil & Gas		300	300	300		12100	
5	Manridge Explor o		13	13	13	− ½	3500	
15	Manson C o		22	28	23		nt	
24	Manufactrs Lf p A	1.813	$24	24	24		400	
37½	Maple Leaf Gardens	40	$44⅛	44	44¼		1681	
13	Maritime Elec	84	$13⅞	13⅞	13⅞		600	
21	Maritime Life p A	2.188	$21½	21½	21½	− ¼	100	
15¾	Maritme T f	1.08	$17⅛	17¼	17⅛		3804	
8	Maritme T 7.1% p A	71	$8⅛	8⅛	8⅛	+ ⅛	740	
9⅛	Maritme T 8.6% p B	84	$9¾	10½	10		nt	
8¼	Maritme T 7.65% p D	765	$9	9	9		700	
25	Maritme T p E	1.862	$24¼	25¼	25½		nt	
7¼	Mark Resources		$10	9¼	9⅜	+ ⅛	22193	
16	Mark Resources D			see below				
16	Marks Work Wrhs f		240	240	240	− 5	10000	
10	Marshall Steel A f		325	350	350		nt	
10	Marshall Steel B		325	375	370		nt	
10	Matachewan Cnsl Mn		15	17	15		nt	
15	Mavtech Hldgs		45	45	45		500	

10½	8½	Nfld Cap B
75	15	Nfld Expl
17⅜	16⅞	Nfld Tel 7.25 p A
20	19½	Nfld Tel 8.85 p C
21	19¼	Nfld Tel 9.75 p B
425	160	Newhawk Gold Mines
49	17	Newscope Res
25½	24½	Newtel p A
20¼	17⅝	Newfel Enterprises
44	10	Nexus Res o
45	25	Noble Mines & Oils
16⅛	8¼	Noma Inds A f
16	8½	Noma Inds B
79	37	Noramco Mng o
5½	½	Noramco Mng w
16¾	12¼	Noranda Forest
25½	24¾	Noranda Forest p A
28¾	20¾	Noranda
32¼	25½	Noranda 7.75% p C
35	28	Noranda Fxd/Ftg p
28⅛	22	Norcen Ener
25⅝	22½	Norcen Ener 8.12 p
27⅛	20½	Norcen Ener A f
25	18¼	North Cdn Oils
23⅜	17¼	N Cdn Oils 7 p D
21¼	18½	N Cdn Oils 6 p C
69	15	Northair Mines o
350	275	Northern Cda Mines

TSE listings, Thursday, April 12, 1990.

VII

Purgatory:
The Fight for HEB Ltd.

PRESS RELEASE
RELEASE: *Immediate*
TSE: MLG
FROM: *Maple Leaf Gardens, Limited*
CONTACT: *Rosanne Rocchi, Miller Thomson*
        595–8500 or 595–8532

Donald P. Giffin, Steve A. Stavro, and J. Donald Crump, Executors of the Estate of the late HAROLD E. BALLARD announced today a summary of the terms of the Last Will and Testament of Harold E. Ballard. The Last Will and Testament was dated March 30, 1988 and application for Letters Probate was filed with the Surrogate Court for the Judicial District of York on April 12, 1990.

1. The Executors are directed to deliver to the Hockey Hall of Fame and Museum such memorabilia as they shall select.

2. All remaining articles of personal use are to be divided among Mr. Ballard's children and grandchildren.

3. The shares owned by Mr. Ballard in Harold E. Ballard Limited ("HEBL"), the corporation which owns approximately 80% of the shares of Maple Leaf Gardens Limited ("MLG") are to be transferred to the Trustees of the Harold E. Ballard Trust (the "Trust"), some of the terms of which are described below. These shares comprise 99.98% of the voting shares of HEBL.

4. An annuity of $50,000 per year is to be paid to Yolanda MacMillan until her death or marriage, whichever first occurs.

5. The residue of the Estate is to be transferred to the Harold E. Ballard Foundation (the "Foundation").

The Foundation was established by Mr. Ballard during his lifetime and will be used to carry on the traditions of the charitable activities which Mr. Ballard supported during his lifetime. Application will be made to Revenue Canada (Taxation) to have the Harold E. Ballard Foundation registered as a registered charity.

The Trust was established by Mr. Ballard during his lifetime and was designed to govern the terms under which the controlling

interest of MLG would be held and eventually transferred. The Trustees of this Trust are the same individuals as the Executors of the Estate. The Trustees are directed to retain and vote the shares of HEBL and MLG for a period of time considered appropriate by the Trustees, but not exceeding 21 years. The Trustees are directed to serve as directors of HEBL and MLG during this period and to operate the business affairs of MLG. Following a sale of the shares of HEBL or the dissolution of HEBL following a sale of the shares of MLG or the assets of MLG, the proceeds of sale are to be transferred to the Foundation.

While the shares of HEBL are held in the Trust, the Trustees have broad discretions and powers. Any income generated may be paid to certain beneficiaries or accumulated in the Trust. The various beneficiaries of the Trust are charitable, humanitarian and non-profit organizations and purposes. Among other things, under the terms of the Trust, the Trustees are to establish the Maple Leaf Gardens Scholarship Fund, a special fund for the benefit of employees and former employees of MLG and their children and grandchildren.

The Executors and Trustees announced that they are aware of the provisions of the *Charitable Gifts Act*.

The Executors and Trustees further announced that they do not currently anticipate any changes in the corporate structures or business affairs of either HEBL or MLG in the near future.

In accordance with Mr. Ballard's wishes, the decision as to the ultimate disposition of the controlling interest of MLG is to be made by the Trustees.

Donald Giffin became the president of HEBL. Steve Stavro, who was appointed by Ballard to the Board of Directors on September 24, 1981, after the death of another director, Lorne Duguid, was the second executor. Donald Crump, the Commissioner of the CFL and another board member, was the third. They also controlled the estate, and in matters of disagreement between the three men, majority ruled. In matters of the Leafs, it was business as unusual.

At the time of Ballard's death, Maple Leaf Gardens had debts of more than $60 million, a huge sum given the financial success of the "business." Most of this debt, incurred by Ballard during his final takeover bids in the late '80s, put the three executors in an awkward position. They were supposed to sell all of Ballard's stock and give the proceeds to charity,* but at this time the estate was up to its eyes

---

* "Princess Margaret Hospital; Wellesley Hospital; Ontario Crippled Children's Centre; Canadian Association for the Mentally Retarded; the Salvation Army; Charlie Conacher Throat Cancer Fund; Maple Leaf Gardens Scholarship Fund; Hockey Canada; any charitable organization as selected by the

in debt. Ballard's three principal properties (the house in Etobicoke, the condominium at 130 Carlton Street near the Gardens, and the cottage at Thunder Beach near Georgian Bay) had to be sold for $2,720,000, all of which was sucked up by the estate to help pay off the debts.

Stavro, Giffin, and Crump agreed that their most important task was to restore the reputation and performance of the Toronto Maple Leafs. As president, Giffin had a huge job ahead of him, so he wasted no time. He reopened Conn Smythe's office, used by Ballard only as a storage room for Yolanda's furniture.* In May, just a month after Ballard's death, "new" Stanley Cup banners were hung in the empty, ghostly Gardens. Eleven banners, one for each Leaf victory, were silently raised to the rafters to commemorate what Ballard detested — past greatness. In the Conn Smythe era, banners for the Leafs had already been raised, as well as others honouring the Marlies and the Toronto National Sea Fleas. Ballard had had them removed and thrown out. Some were used by painters as drop-sheets, others never became so usable and were simply put out the back door on Wood St. to be disposed of by the garbage collectors.

Giffin's next move was to fire Guy Kinnear, the Leafs' trainer of 21 years. Kinnear began his Leaf life when Ballard hired him to work for the Marlies in 1967. He was promoted to the Leafs two years later. A boat mechanic by trade, Kinnear first became acquainted with Ballard in the summers while helping him do odd jobs at his cottage. He was regarded as Ballard's ear in the Leaf dressing room and was not missed by many of the players. Giffin brought in 24-year-old Chris Broadhurst, a fully qualified graduate of Sheridan College's sports therapy program, and an enthusiastic, outgoing trainer with a fresh attitude.

Giffin had a tunnel built from the Leaf dressing room to a new exercise room under the Hot Stove Club.** The old Marlie dressing room became a waiting room for wives and girlfriends, and a new media room named in memory of long-serving Leaf publicist Stan Obodiac was built. As well, the beautiful Art Deco brick exterior of the Gardens was chemically cleaned.

Trustees; any non-profit organization operated exclusively for social welfare, civic improvement, pleasure, or recreation selected by the Trustees; any Canadian amateur athletic association selected by the Trustees; any Canadian university, college, or other educational institution selected by the Trustees."

* Yolanda took the Estate to court over Ballard's will, claiming that she had lived with Ballard since 1980 and he had not made "adequate provisions." She sought $500,000 a year. Crump submitted a detailed report that provided the Court with 79 points of question about Yolanda's character. Her annuity was not increased.

** During this construction, bottles, dishes, and a bedpan all from the 19th Century were discovered, leading the Ontario Heritage Foundation to believe the corner of Carlton and Church was witness to fighting during the Rebellion of 1837 led by William Lyon Mackenzie.

On April 19, 1990, right after the season had ended and Ballard had been buried, Giffin confirmed Floyd Smith's position as the man in charge of all hockey operations. Smith was given free reign to work as general manager to make the club respectable. With Doug Carpenter as coach, the team was coming off its first .500 season in more than a decade, so it seemed a corner was being turned even while Ballard was dying. Smith fired assistant coach Gary Larrivière. Paul Gardner, the four-year coach of the Newmarket Saints, was also fired. The farm team had been losing $1 million annually and its on-ice performance was similarly dismal. Frank Anzalone was hired as his replacement, a gregarious American who brought a vigorous spirit to a stale atmosphere. Most important, though, was Smith's hiring on May 8, 1990, of Pierre Dorion as the team's chief scout. Dorion had been working in the NHL's Central Scouting Bureau and had a thorough knowledge of talent worldwide. He was dedicated, intelligent, and effective, three qualities hard to find at the Gardens during Ballard's tenure. Dorion took over the responsibilities Smith had handled coincidentally with the GM duties in '89–'90, and became an integral part of the Leafs' future. His word on a player's potential became sacrosanct.

Smith then rehired Doug Carpenter. He had no choice. After such a successful season, at least against the backdrop of previous Leaf seasons, the job was Carpenter's to lose. For the first time in Leaf history, he was even allowed to hire an assistant coach *on his own*. He chose Tom Watt, recently fired by Cliff Fletcher in Calgary, for the position. In August 1989, Ballard had reluctantly hired Carpenter as coach, a man destined for the job since Imlach hired him for the farm team almost a decade earlier. Under Carpenter, the team played wide open hockey in his first year ('89–'90), winning games by preposterous scores such as 8–5 (over St. Louis), 8–6 (Pittsburgh), 9–6 (Chicago), 7–6 (Boston), and losing games in much the same way — 9–6 Chicago, 12–2 to Calgary, 7–4 to Philadelphia. Goals were scored in record numbers, led by Gary Leeman's 51, and a total absence of defence was both fun for the lazy players and successful in the won-lost columns. Fans had plenty to cheer about even during defeat, but the team finished weakly down the stretch and was easily eliminated by St. Louis 4–1 in the first round of the playoffs, when the Blues' defence overcame the Leafs' offence with the greatest of ease. Typical of the season, the only time Toronto

scored more than four goals in the series was in a 6–5 overtime loss. While the Leafs scored a record number of goals, they still gave up 21 more (337–358), and the goalies' averages looked like the price of beef, not eggs: Peter Ing 5.93, Alan Bester 4.49, Jeff Reese 4.41, Mark LaForest 3.89.

The 1990 draft was held on June 16 at a packed Pacific Coliseum in Vancouver. It was there that Smith made one of the most important decisions for the new Leaf era. For his first-round selection, 10th overall, he had a choice of two great prospects. Drake Berehowsky was a big, strong defenceman for the Kingston Frontenacs of the OHL. His toughness and defensive-mindedness were just the kind of attributes the Leafs needed. He was a stay-at-home blue-liner who could probably make the team next training camp. Trevor Kidd, though, was the top-rated goalie in Canada, playing for the Brandon Wheat Kings in the Western Hockey League. He was a member of Dave King's National Team and the kind of player who could win a game on his own. Goal is always the first place from which to build a team, and Smith most certainly needed to build. It was a tough choice.

Smith gambled a bit and went for Berehowsky; Calgary took Kidd next, 11th overall. The Leafs didn't get another selection until the next round, 21 players later and 31st overall. To make amends for leaving Kidd behind, Smith went for the best available goalie still left — a kid out of Chicoutimi in the Quebec juniors named Felix Potvin. Potvin was Kidd's backup for the 1990 World Junior Championships in Finland and was also highly coveted by Pittsburgh. This was the highest choice the Leafs had ever used to get a goalie, but if Smith did nothing more in his time with Toronto, his place in Leaf history would already be secure. Potvin has proved to be a franchise player, the cornerstone of the Leafs for the next 10 years or more.

While Giffin as president and Smith as manager were going great guns to rebuild the organization, Smith as player general and Carpenter as coach were undermining these attempts. They believed that the three goalies in camp fighting for jobs — Jeff Reese, Alan Bester, and Peter Ing — were collectively competent. Carpenter was fully confident in using the three-goalie system, even though no team had ever done this successfully. In pre-season the team was a promising 5–3–2, and all looked good for a repeat of, or improvement upon, last season. But looks can be deceiving, and one road trip out west to open the '90–'91 season confirmed the changeability of that fair maiden Success. The Leafs were blown away 7–1 in Winnipeg, lost 4–1 in Calgary two nights later, and then edged 3–2 in Edmonton the next night. Four days, three losses. Each goalie played in a game — Reese then Bester then Ing.

The home opener was on October 10, and a return to great Maple Leaf tradition was inaugurated by a ceremonial faceoff. Ballard had detested these moments of civic politeness and generosity, but Giffin and Smith thought them essential. They were right. Dropping the

puck were Ace Bailey, Harrold Darragh, Frank Finnigan, and Red Horner, four octogenarians who had played in the very first home game at Maple Leaf Gardens on November 12, 1931.

The score wasn't as honourable as the pre-game ceremony, a sloppy 8–5 loss to Quebec to drag the Leafs' record to 0–4. While an 8–5 loss during a .500 season is easily forgotten, for an 0–3 team to score five goals and lose the game looked considerably worse. After a 3–3 tie with Detroit, Toronto quickly lost two more games, to Hartford (3–1) and Chicago (3–0), to drop their record to 0–6–1. A 6–2 win over the Blackhawks, however, did not alleviate what was quickly becoming a disastrous situation. Their next game, a 5–1 loss to the Rangers, prompted one veteran player to spew anonymously, "You know what the problem is," referring to Carpenter. "This team was in trouble with 20 games to go last season." Indeed, although the team had played .500 the year before, they finished with a weak 5–9–1 record for March before being eliminated by St. Louis in the first round of the playoffs. The poor start to Carpenter's second year was not an aberration so much as a carryover from the previous season's end.

Two consecutive drubbings by the Blues at the end of October, 8–3 and 8–5, left the team 1–9–1. An appalling 54 goals against in 11 games was clear proof that the three-goalie system wasn't working. The defence was on vacation, and the glorious 337-goal offence had scored but 28 times. Smith had to do *something*, so he did the obvious and fired Carpenter. The season was already in tatters, their promising .500 coach out the door a month into the supposed turn-the-corner year. Operation Salvage was implemented.

Ironically, Carpenter's decision to hire Tom Watt as his assistant had undermined his own cause. Watt came to the fore in 1965 as coach of the University of Toronto Blues. Over the next 14 years he brought 11 Conference Championships and an unheard of nine National titles to Varsity Arena.* He coached in Vancouver and Winnipeg and had a great deal of international experience. He, like Carpenter, had long been touted to coach the Leafs and his arrival as assistant signalled as much. Watt was, in short, too good, too inevitable, to be an assistant. If Carpenter went even a little awry, his replacement could not be more easily found.

Tom Watt took two steps to the left behind the Leaf bench and, *voilà!*, he was head coach. The team played better in its first game under him, but they still lost 3–1 to Buffalo. A record of 1–10–1 and talk of missing the playoffs began in earnest. To make matters worse, a trade by Smith the year before had become the subject of constant ridicule. He had acquired Tom Kurvers from New Jersey for the

---

* The U of T's coaching history is impressive by even the finest NHL standards: Conn Smythe, 1923–26; Prime Minister Lester Pearson, 1926–28; Ace Bailey, 1935–40 and '45–'49; Judge Joe Kane, 1962–65; Mike Keenan, 1983–84; Watt, 1965–79 and '84–'85.

Leafs' number one draft pick in 1991. The number one pick would be Eric Lindros, and whichever team finished 21st overall would get him. Kurvers' play was far from stellar, and the Leafs' horrible beginning gave every indication they were bad enough to finish dead last. But if they did, there would be no Lindros compensation for the misery; their pick would go to Jersey and the Leafs would be left with much pie on their face.

During a 7–3 loss to the Flames at the Gardens next time out, one fan displayed a sign that read "Help wanted: hockey players with heart. Should be able to self-motivate. Apply to Leafs' GM. Fast." When the team was 2–12–1, the Board of Governors held an emergency meeting and concluded something more had to be done. They couldn't fire Watt yet, so they had to think of something else. Giffin maintained complete confidence in Smith's ability to do whatever it took to get the club moving. The Leafs lost three more, and their 2–15–1 record was the worst start ever for a Leaf team. Smith then rolled up his sleeves, pulled out his little black GM-phone directory, and over the next month traded half the team.

Gone were John McIntyre, Mark Osborne, Ed Olczyk, Scott Pearson, Lou Franceschetti, Brian Curran, John Kordic, and the infamous Kurvers. Arriving were Mike Krushelnyski, Dave Ellett, Paul Fenton, Michel Petit, Aaron Broten, Lucien Deblois, Mike Foligno, and Brian Bradley. Smith's changes were only lateral. He didn't engineer any "steal" in which he was able to actually improve the team very much. The chemistry was better, the Leafs won a few more games, but the playoffs weren't any more in sight now than they were opening night. Nor were his trades made with any thematic purpose. At one moment he looked to be acquiring experience in Deblois (33 years old), Foligno (30), Broten (30), Fenton (31), and Krushelnyski (30). Later, he seemed more interested in youth, trading for a 5th, 6th, and 8th round choice in the upcoming draft. He got Paul Fenton from the Jets in the Olczyk deal and then traded him to Washington two months later, even though he had become a gritty, effective checker, the stuff of which a good fourth-line winger is made.

By the beginning of December, Giffin was becoming increasingly frustrated. He had put his trust in Smith, but clearly that hadn't been enough. He was determined to hire a hockey man to control the whole operation, a president and CEO who would be given the clout to change *everything*, so long as a winning hockey team was the goal and result. To this end he began a methodical, patient, and determined hunt. His first candidates were Jim Gregory and Glen Sather, then Harry Sinden and John Ferguson. The Leafs could afford the best, and the fans deserved the best — he would not settle for anything less.

While Giffin was looking for a Leaf president, Steve Stavro and Bill Ballard were duking it out in the boardrooms and courtrooms of Hogtown. Bill was still contending that he should be given the

chance to buy his brother's shares, the ones sold to Harold and now owned by the estate. Furthermore, Molson's had extended its October 30, 1990, deadline on repayment of the loan it had made to Ballard in 1980 because the last thing the company wanted, ironically, was to own only 19.99% of HEBL. If it did, Molson's would risk having to sell the Canadiens because of a too obvious conflict of interest. It would gladly have done this if it could have been assured of full ownership of the Leafs, but Molson's didn't want to risk being frozen out of both the Gardens' picture (19.99% does not an owner make) and the Montreal Canadiens as well.

Steve Stavro was a perfect example of Canadian success. His family immigrated to Canada and his father opened a small grocery store on Queen Street East near the Greenwood racetrack. Steve and his brother Chris worked there constantly and got to know everything about the business. In 1949, Steve opened his own store at 425 Danforth Avenue, and the rest is history. Today you can see a two-page advertisement in the *Star* and *Sun* every week for his Knob Hill Farms chain of food stores, and his Cambridge Terminal is enormous — eight acres. Yet he remains the quintessential entrepreneur: the Ed Mirvish of food and sport (rather than merchandise and culture) who still gets up insanely early in the morning to inspect the produce his stores sell. He is happy to talk about bananas or roast pork, but not the business manoeuvrings that got him the Maple Leafs.

Stavro had it in for Giffin just about from the word go. He vehemently opposed bringing in a *hockey* man to oversee the *whole* Gardens operation. He thought the task too onerous and too foreign for one man. He wanted two. The first man on his list was his friend Lyman MacInnis, a former Anne Murray accountant, a senior executive at Labatt's, an associate of Alan Eagleson's, and at the time a possible successor as head of the NHLPA. MacInnis would operate the *business* side of the Gardens. The second person would be the hockey man, who would worry only about the Leafs. Speculation ran rampant on June 9, 1991, when MacInnis announced his resignation from Labatt's, effective August 21, 1991, three days after a scheduled Maple Leaf Gardens shareholders meeting at which it was expected Stavro would try to hire him.

To complicate matters further: while there were three executors of the estate of Harold Ballard, there were seven members of the Board of Directors which oversaw the Leafs: Stavro, Giffin, Crump, Thor Eaton, Ted Rogers, Edward Lawrence, and Frederick McDowell. Stavro and Crump wanted to dump Giffin from the board, but they didn't have the support among the other directors to do so. Giffin was well-liked and highly respected, a man honourable to a fault. The tension between the three men and the two controlling groups was great. As president of the Board of Directors, Giffin earned $300,000 a year. He could not be removed from this post, and as Stavro had only Crump as an ally on the board, Giffin was free to do as he liked. But with matters pertaining to the *estate*,

Ballard's will stated that "if at any time my Trustees are unable to agree regarding any matter in connection with my Estate, I declare that the decision of a majority of my Trustees shall govern and be final and binding." Stavro had Crump's support in that capacity, and with a two-out-of-three majority *he* controlled HEBL, the estate. But the estate's concerns were purely financial and had nothing to do with hockey. Hockey was the board's bailiwick.

On March 1, 1991, two major court rulings were handed down that began to affect the connection between these two bodies of power. First, Mr. Justice Richard Trainor ruled Stavro was allowed to pay off the estate's debt of $22.7 million to Molson's by April 15, 1994. In return he won the right of first option held by Molson's to buy *all* of HEBL's stock. Second, Bill Ballard gained more power. Mr. Justice James Farley ordered the removal of Crump and Giffin from the board of HEBL, to be replaced by Ballard himself and one neutral nominee. Farley ruled that they had neglected the rights of Bill. Even though he was a minority shareholder, his potential greater interest was being ignored. He won equal power rights within HEBL until his legal battle over ownership of Harold Junior's shares had been decided. But Bill Ballard still had no say in matters pertaining to his father's estate, and none on the Board of Directors at the Gardens. The decision was more a symbolic than real victory and didn't give him any true power to use as leverage against Stavro's takeover plans (which had been greatly strengthened by Justice Trainor's ruling).

The first decision was vital because it gave Stavro legal permission to acquire Maple Leaf Gardens — if he could. Giffin argued that this was a serious conflict of interest. As executors to Ballard's estate, Stavro, Giffin, and Crump were responsible for selling all of HEBL within 21 years and giving the money to specified charities. Their first responsibility was to HEBL (and, by extension, the charities) to get as much money as possible for the shares. But as buyer, Stavro would want to pay as little as possible for them. Thus the conflict of interest.

Ballard's will left the door open for one or more of the executors to buy HEBL and, for all intents and purposes, the Gardens. The will stipulated that if this were to happen the executor(s) buying the shares would have to do so at fair market value (i.e., the most money in a free, unrestricted market). The Board of Directors, however, had to think of the good of the hockey club, not just the value of the shares. Establishing ownership would certainly help stabilize the franchise (healthy management, healthy hockey team) but quite possibly at the expense of the value of the estate. If Stavro bought the Gardens for a low price (definitely a conflict) and improved the team, the charities would lose money but the franchise would be more stable. In the short run, the shares would be lower, but with the improvement of the team the shares would rise over time (but the charities wouldn't reap the benefits). If the ownership question were not resolved, the value of the shares would probably increase

more quickly, but the team would certainly continue its downward spiral. Which was more important, the Maple Leaf hockey club or the stock market price of MLGL shares?

Stavro, by virtue of his being on the inside, could force the estate (which he controlled through his alliance with Crump) to sell him the shares in much the same way Harold had done with Stafford's shares in 1972. That no one could stop him was the point Bill Ballard and Giffin were making. Bill had made a financial proposition regarding the Molson's shares that was $2 million better than Stavro's, but his offer was rejected. However, Harold had made it clear he wanted his children to have nothing to do with the owner-ship/management of the Gardens (he had, after all, *not* gotten married for this very purpose). Stavro was, in some strange way, operating in the spirit of Ballard's last wishes, while serving his own ambitions.

Stavro's planned takeover was held in check at the next Board of Directors meeting on March 25, 1991, set up in part to discuss Giffin's one-year term as president which was soon to end. Stavro attended the meeting with every hope in the world of ousting Giffin, but instead Giffin was given a vote of confidence by the directors and his contract was renewed for another year. At the meeting, Giffin declared his intention to hire a new man in charge of hockey operations by the summer and stepped up the intensity of his search.

The turmoil in the backrooms was being rivalled, if not eclipsed, by the turmoil at centre ice. The only bright spot in this dour season was the All-Star Game performance of Vincent Damphousse in Chicago, where he scored four goals and was chosen the game's MVP. Otherwise, the team continued to play miserably and was for all intents and purposes out of the playoffs midway through the season. It took the Leafs 28 days and 11 games to win their first game in the calendar year 1991. Two weeks into January, Al Iafrate (who was, on more than one occasion, referred to as I. Alafrate by a local play-by-play man) demanded to be traded. Smith acceded two days later, sending him to Washington for Peter Zezel and Bob Rouse, two men full of the character and grit that the more-talented Iafrate so sadly lacked. This was to be Smith's best trade, as proved by both Zezel's and Rouse's excellent contributions in the '93 and '94 playoffs.

Meanwhile, Gary Leeman's name came up in trade rumours almost daily. Coming off his 51-goal Carpenter-year, he was strug-gling as much as the team from both injuries and a long scoring slump. One rumour in particular was fascinating. Glen Sather in Edmonton had apparently offered the Leafs Grant Fuhr in exchange for Leeman, Damphousse, and Ing, but the trade was scuppered when it was leaked to the media. Once the deal became public, both Smith and Sather backed out.

Cliff Fletcher in Calgary was another interested party who was talking to the Leafs. He wanted Wendel Clark and seemed willing to

part with Doug Gilmour to get him. One *Star* headline in November 1990 ran: "Flames' Gilmour on Leafs' list as trade kettle still on the boil." But Wendel always seemed to epitomize what the Leafs would look like as winners, and he would never be traded while the team was so weak. His value to the club and fans was always more in spirit and emotion than what Smith could have gotten for him in skill. The talks subsided.

Smith had much greater success reorganizing the corporate image of the Gardens than improving the won-lost record of the hockey team. In another wonderful move to resurrect the prideful ghosts of Gardens past, Giffin and Smith announced the inaugural King Clancy Cup game to be played March 22, featuring the best of the Leaf old-timers and the best of the Montreal old-timers. Sittler, McDonald, Shack, Ellis, Tiger, Palmateer, Richard, Savard, Ferguson, and Dryden all happily participated to make it a great night and raise about $50,000 for Leaf Alumni in the process. The nostalgic feeling was wonderful, the Gardens alive and laughing, and the Leafs won 5–1. They were presented with the King Clancy Cup which was, in fact, the long-ignored Bickell Cup spruced up with a new base.

With this game, the Leaf Alumni was officially organized, Frank Mahovlich presiding. For years players such as Keon, Henderson, Ellis, and the Big M refused to even enter the Gardens, so insulted were they by Ballard's disrespect for former players. As Bob Nevin bluntly put it, "When Harold was around, it was like we never existed." Now, the heroes and victors of the past would imbue the building with a much needed sense of pride, harmony, family history. They could drop by to say hello, hold autograph sessions, attend games, happily talk about the game they loved to a new generation of players and fans. The Leafs, established in February 1927, became the *21st* team in the NHL to form an Alumni.

Changes, there were a few. In April, the Board of Directors built 16 new corporate boxes on the west side of the Gardens, a move which resulted in the removal of 425 Grey seats.* These boxes did much to emasculate the feeling of closeness, intimacy, and personality at the Gardens, but the salary explosion demanded that any new source of revenue be exploited. On May 2, the Leafs announced that they would move their farm team to St. John's, Newfoundland, for the '91–'92 season, following up a Crump suggestion initially made in 1989, thereby removing yet another unpleasant reminder of the Ballard years — the pitiful Newmarket Saints.

By this time, of course, the Leafs had turned on their television sets, pulled up their chairs, and started to watch the playoffs. A 23–46–11 season will give you that opportunity. But the pressure was off in one respect. The Nordiques went into the tank, winning only 16 times all year and finishing last overall for the third successive

---

* Which went on sale in the Gardens lobby for $25 each.

year. They had the number one draft pick, Eric Lindros. The Devils, picking for the Leafs 3rd overall, selected Kamloops defenceman Scott Niedermayer. Smith (and Kurvers) were off the hot seat.

The Leafs had weathered a terrible storm during their first post-Harold year. Under Giffin and Smith, they had turned a corner by, if nothing else, eradicating much of what Ballard had done. The team had improved somewhat under Watt (21–31–10) after the horrible beginning, and Smith had moved out many of the players from Ballard's days who had that complacent attitude of "losing well." Many office moves had been made to bring the team into the post–Original Six era, and Leafs-oriented decision-making was being allowed for the first time since Conn Smythe was in charge.

On May 16, 1991, the heavens opened wide to reveal white clouds, bright sun, and blue blue sky. Cliff Fletcher, after 19 years in the Calgary/Atlanta organization, announced his retirement, saying, "I was stale and I felt that at my age, if I was going to have a career change, this was the time to do it. I'm looking forward to a new challenge." Giffin got on the phone as soon as he heard the news. Over the next two weeks he talked several times with Fletcher about the Leaf situation and his suitability to it. Giffin also consulted with all the right people about Fletcher. League President John Ziegler told him Fletcher was the best possible man any team could hope to land, bar none, as did Jim Gregory, Alan Eagleson, and a host of other reputable hockey-minded people.

Giffin and Fletcher met for the first time at the Gardens on Tuesday, June 4, and the next day Fletcher's employment as President, Chief Operating Officer, and General Manager was confirmed. At the press conference in the Hot Stove Club to announce the hiring, Donald P. Giffin smiled proudly and declared, "This is a great day in the life of the Toronto Maple Leafs."

MAPLE LEAF GARDENS
LIMITED

CORNER CARLTON AND CHURCH STREETS
TORONTO 2.
ONTARIO

Toronto St. Pat's, 1927.
HOCKEY HALL OF FAME

VIII

June 4, 1991:
The Renaissance Begins

*"This is the greatest franchise in the National Hockey League. . . .
I want to reconfirm the pride and tradition of this great hockey
club."*

— Cliff Fletcher, June 4, 1991

Donald Giffin's finest assets as president were his honesty and integrity. He knew little about how to run a hockey club and he openly admitted it (unlike Ballard who knew far less than nothing but never admitted as much). He was also astute enough to realize that someone had to run the club, and as he had been put in charge of the estate it was up to him to find the right man.

Cliff Fletcher was capable of making the Leafs a proper organization again, but first he needed — demanded — independence. "I want to be in full control of both the business and the hockey side of things. . . . I want to build an off-ice organization second to none in the National Hockey League." To this end, Giffin resigned his own post as president and gave Fletcher a five-year, $4 million contract with a *very* expensive buyout clause in the event someone (i.e., Stavro) wanted to ditch the Silver Fox. In other words, Fletcher wouldn't be working anywhere else for the next half-decade.

Fletcher began his career in the Montreal system in 1956 as the manager of the Verdun Blues, one of 10 teams in the Montreal Metropolitan Hockey League, the precursor to the Quebec Major Junior Hockey League. He then managed the Montreal Junior Canadiens for a year before becoming responsible for scouting the whole junior system in Quebec.

In 1967, Lynn Patrick in St. Louis hired him as the Blues' chief scout for Eastern Canada, and three years later Fletcher became the assistant GM to Scotty Bowman, who doubled as the Blues' coach. In 1971, he and Bowman were both fired when, for the first time in the young franchise's history, the team failed to make it to the Stanley Cup finals. The next year he became the General Manager for the newest member of the NHL, the Atlanta Flames. In their first year, the team set a record for most points by an expansion club. By their third season they were a better than .500 hockey team and have

finished below that mark only twice since (and then barely).* When the Flames moved from Atlanta to Calgary in 1980, the team kept improving, primarily through Fletcher trades that saw them acquire Lanny McDonald from Colorado, Joe Nieuwendyk from Minnesota (as a draft), and Joe Mullen from St. Louis. The Flames got to the finals in 1986, where they lost to Montreal in five games, and again in 1989 when they won the Stanley Cup by beating those same Habs in a six-game classic (4–2 in the deciding game).

General consensus held that Fletcher had committed but one major sin in all his GM years. In March 1988, he traded Steve Bozek and Brett Hull to St. Louis for Rob Ramage and Rick Wamsley. Hull was often scratched from the Flames' lineup by coach Terry Crisp, who questioned his commitment to conditioning, defence, and winning. Crisp's assessment was bang on, and Fletcher's trade helped bring a Cup to Calgary the very next year. Hardly a high price. In fact, given the kind of player Hull is, it might be argued the Flames never would have won the Cup *with* him (or without Ramage and Wamsley — take your pick).

Since Hull's arrival in St. Louis, the Blues have never won more than one round in the playoffs. He has scored buckets of regular season goals, but never won anything of team significance. His abilities in St. Louis match those of Leeman and Vaive in Toronto's '80s. The stats sound great, but there's nothing to show for them. Hull is the kind of selfish player who gets 70 goals and 30 assists, whose idea of contributing involves loafing at the fringe of the play waiting for a loose puck. He has an incredible shot and a quick release, but unlike Mike Bossy or Phil Esposito, he will never win a Stanley Cup. His defection from Canada to Team U.S.A. for the '91 Canada Cup was precipitated only by the knowledge he couldn't have made the first cuts at Team Canada's camp to save his ego. He will never contribute to a winning cause.

Fletcher's priority in Toronto was to provide stability to the organization. Typically, however, his first battle was not with the draft or player contracts or anything connected to hockey. It was with management, particularly Steve Stavro. The appointment of Fletcher was approved by a vote of 5–1 by the Board of Directors at Maple Leaf Gardens, the lone vote of dissent being Stavro's (Crump abstained). His very public objection to the hiring lay not so much in his opinion of Cliff Fletcher as in his antipathy to Donald Giffin. Stavro seemed unconcerned at this point by Giffin's honest search for a hockey leader and the league's general consensus of Fletcher's ability. He was more concerned with doing business his way. After the board approved Fletcher's contract, Stavro commented, "As long as I have a say Cliff Fletcher definitely won't have carte blanche. I know all the particulars of the deal and in my opinion he was given far too

---

* 1981–82: 29–34–17, and 1982–83: 32–34–14.

much power. That I won't stand for." Chilling words from a man who knew relatively little about Fletcher's hockey abilities, but a great deal about wielding power. Fortunately, as time would show, this resentment was placated by both the vast improvement the club would make in a short period of time and Stavro's own good common sense.

The summer months were red alert days for Fletcher, but he had a few advantages working for him. While it became increasingly obvious that Stavro would eventually take control of HEBL's shares, it was in Fletcher's favour that the taking of this control be as protracted a process as possible because in the interim Stavro could not do anything to influence or dictate Fletcher's job. That meant the new Leaf boss had time to establish himself before Stavro's takeover was complete. In the three short months he had between taking office officially (July 1) and opening day at the Forum (October 3), Fletcher turned the team around with extraordinary speed. On the day he was hired, he confirmed the return of coach Tom Watt and assistant Mike Kitchen, and offered Floyd Smith the position of Director of Player Development. He then fired the American Frank Anzalone as the Newmarket coach and hired Belleville native Marc Crawford, a 30-year-old who would set up shop as the team moved to a fresh start in St. John's and called themselves the Maple Leafs (good riddance Newmarket Saints). He also hired former Leaf Joel Quenneville as a player/assistant coach to Crawford on the Rock.

Fletcher hired Mike Murphy as a second assistant coach to Watt and added three new scouts to bolster the most understaffed club in the league: Anders Hedberg, based in Stockholm, would cover Europe; Garth Malarchuk, Western Canada; and Peter Johnson, son of the late Calgary/Penguin coach Badger Bob Johnson, the States. Later in the fall he hired Bill Watters as his assistant to help with contracts, budgets, and administration. All of a sudden the Leafs' offices were full of productive, intelligent people.

Fletcher knew that, while he was coming to a disastrous organization, Toronto was the hockey capital of the world. Night after pitiful night for more than a decade, 16,382 faithful fans came to the games, despite the turmoil, the losses, the hopelessness. He knew it was not a matter of establishing the team from the ground up as would be necessary in Florida or California, but of redeveloping the decades of tradition that had been ignored. Motivated by this knowledge, he hired Brian Conacher, son of the Big Train, Lionel, as Vice-President of Building Operations for the Gardens. He also brought in John McDermott as the official anthem singer to add a little class and pleasure to the pre-game adrenaline ritual.

Fletcher also had to contend with massive player problems. Thirty-one contracts in the organization had to be renegotiated, first and foremost among them Wendel Clark's. Also, Rob Ramage had been left unprotected in the expansion draft and was claimed by Minnesota, leaving the Leafs without a captain. However, everyone knew

Red Kelly's sweater.
DOUG MACLELLAN / HOCKEY HALL OF FAME

that if Clark stayed with the team he'd certainly be given the hallowed "C." On August 8, Fletcher made his most important move to date by signing Wendel Clark to a one-year contract with an option year at $600,000 a season, making him the highest paid Leaf of all time, and naming him the team's 16th captain. Darryl Sittler was also officially back as a Maple Leaf to work in marketing, public relations, Alumni relations, and hockey operations. These efforts indicated that Leaf players would be treated with appropriate respect, and that Alumni would be acknowledged for their past performances on ice and asked to make future contributions toward the continuance of tradition and success off it.

Another great intangible that factored into the Leafs' resurgence was the 1991 Canada Cup. Maple Leaf Gardens was the training camp for Team Canada as well as the site for many of the tournament games. The excitement in the city was electric and was further enhanced by the invitation of four Leafs — Clark, Damphousse, Ellett, and Leeman — to Canada's camp. The Gardens was abuzz in August as it hadn't been for many a long dark year as the prospects emerged of at least *one* Leaf making the team and perhaps even repeating Sittler's '76 heroics.

In about six weeks, Fletcher had established a front office that could finally cope with the expectations of a professional hockey team. As he worked his way through contract negotiations, he began to concern himself with exactly what sort of a team would represent

the '91–'92 Leafs. He drew two conclusions: (1) you build a team from the goal out; (2) Peter Ing and Jeff Reese were not the goalies upon which to build such a team. So he went looking for a star between the pipes and gave himself a list of the four finest names in the game: Grant Fuhr (Edmonton), Sean Burke (New Jersey), John Vanbiesbrouck (Rangers), and his formerly-own Mike Vernon (Calgary). Trade rumours were rife as soon as Fletcher's plans became known. Fuhr and Burke were in Team Canada's camp, Vanbiesbrouck in the U.S.'s, and Vernon a very known and respected quality to Fletcher from their Flames days. At one point the Leafs were rumoured to have made a big offer to get Vanbiesbrouck, but Fletcher squelched it. "I can tell you right now we're not even considering trading Gary Leeman and Luke Richardson" for the Manhattan goalie, he insisted.

However, he did admit to backing out of a deal with Sather that would have made Fuhr and Kevin Lowe Leafs in exchange for Damphousse, Richardson, Pearson, and Potvin. The Leaf GM balked because of Potvin's inclusion. While he was desperate for a goalie, Fletcher would not trade away the fortunes of future Leaf teams for a stopgap present solution. Although Fuhr was the best in the game, he wouldn't be around in half a dozen years, and that was when Fletcher's real plans would be just kicking in.

All four Leafs were eventually cut by coach Mike Keenan, but Team Canada still sailed to another victory. During the month-long tournament, one fact became patently clear: Bill Ranford, the Oilers' "other" goalie, was the star of the world in Canada's net. He beat out Fuhr for the number-one spot on the team in camp, and made unbelievable save after unbelievable save during the round robin. He was undoubtedly the most outstanding player in the two-game finals sweep of the Americans and was selected the tournament's Most Valuable Player. Ranford established himself as heir to Grant Fuhr's Edmonton throne, a throne he was evidently capable of inheriting *now*.

Glen Sather knew he didn't have a number one and a number two goalie on his Oilers team. He had a number one goalie and a second number one goalie. He would have been crazy not to trade one of them to strengthen the team on defence and up front. Slats deemed Fuhr more expendable because his market value was higher and he was four years older than Ranford. Three days after Canada swept the States 2–0 in games (by scores of 4–1 and 4–2) at Copps Coliseum in Hamilton, courtesy of a Gary Suter error that turned into a Steve Larmer breakaway goal, Fletcher got the goalie he wanted and Slats got the mixture of players he was after. The Leafs traded for Fuhr, Glenn Anderson, Craig Berube, and future considerations (Ken Linseman); the Oilers got Damphousse, Richardson, Ing, and Scott Thornton. One clever condition went along with Anderson's transfer, and proved how savvy a trader Sather was. He wanted to ditch Anderson because his best years were over and the off-winger was still looking for a big contract. But, he didn't want to

give away a possible excellent year or two that might be left in Anderson's legs. The stipulation was that if Anderson scored 70 goals in two years, regular season and playoffs combined, Fletcher would have to give up a first-round draft choice; 50 goals meant a second-rounder; fewer meant nothing would be given. As it turned out, Anderson scored 46 times, so the Leafs were off the hook, proving that Fletcher was every bit as savvy.

From the Oilers' perspective, the deal made perfect sense. They got a top-flight left-winger (Damphousse), a rugged stay-at-home defenceman (Richardson), a possible backup goalie (Ing), and a prospect of unknown talent (Thornton). They gave up a top-flight goalie (Fuhr) whom they could afford to lose, a winger who was on the backside of a superb career (Anderson), a replaceable tough-guy fourth-line winger (Berube), and a player they had no use for (Linseman).

The Leafs picked up the best "money" goalie in the NHL, a man who could stop the haemorrhaging that goes with constant losing night after night. As Fletcher said, "Now we have a goalie who can give us a chance to win any time he puts on the pads." In Fuhr and Anderson, Fletcher also acquired a new attitude, one that had a combined 10 Stanley Cup rings and a much needed positiveness to it. The Leafs gave up talent in Damphousse and Richardson, but Ing had played himself out of a Leaf uniform and Thornton, Fletcher felt, wasn't going to light up the banal Edmonton sky (a nuclear reactor couldn't do that).

The ensuing fortunes of the players involved in this mega-trade proved Fletcher clearly got the better of the deal. The Leafs eventually traded Fuhr and future considerations to Buffalo for Dave Andreychuk, Darren Puppa, and the Sabres' 1st-round pick in 1993 (Kenny Jonsson). For Anderson and a '94 4th-rounder, the Leafs got Mike Gartner. And for Berube, taking into account the complexities of the later deal with Calgary, the Leafs got Kent Manderville. For Damphousse and a '93 4th-rounder (Adam Wiesel), Sather got Shayne Corson, Brent Gilchrist, and Vladimir Vujtek from Montreal (Gilchrist was later traded to Minnesota for Todd Elik). For Ing, the Oilers got but a 7th-round draft pick in '94 (Chris Wickenheiser) and future considerations from Detroit. Scott Thornton has struggled to crack the Oiler lineup and has played more for their AHL affiliate in Cape Breton than at the Northlands Coliseum. Richardson, however, has been a reliable, rugged defenceman who has stayed on the Edmonton blue-line since.

By the end of training camp, while the Lindros family was making a mockery of the NHL and asses of themselves, the Leafs looked as though they had turned a corner. They were a stable club with a competent front office, they had a world-class goalie, and their pre-season record was an impressive 5–2–2. Fletcher and Fuhr were two new "f" words Leaf fans could finally use to replace the old, '80s version. Re-establishing tradition was also made easier by virtue of

the fact that the upcoming season was the NHL's 75th. All of the Original Six teams wore their original uniforms and played in their dark jerseys for home games (during the last half of the year) as they had done before the 1970–71 season. This was the year that history was in vogue, and if there was one place the Leafs looked the best, it was in the past. As a celebratory gesture to the olden days, the Leafs met at Union Station the day before the 1991 season opened to take the train *en masse* to Montreal for the game. All the players wore suits and fedoras and looked every bit the '50s group of Chadwick, Hannigan, Sloan, and Bolton. The mood around the league was one of looking back and waxing nostalgic, which helped Fletcher establish the kind of atmosphere he needed if he were going to succeed.

The opener at the Forum was special. The referees wore their old off-white sweaters, the Leafs and Habs their old jerseys. Not for years had the rivalry seemed so important, the urge, the life-dependent *need* to beat and hate and play the Habs so great. The crowd was unusually raucous, and as always as vocal for the Leafs as the hometown Club. The blue and white lost a thrilling game 4–3, but atoned a couple of nights later at their home opener against another Original Six team, the Red Wings, winning 8–5. Two nights later, they beat St. Louis 3–0 with Fuhr in net for the shutout. The star of these opening three games was the new captain, Clark, who scored five goals and nine points to lead the league at this early stage. But in the St. Louis game he injured his knee and missed the next 10 games. Without him, the Leafs lost their next seven straight. Clark came back too quickly from his hurt and played just three more games before being sidelined for the next 24. His effect on the team was dramatic when he played and equally so when he didn't. If the Leafs were to win regularly, Clark would have to play regularly.

In mid-November, tragedy struck when Grant Fuhr suffered a groin injury. Goal was the Leafs' big vulnerable, and as Fuhr went so went the goals against. Fortunately, backup incompetent Jeff Reese had the flu, so Fletcher called up 20-year-old Felix Potvin from the Rock, a no-choice emergency move that ended up producing a glimmer of hope for the Leafs' future. With Potvin in net the Leafs lost 3–0 to Chicago and 3–1 to Hartford, and tied the Blackhawks 2–2 at the Gardens. However, in the process of going 0–2–1, Felix was stunning. His nickname was the Cat, and after three games with the Leafs no one called him Potvin any more. Although his style was unorthodox and his positioning erratic, his sheer quickness more than compensated. He gave every indication of being capable of stepping into the goal crease of an NHL building every night. Fuhr recovered, Reese got better, but no one forgot about the feline goalie they shipped back to St. John's — Felix Potvin.

The first half of the season produced a strange feeling at the Gardens. The Leafs weren't winning many games, yet everything was enthusiastic, positive, and forward-looking. An open skills com-

petition at one practice produced a crowd of 10,000 kids; Fletcher was preparing for the winter meetings at which he hoped to get Toronto and Montreal back into the same division; Wayne Gretzky and the late great John Candy were looking into getting an OHL franchise to play out of the Gardens again. The very fact that Fletcher was able to get Grant Fuhr had already legitimized both his intentions and his abilities as GM. Whether Fuhr had an average of 2.87 or 3.92 was immaterial. This was the same goalie who played with Messier and Gretzky in Edmonton. He had *five* Stanley Cup rings and a Canada Cup. He had won it all. He was the quickest of the quick, the hero of heroes, the best of the best. And now, he was in a Leaf uniform.

In early December, Fletcher turned the new Leaf class into Grant Fuhr cash, making him the highest paid goalie in the league. The goaler was given a four-year, $6.4 million contract that reflected not his won-lost record but his reputation in the NHL and provided financial respect for the team's marquee player in a way unfamiliar to great Leafs of the Ballard years. Symbolically, it showed all the players in Toronto, in the NHL, in all the minor and junior leagues, that the new Leaf management was not reluctant to spend money to win. Fletcher was prepared to bargain in good faith with the players and the fans.

At the same time, he was keenly aware that more trades would have to be made to salvage the season in the short term and establish a higher level of play long term. This was especially clear after a terrible 12–1 loss to Pittsburgh on Boxing Day, tying the Leafs' mark for worst margin of defeat, an 11–0 embarrassment to Boston on January 18, 1964. Don Simmons was in for all 11 that night, and Fuhr was in net for the whole dozen now. If not for him, though, Mario Lemieux's seven points could easily have turned into a Sittler-tying 10-point night.

Meanwhile, Stavro was slowly wending his way into power, thanks largely to the fact that by opening day MLGL was still $37 million in debt. On September 20, 1991, Bill Ballard finally gave up the good, unwinnable fight and agreed to sell his 25% of HEBL shares for $21,075,000, a sum the estate was able to pay thanks to a loan from the TD Bank. The two parties also agreed to end all litigation against each other. The ownership pie now looked like this:

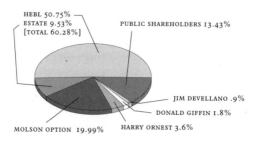

HEBL 50.75%
ESTATE 9.53%
[TOTAL 60.28%]

PUBLIC SHAREHOLDERS 13.43%

JIM DEVELLANO .9%

DONALD GIFFIN 1.8%

MOLSON OPTION 19.99%   HARRY ORNEST 3.6%

These moves gave Stavro a clear opening to take full control of the Leafs at the next shareholders' meeting a month later. On October 22, Stavro replaced Giffin as Chairman and CEO of MLG Ltd., and deposed four other board members — Rogers, Eaton, Lawrence, and McDowell. Using the estate's power with allies Crump and Kelly, Stavro then elected the three of them and four close friends* to form the new board.

Manoli Stavroff Skoldas, 64 years old, born in Gabresh, Macedonia, was now in full control of the Toronto Maple Leafs hockey club. By this time, he had seen Fletcher in action long enough to know the team was headed in the right direction. Stavro had begun the Eastern Canada Professional Soccer League in the early '60s, a minor pro gig that had four teams — Toronto City,** Toronto Italia, Hamilton Steelers, and Montreal Cantalia. Though the league didn't flourish for long, Stavro did have an inkling about building a team. He was also smart enough to see how warmly the players, organization, fans, and media had embraced the new Fletcher era of hope and prosperity. Peace was made. Fletcher kept his job.

"The fans spoke, and I listened," said Stavro. Sage and humble words that said more of his fruit market character than any thirst for power he might have possessed. His house, Sevendon, on Teddington Park Avenue, attested to his business acumen; his retaining Fletcher attested to his common sense.

---

* Ron Pringle, Ted Nikolaou, Brian Bellmore, and George Whyte. For the 1994–95 season three new members were added: Robert G. Bertram and George J. Engman from the Ontario Teachers' Pension Plan Board, and William T. Brock from the TD Bank.

** City was operated by Stavro and featured the ageing British hero Sir Stanley Matthews in 1961.

GRAIG ABEL

IX

The Trade

On the morning of January 2, 1992, Cliff Fletcher woke up and took notice of three items in the sports section of his newspaper. First, his rebuilding Leafs were in fifth and last place in the Norris Division with a record of 10–25–5. Minnesota was the nearest club, in fourth and final playoff spot, ten points ahead with an astounding five games in hand. Second, the team's leading point-getter was Peter Zezel with 30 in 40 games, exactly half the season. For the Leafs' leading man to be on course for a 60-point season pointed all too obviously to the team's woeful offence. And then the third item. The headline read:

IRATE GILMOUR
LEAVES FLAMES
IN CONTRACT SPAT

The day got better and better and better for Fletcher. By bedtime he had orchestrated the single largest trade in NHL history and the most one-sided deal ever made by the Toronto Maple Leafs. For ever more it will be referred to simply as "The Trade." Coming to Toronto were Doug Gilmour, Jamie Macoun, Ric Nattress, Kent Manderville, and Rick Wamsley. Going to Calgary were Gary Leeman, Michel Petit, Alexander Godynyuk, Craig Berube, and Jeff Reese. The results were as disastrous for Doug Risebrough's Calgary team as they were miraculous for Fletcher's Leafs.

The story began in 1990. After taking the Flames to a Cup victory in 1989, Terry Crisp coached the Flames to an excellent 99-point season for his encore (42–23–15). That, however, was 12 wins and 18 points down from the amazing Cup year (54–17–9, 117 points) and was followed by a quick 4–2 loss to L.A. in the first round of the playoffs. The glory was fleeting. Fletcher, the Calgary GM, fired Crisp and assistant coach Tom Watt after the loss to L.A. He named Doug Risebrough, his assistant for the past year, as new head coach. Just a year later, Fletcher came to the Leafs and the Flames gave Riser, despite his vast inexperience, the GM portfolio to go with his coaching duties (before his year as assistant GM, he was Crisp's assistant coach for two years).

Risebrough was inheriting a big and talented team, but one with at least five players who were either playing out their option or who

were discontent with their level of pay. Gilmour, Macoun, and Nattress were among the latter. Because he wanted to make his own mark on the team, Risebrough was willing to trade anyone not happy or motivated enough to play at his highest level. To make matters worse, the Flames started the '91–'92 season slowly, going a mediocre 12–10–5 over the first two months of the season. Risebrough had seen what had happened to Crisp the year before, with a much better record, so no one had to tell him the heat was on. He phoned his friend and mentor Cliff Fletcher in Toronto and asked about Gary Leeman. Fletcher in turn asked about Gilmour, whom he was pretty sure Risebrough, the former Montreal centre, was willing to trade. The year before, while Risebrough worked under Fletcher in Calgary, Cliff himself had offered Gilmour for Wendel Clark.

Why Risebrough was interested in *Leeman*, and not Clark, is difficult to understand. Leeman had the same pursed lips and scrunched brow as Darryl Sittler, but that's where the similarities ended. The Leaf winger did have one excellent year, but that had been a year and a half ago under a happy-go-lucky, goal-hungry coach. Leeman had done nothing before or since to distinguish himself as a superior NHLer. Gilmour, on the other hand, had averaged more than a point a game over nine and a half years and 656 games. The most plausible explanation for Risebrough's interest seems to be that Leeman was the best forward Fletcher had or was willing to talk about, and if Risebrough was going to talk trade he'd like to do it with someone he knew. As Fletcher's assistant the year before, he would not have gotten to know many general managers directly as equals, so Fletcher was the safest (though not necessarily the best) bet.

Gilmour's unhappiness was motivated at first by money, but over time pay became the least important reason for his leaving the Flames on New Year's Day, 1992. His contract had expired the previous spring, and he decided to take his case to arbitration. He submitted a demand of $1.2 million; Calgary countered with $550,000, a small increase over the $391,500 they paid him in 1990–91 when he scored 81 points. On November 12, 1991, the day before his arbitration hearing, the Flames played a home game against Detroit. In the press box sat Al Coates, the new assistant GM of the Flames, and by his side was Gary Schreider, the supposedly "independent" arbitrator who would decide Gilmour's case in less than 24 hours! At the hearing the next day, Gilmour's eyes were opened further, this time by the evaluation of him that the Flames presented to Schreider. Gilmour was shocked: "They said my skills have gone downhill. . . . They felt that my skills had diminished from my first year in Calgary to last year. I was not going to accept that." It was a demoralizing process, made more so by the arbitrator's decision, handed down December 8. Not surprisingly, Schreider decided on a salary of $750,000, well below Gilmour's expectations. The next day, upset by all that had happened, he asked to be traded.

"He [Risebrough] has not made any impact trades since he has become general manager. Knowing how unhappy I am, he now has an excuse to trade somebody. And if the trade doesn't work out, then he doesn't have to take the blame for it."

It didn't and he did. In announcing the deal, Fletcher simply said, "Not many 10-player deals are made, especially one that can help both teams now and in the future." The result is reminiscent of one of Don Cherry's favourite stories, involving a Bobby Orr goal against Calgary's precursor, Fletcher's Atlanta Flames:

> Bobby got the puck behind our net and slowly moved up along the right boards. None of the Atlanta players dared run at him at the time because they knew they would be deked and caught out of position, so they all sat back as he moved up the side. He crossed our blueline, the centre red line, the Flames' blueline and then moved into the corner near the Atlanta net. Now the Flames figured that they had him trapped — literally in a corner, so the whole team ran at him, including the goaltender. Suddenly Bobby accelerated, went behind the net, came out the other side and put the puck into the twine on his backhand while the entire Atlanta team was flat on the ice!
>
> Most players would jump around or hot-dog it after scoring a goal like that, but not Bobby. As soon as the red light flashed he put his head down because he knew he had embarrassed the entire Flames team; he hated embarrassing people.

After the trade, Fletcher put his head down and went back to his office. He had embarrassed Risebrough and the Flames. Badly.

The trade broke down into four parts. Clearly the heart of it was Gilmour for Leeman. Leeman became instantly unpopular in Calgary, and his play did nothing to make the fans apologetic for their animosity. A month into his stint with the Flames, he was loudly booed during pre-game introductions at the Saddledome. He finished the year with two goals and seven assists in 29 games and was traded for Brian Skrudland a year later, after scoring just nine more goals in 30 games. Calgary lost Skrudland to Florida in the expansion draft in 1993, so in effect the Flames gave Gilmour away and got absolutely nothing in return.

Rick Wamsley for Jeff Reese was an obvious trade-within-the-trade. By mid-December, Wamsley had dressed for only three games in Calgary as Risebrough clearly favoured Mike Vernon as the number-one goalie. In Reese the Flames got one of the worst goalies ever to wear a Leaf uniform. Unconventional, erratic, inconsistent, with undisciplined legs and slow hands, Reese was as replaceable as a deflected puck that goes into the crowd. Wamsley didn't figure in the Leafs' goalie plans, as it turned out, but retired and became the goaltending consultant for the whole Leaf organization. In the summer of 1994, he was appointed full-time assistant coach to Pat

Burns, another example of Fletcher working a Leaf Alumnus into the club's front office once his playing days were over. (Reese was traded to Hartford for Dan Keczmer a year-and-a-half later.)

The defencemen made another pairing in the trade: Macoun and Nattress for Godynyuk and Petit. The Flames' pair was one of the most reliable defensive units in the league. They had played together for the better part of four years and knew everything about each others' moves and styles, critical factors with blue-line partners. They were a rare tandem of almost unparalleled quality in their own zone — fierce in the corners, tough when the going got rugged — stay-at-homers who could keep the front of the net clear and move the puck out of their end effectively. In Godynyuk, Risebrough got an unknown, unproven quality and was likely mollified by the allure of the Russian name. Not all Russians, as it turned out, were caviar; Godynyuk was strictly canned tuna. He too was left unprotected in the '93 expansion draft and claimed by the Panthers. Petit is the only one of the five who endured, but he left the team as a free agent, signing with L.A. in August 1994.

Manderville and Berube seemed almost an aside, a suggestion made by Fletcher who was amazed that Risebrough was willing to trade so many players all at once to one team. Berube added a little toughness to a team that was becoming less and less tough with the passage of each long-distance minute Risebrough talked to Fletcher on the phone. Berube was traded to Washington for a 5th-round selection in 1993, which Risebrough used to select 20-year-old prospect Darryl Lafrance. Manderville was a Canadian Olympian of unknown potential who has turned out to be another little steal, a fine fourth-line winger who could kill penalties, check, grind, plant himself in the crease, dig in the corners, scrap. He has been a valuable commodity who won't get any television deals or million-dollar contracts, but without whom Stanley Cups can't be won.

In Gilmour the Leafs got a franchise player who literally changed the fortunes of the entire organization. He became the best two-way centre in the game, playing superbly with and without the puck. He killed penalties and directed the power play and his passing equalled Gretzky's or Lemieux's. Most important of all, he brought the attitude and character of a Stanley Cup champion to the dressing room. Losing a tough game was no longer acceptable to the Leafs. Trying "really hard" and coming "really close" were no longer measures of success. Winning and getting two points were what counted.

Gilmour's skating style recalled Darryl Sittler's; short, choppy strides, skating from the hips, head up, both hands always on the stick, puck in front, looking to pass rather than deke and risk a two- or three-on-one the other way. The way he used his stick was magical. He had the ability to go into the corner and somehow strip a much bigger player of the puck. He intuitively knew where his wingers were or when a defenceman was slipping into the slot. He could read a

Gilmour's early days, in St. Louis.
GRAIG ABEL

game beautifully, and knew exactly when to be tough and when to
"fall" to draw a penalty, knew when a penalty "should" be called.
He was a master of self-preservation who could throw a check with
the best of them or land on his back after the slightest contact.
Gilmour hearkened back to the days of the good ol' boys, class of
'67. Like Davey Keon, he used a perfectly straight stick. The gap in
the front of his mouth, courtesy of a little stickwork, rebuffed the
image of the "pretty boy" NHLer of the '90s. His slapshot was
innocuous, the showy shot not a part of his repertoire at all, his size
was more '60s than '90s, as was his tenacity. It's as though he
represented the answer to the question so often asked about how a
player like Keon would fare in today's game. Just look at Dougie.
He'd fare just fine, thank you.

During their St. Louis days together, Brian Sutter had thought Gilmour looked like Charles Manson and with that inimitable hockey humour nicknamed him "Killer." The name stuck, but a far more appropriate reason for the moniker can be found by looking at Gilmour just before he is set to take a faceoff. He looks to see where his teammates are setting up, checks the other team's lineup, looks at the linesman's hand, stares far away somewhere with the most determined concentration. He looks *through* the player, the boards, the stands. His eyes are like bullets, his look fierce and intense. The love of competition, the desire to prove he is better than the opposition each and every moment, is what makes him a Killer. And the teeth!

Gilmour played two seasons for the Cornwall Royals of the OHL (1981–83). In his final year, he scored 70 goals and had 177 points, and won the Red Tilson Trophy as the league's MVP. The previous summer, however, he wasn't drafted until the 7th round by St. Louis, 134th overall, because most scouts felt his lack of size would work against him in the big NHL. He was thought to be one of those phenoms who can put big numbers on the board in junior, but fade sadly when the strength and size of the NHL are at hand. In his first three seasons with the Blues under coach Jacques Demers, Gilmour produced very modest, if consistent, point totals of 53, 57, and 53. He became known as a defensive specialist who could do wonders stopping the other team's best centre and score the occasional goal himself when the chance arose.

The '86–'87 season proved to be a watershed year for him. Demers jumped ship to join the Red Wings, and Jacques Martin was named the new Blues coach. He gave Gilmour more ice time and greater responsibility: number 9 responded in spades. He finished with an incredible 105 points, fifth in league scoring, and St. Louis finished first in the Norris Division. The next year he scored 86 points before Cliff Fletcher brought him to Calgary with Mark Hunter, Steve Bozek, and Michael Dark for Mike Bullard, Craig Coxe, and Tim Corkery on September 6, 1988. A steal even then.

In Calgary, Gilmour blossomed into a *bona fide* star centre. It was he who scored the two biggest goals of the '89 finals that Calgary won over Montreal. With the teams tied 2–2 going into the third period of Game 6, Gilmour scored the game winner and the insurance goal as the Flames won 4–2. The Cup was Calgary's and Dougie the hero.* After Fletcher traded captain Brad McCrimmon in the purge of '90, Gilmour was one of four players to wear the "C" that year, and if it hadn't been for his contract troubles he was probably set to be elected to the job full-time the following season. In his 266 games as a Flame, he recorded 295 points, all the while maintaining his superb defensive responsibilities to a fault. Many of the great

---

* Although Al MacInnis won the Conn Smythe.

centres of the game today couldn't describe what the inside of their own blueline looks like, but Gilmour was as likely to be found behind his own net checking the offensive centre as he was behind the opposition goal looking to pass to a man out front. Never could he be seen floating at his blueline waiting for the "Showdown" break-away pass. If he were on the ice in the last minute with the other goal empty, he knew he was there to preserve a one- or two-goal win, not to try to pot a selfish empty-netter to pad his own goal total. In the modern breakaway world of Gretzky, Gilmour still practised the ancient art of backchecking. Nor did he shy away from skating along the boards to avoid being checked, or cower when the going got tough. From day one of his career he had to prove that heart and skill outweighed any size deficiency, and in fact it is *because of* his size that he has developed the intensity, the belligerence, and the indomitable perseverance that make him so great. His size didn't work against him. It worked *for* him.

To be fair to Risebrough, Gilmour was not the player in Calgary that he became in Toronto when he put on number 93 for the Leafs. It's just one of those unexplainable blips that occur in sports. He was obviously trying his hardest with the Flames, but somehow Toronto — the fans, the coach, the building — brought more out of him in the same way the intensity of a Game 7 of a Stanley Cup final is greater, more dramatic, than an average regular season game. For Gilmour in Toronto, every game became a Game 7.

The Trade had major effects on both clubs. Calgary went on a mini-win streak right away (4–1–1) and then collapsed completely. Two weeks after the trade the Flames were 20–18–6. They finished the year 31–37–12 and missed the playoffs for the first time since 1975. On March 1, they lost 11–0 to Vancouver, the club's worst defeat ever, and two days later, under relentless pressure, Risebrough removed himself as coach and put Guy Charron in his place (i.e., he fired himself as coach to keep his more secure job as GM).

Meanwhile, the Leafs came to life. The day Cliff Fletcher started in the summer of '91, the team had only one player who had been on a Stanley Cup–winning team (Mike Krushelnyski). By January 3, 1992, they had seven (Fuhr, Gilmour, Macoun, Nattress, Wamsley, Anderson, Krushelnyski). The experience, the maturity, the depth, paid off instantly, though Macoun was quick to suggest patience be the order of the day. "This is a two- or three-year project. Hopefully the fans understand after 20 years of neglect — maybe that's not the right word — after 20 years of misdirection, Cliff is here to show the right way." Sage advice for a newcomer, but he was dead wrong about one thing: "neglect" *was* the right word.

The Leafs began to win games they would never have even been in a few weeks earlier. At the Joe Louis Arena in Detroit, down 3–1, they came back to tie. Then in overtime Gilmour stripped Yves Racine of the puck behind the Detroit net and whipped it out to Anderson who scored the winner. The next night they beat Montreal

6–4. Two nights later they scored two in the third to beat the Red Wings again, this time 4–3. A crucial weekend came at the end of February. While the Leafs were developing chemistry and confidence, the Stars were holding their own. By February 29, Toronto was still nine points behind Minnesota for the final playoff spot, although the Stars had only one game in hand now. That Saturday night at the Gardens the Leafs pulled a rabbit the size of an elephant out of a hat the size of a thimble. Down 5–2 to Chicago in the third, they scored three unanswered goals to tie the score, and Captain Clark got the winner in overtime. The next night they thumped the Stars 6–2, and all of a sudden they were just five points back and coming on strong. The season had all the makings of a 1959 repeat, but this time it would be Gilmour rather than Imlach who would lead the way if the comeback were to be completed.

The team went on a five-game road trip out west, a beautiful part of the country to be sure, but traditionally inhospitable to the Leafs' fortunes. Earlier in the year, pre-Dougie, they had lost three in a row without much of a fuss, 6–4 to Calgary, 4–2 to Winnipeg, and 4–1 to Vancouver. That was then. This time they went into the Northlands Coliseum and beat Edmonton 5–2 and the next night staged a great comeback in Calgary. This was the first trip to the Saddledome for the new-Leaf fivesome, two months after Dougie *et al.* came to T.O. Watt started Wamsley in goal, figuring the revenge factor would be great, but with four minutes to go in the game the Flames had chased him from the goal and held a comfortable 4–2 lead. Then Dougie took over. He set up Daniel Marois at 16:08 to make it 4–3, but Ron Stern came right back to make it 5–3 Calgary with 2:06 remaining. The fans trickled to the exits, figuring the two points were in the bag. The Flames didn't need Gilmour that badly. But with Fuhr on the bench, Dougie scored in a mad scramble at 19:13 and then made a perfect pass to Rob Pearson who tied the score 5–5 with just nine seconds to go. The overtime was all Leafs, and it was Toronto that had to "settle" for a tie. It was vintage Gilmour, and the Calgary fans were left to hiss at new coach Charron and the hometown players, their venom really intended for the other Doug in the building — Risebrough.

The Leafs were finally doing what any good team has to be able to do — pull victory from the deadly jaws of defeat. The attitude of the Salmings, Leemans, and Derlagos of the '80s was being replaced by a refusal to accept defeat. Playing poorly happened on occasion, but you still had to win those games somehow, anyhow. Good teams found a way.

However, a few wins and decent play does not a season make. There was still plenty of work to be done with this '91–'92 team if the schedule was going to extend to the playoffs. The two wins in western Canada gave way to two 4–1 losses in California to San Jose and Los Angeles, lapses in team concentration the Leafs could ill-afford. They finished the road trip with an essential 3–0 shutout of their rivals, the North Stars, in the Twin Cities, with Fuhr at his acrobatic best, but the Leafs were still six points back.

While the team was improving on ice, Fletcher was also making sure its salary structure moved out of Ballard's Museum and into Stavro's Modern. The players deserved their due respect in the Alumni room but also at the bank. Macoun signed a four-year, $2.4 million contract, doubling his salary, and Gilmour was given a four-year, $4 million contract, thereby ensuring that both would likely end their careers as Leafs. Gilmour was ecstatic: "This is the first place I wanted to go. Now I want to stay here a long time. . . . I'd love to retire here."

As the season wound down, the first ever modern-day players' strike became a greater and greater possibility. On March 28, the Stars lost 4–3 to Calgary while the Leafs beat the Blues 3–2. The teams were now only two points apart. But the momentum subsided once again. Minnesota beat Buffalo the next night 5–3 to move four points up, and then the dreaded strike occurred. For 10 days it seemed there would be no resolution to the Leafs' comeback and the Stanley Cup would not be contested for the first time since the influenza epidemic of 1919 cancelled the finals between the Canadiens and the Seattle Metropolitans. Money, politics, and lawyers took control of a playoffs promising drama, tension, and excitement.

The strike was also terribly disappointing for the Leaf Alumni. On April 1, the Leafs were to honour Ace Bailey (number 6) and Bill Barilko (number 5) by officially retiring their numbers and raising commemorative banners in their honour. The strike postponed the game against the Islanders indefinitely, and six days later Ace Bailey died at age 88. He knew the honour was awaiting, but what a thrill it would have been to have seen him at centre ice as the banners slowly sailed to the rafters of Maple Leaf Gardens. Instead, the ceremony went on without him before the October 17 game versus Chicago near the start of the '92–'93 season.

After just 10 days, on April 10, the players and owners ratified a new collective bargaining agreement. The players agreed to an 84-game schedule, with the two extra home games to be played at neutral sites. The owners agreed to reduce the age of unrestricted free agents from 31 to 30, and an agreement for long-term merchandising rights was reached. This last was a key issue because everything from hockey cards to clothing was soaring in popularity, collectability, and value, but the players were still receiving Imlach-like profits from the revenues.

The strike was over, the season was on again, but the Leafs weren't

HOCKEY HALL OF FAME

able to rekindle the fire in the ensuing days. They lost 6–2 to the Islanders their first game back, assuring Minnesota of the final playoff spot in the Norris Division. While the disappointment at falling short was great, a recapitulation of the year as a whole produced nothing but hope and optimism. Fletcher had made remarkable progress with the club and the future was actually something to look forward to.

In retrospect, the '91–'92 season represented the growing pains of a changing club. By the summer of 1992, Fletcher was way ahead of schedule in reorganizing every facet of the Leaf organization, a result of both his talent and the independence he was given. No one else in MLG or HEB or RCMP or CSIS or TTC had any input or disruptive influence in his decision-making. "The Trade" was a once-in-a-lifetime deal, like winning the lottery, and improving the Leafs beyond Gilmour was going to be a slower and tougher process.

Although the team missed the playoffs, so many player changes had been made that it would have been impossible to achieve greater cohesion more quickly. Only eight players from the year before were still with the Leafs, and Fletcher had brought in 14 others, including three young players from the '92 Albertville Olympics: Kent Manderville (Canada), Joe Sacco (U.S.A.), and Dmitri Mironov (Commonwealth of Independent States). The in-and-out-of-the-lineup Clark also played havoc with the team's consistency; the longer he played the better the Leafs played, but over the year his injuries proved costly to a team skin-thin in depth. He played in 3 games, missed 10, played 3, missed 24, played 6, missed 3, played 31. It was during that final stretch of 31, when he and Gilmour were both in the lineup, that the team excelled. They went 16–13–2 over that stretch and 20–18–2 over the last half of the year, doubling their win total of the first 40 games of the season (10–25–5).

By the end of the year, the Leafs had a great goalie (Fuhr), a great prospect (Potvin), a solid defence core (Macoun, Nattress, Rouse), a rugged winger (Clark), a scoring centre (Gilmour), a great checking centre (Zezel), and great potential (Manderville, Sacco, Mironov, Pearson). Glenn Anderson, who had just 13 points in the first 40 games, scored 44 in the second half with Dougie as his centre. The next season couldn't start soon enough.

The future also looked bright on the farm. The St. John's Maple Leafs went to the 7th game of the Calder Cup finals before losing to the Adirondack Red Wings 4–2 in an odd series that saw all seven games won by the visiting team. The farm is where the prospects are, and St. John's gave every indication the big team's success was catching on.

From the office, Fletcher continued his massive restructuring. He made plans for more luxury boxes in the Gardens to increase revenue, sold board advertisements for $150,000–$200,000 a year, and used on-ice ads to further supplement the Leaf cash reserves. He was also actively working to get wine and beer into the Gardens,* the revenue from which would go toward improving all facets of hockey operations. His attempts proved to be a red-tape headache, however, as the Ontario Liquor Board's Licence Act applied to baseball, football, and soccer, but *not* hockey. It was an extraordinary omission that required the Act itself to be amended before the City could give final approval to license the Gardens.

Fletcher also sought to improve Toronto's schedule — something Floyd Smith had refused to do — which was fraught with undesirable dates. Too often the Leafs would play a road game on a Friday and come home to play at the Gardens on Saturday night against a team that had enjoyed the previous night off. Fletcher didn't want the visiting teams to have such an advantage, sitting in Toronto for a day while the Leafs played and travelled and wore themselves out. Traditionally, the Leafs wanted to play as many Saturday night games as possible, but Fletcher thought sacrificing three or four choice dates a year for six or eight crucial points in the standings would be plenty worth it for fans who wanted a winning team.

The Leafs also presented a 70-page report to the NHL proposing that the 1995 All-Star Game be held in Toronto, a wonderful idea in light of the fact that the Gardens hadn't seen All-Stars since they last saw the Stanley Cup, while many less deserving cities had hosted it in the interim.

Even though the Leafs weren't in the playoffs, May 1992 was a tense and dramatic month for Fletcher. On May 4, he made his toughest decision as general manager when he dismissed Tom Watt as coach and reassigned him to the position of Director of Player Development. In explaining the move, Fletcher said: "This is part of the ongoing attempt to rebuild the structure of Maple Leaf Gardens. We're looking down the road, not short-term, and I just feel over the long haul that now would be the time to bring in someone who could grow with the team." He promised to have a new coach by draft day, June 20, but immediately two men were rumoured to have the inside track — Dave King and Leaf assistant Mike Murphy.**

As coach of Canada's National Team since 1983, King was based in Calgary and the team often played and practised at the Saddledome. He was, therefore, a well-known quantity to Fletcher and was generally considered the best coach *not* in the NHL. He was a patient,

---

* Toronto and Ottawa were the only stadiums or arenas in North America not licensed.

** Although the Blues had fired their coach Brian Sutter on May Day, Fletcher wasn't interested.

controlled coach, not given to fits of screaming, who worked very well with younger players and helped them reach their potential in a way that translated to game success. His popularity and moderate success at the international level always made his position with Team Canada secure. He was never going to be fired, and he always had the excuse of "young players" or "lack of experience" or "make-shift squad" in the event of a loss. King's Canada's juniors would never lose games to countries they shouldn't lose to. Such is the level of competition worldwide that the weak teams — Switzerland, Italy, Germany, France — were so inferior that even the poorest performance would be enough for Canada to win. A loss to a strong team — Sweden, Russia, Finland, Czechoslovakia — wouldn't be such a surprise as to merit King being fired. As well, motivating a 17-year-old kid to play for his country is much easier than motivating a 10-year veteran to play well in game number 42, 63, or 78 of another NHL season. As National Team coach, King looked as good as he was ever going to get.

King's assets were also his weaknesses. He had no NHL experience, and that was an important fact to consider for a team like the Leafs that Fletcher was trying to develop. He wanted a strong, knowledgeable man behind the bench to provide confidence and direction. The last thing the Leafs needed was to train an NHL coach by giving him the experience with them. King was born to coach at the junior level, not at the NHL level. He was a tutor.

On May 21, he agreed to join the Flames as head coach. The very fact he did so attests to his qualities. On the one hand, he was being loyal to Calgary. For King, this was the obvious choice of team. At the same time, it was almost as if the challenge of Toronto was too daunting, too big-time professional, too foreign. He was born in Saskatoon and his whole hockey life had been limited exclusively to the Prairies (University of Saskatchewan Huskies, Saskatoon Junior B Quakers) before he began coaching the National Team. The pressure in Toronto would have been greater, the fans harder to please, the expectations higher, the atmosphere unfamiliar and intimidating. Not so in Calgary. King was as familiar with the dressing rooms in the Saddledome as he was with his own living room. It was the obvious choice, to be sure, but also the safest. The same logic holds true for Fletcher's coach considerations. Hiring King would have been the safest, most obvious move Fletcher could have made. No one could have criticized him or second-guessed him. Just the opposite. Fletcher would have been lauded yet again for luring more world-class talent to the Leafs. But, in truth, it was a godsend King signed with Calgary.

Over the next two years, King led the Flames to excellent regular season records with 97 points each year, but both times they were eliminated in the first round of the playoffs. In 1994 they were leading the Canucks 3–1 in games before losing three consecutive heartbreakers in overtime, the last one 4–3 in the Saddledome. The

pressure of such games is simply much different from playing for a gold medal in some small village in Poland or Finland. More important or less important is not the point: *different.* King was as unfamiliar with NHL pressure as he was familiar with international competition.

Fletcher's patience and luck were rewarded on May 28 when Pat Burns ditched the Montreal Canadiens after being attacked in the press yet again for his failure to produce results in the playoffs after yet another excellent regular season with another below-average roster. Fletcher needed as much time as it takes to dial 514 plus the seven digits to Burns' home to decide that Burns was the man to work with the Leafs long-term. They agreed to terms immediately.

And so, in less than a year as president and general manager, Cliff Fletcher had brought in the most competent, intelligent, successful hockey men around to manage the Toronto Maple Leafs.

DOUG MACLELLAN / HOCKEY HALL OF FAME

X

Burns Takes Control

"In Montreal, they talk about the Canadiens' pride and tradition. Well, if the Canadiens were as bad as the Leafs were for so many years, the Forum would have been two-thirds empty."
— Cliff Fletcher

Montreal fans are, quite simply, the worst in the NHL. They do not love hockey; they love the Canadiens. There is no good reason, in their eyes, why the Habs can't win the Cup every year. This is Montreal, after all. The players put the sweater on, the coach is inspired by tradition behind the bench, victory is assured. A loss is always the referee's fault first, the coach's fault second, and the players' fault third. All three, on any given night, are equally culpable. For the fans, it's not about the love of the game; it's about seeing the Habs win. When that goes, so go the fans.

This is why Pat Burns dumped the unworthy Canadiens. In his first year with Montreal, he took them to the finals before losing to the wonderful Lanny McDonald Flames of 1989. The next three years his Habs won 41, 39, and 41 games in the regular season, but each time lost to Boston in the second round of the playoffs (4–1 in 1990, 4–3 in 1991, 4–0 in 1992). With each loss Burns was not only criticized, but his methods were trashed, and his very integrity ridiculed, primarily by anti-English journalists. The 1992 playoffs were the last straw.

The Canadiens' first-round opponent was the Hartford Whalers, and the series went the full seven games. Russ Courtnall scored at 5:26 of the second overtime to give Montreal the series win in Game 7, but that was hardly good enough for the fans and media. Montreal won the first two games at the Forum 2–0 and 5–2, but Hartford came back to win Game 3 at the Civic Centre 5–2. After the loss, Burns was pilloried for being a lousy coach on the road and for blowing the chance to end the series quickly. Only a sweep would have satisfied the media's itch for perfection and pacified the fans' cry for victory. The loss was called "an embarrassment," the team referred to as the "worst on road since Napoleon."

A second win for the hometown Whalers, 3–1, ensured this would be a long series and incurred the wrath of Montrealers, all of whom felt insulted by having to play so many games to do what everyone knew would eventually be done — eliminate the Whalers. *After* a 7–4

win at the Forum in the fifth game, Burns was again sent before the firing squad, this time for benching Courtnall and Mike McPhee. Game 6, back at the Civic Centre, went into overtime, and when Yvon Corriveau scored after just 24 seconds to give Hartford a 2–1 win, the Montreal fans and press launched a two-pronged attack. They railed against referee Dan Marouelli for his decision to disallow a Brent Gilchrist "goal" in the third period that would have given the Habs the win; and they accused Burns of wanting to lose the game, the series, his job. As for the defence, power-play, fore-checking, line matchups? Nada.

The insult of having to play seven games against a team called the Whalers sent every Habs fan into paroxysms of rage and humiliation. Game 7's OT win wasn't a cause for celebration — the series win had been too ugly, dirty, hardworking a business for that. It only gave the fans the chance to wag a finger Burns' way and say, "The next round had better look easier and prettier, coach."

It wasn't. Boston was coming off an equally tough seven-game win over Buffalo but was by far the superior team. The first game was a 6–4 Bruins win at the Forum, a game in which Patrick Roy looked more than a little shaky. By the third period, the fans were derisively chanting, "Racicot! Racicot!", referring to Roy's inept backup who has had a tough time holding the backup job in Fredericton, the Habs' AHL farm team, before and since. Roy's excellent play over the previous four years was not good enough to allow for an off night. Nor was there any need to support him during this crucial series. He was the best; he didn't need support. He needed derision. Smart fans.

Boston won the next three games 3–2, 3–2, and 2–0 to sweep Montreal, and then the Bruins in turn were swept by Pittsburgh. The Penguins went on to whip Chicago in four straight to win the Cup.

The playoff results clearly indicated Montreal was three vast removes from being an excellent team, yet Burns was expected to win the Cup with players like Mike Keane, Mathieu Schneider, Kevin Haller, Sylvain Turgeon, Benoit Brunet, Paul DiPietro, Stephan Lebeau, Gilbert Dionne, and Courtnall. To call them mediocre is flattery beyond deserve. To say they have the skill to win the Cup is pure rue Sainte Catherine drunkenness. Not once in the English or French press in Montreal were the Bruins given credit for embarrassing a vastly inferior team called the Canadiens.

During the Boston series one writer lampooned Burns' coaching methods and ended his column with this: "Aren't defensive teams supposed to hold on to a lead? . . . 'We've got to play good ol' boring Canadiens hockey to win,' Burns said yesterday with barely a nod to the Canadiens tradition of Richard, Moore *et al.*" Richard? Richard scored 544 goals in his career. Give Burns, or any coach, a player of his calibre and you can be sure there would have been no need to play defensive hockey. Moore? He won six Cups, two Hart Trophies, and is in the Hall of Fame. Did Burns have any such player in his lineup? The article serves only to highlight the huge gap between

Hab-fantasy and hard-core reality in the Montreal psyche as well as to illustrate the daily fight the coach had to endure *before* dealing with what happened with his team on ice.

In Toronto, Burns was given a four-year, $1.7 million contract by Fletcher,* making him the highest paid coach in the NHL. A week later, the two joined players, alumni, and luminaries at an open house at the Gardens to unveil the new Leaf jersey, a combination of the vintage Armstrong sweater and the most recent one. The hearkening back to better days was an instant hit and became an important part of establishing a new tradition in Leaf morale by severing ties with the out-of-fashion losers of the '80s. Looking at pictures of players from the Ballard era, one was struck by the simple blandness of the jersey, the lack of imagination that went into the design, and — most important of all — the hideous memories it conjured.

During the summer Consumer Minister Marilyn Churley gave the Leafs approval to sell beer and wine during games, on condition that four police officers patrol the Gardens and area after the game, sales stop after the second period, and are limited to hockey games. The Leafs' Booster Club was also reintroduced that June and became hugely popular. Fans from as far away as Japan, Australia, Germany, and England joined the local enthusiasm for the revival of big-town hockey success in T.O. While open to anyone, the club is not well advertised so as to keep it reasonably exclusive and encourage intimacy between the players and fan club members. At dinners, for instance, one player sits at every table among the fans, providing a special memory that would be lost if membership were to expand significantly.

The only important player move was another coup for Fletcher, who acquired Sylvain Lefebvre from Montreal for a 3rd-round draft choice in 1994 (Chris Murray). The Habs apparently didn't need a defenceman who could keep the puck out of his own net. For the Leafs, the move was precipitated by the loss of Ric Nattress who opted for an American megabucks contract in Philadelphia. After a rocky few games initially, Lefebvre turned into the Leafs' most effective defensive defenceman, always on the ice against the other team's top scorers, always rock-solid reliable. (Glenn Anderson also agreed to a one-year $900,000 contract, putting off his threatened Swiss-league vacation for the lure of reaching more personal plateaus — 1,000 games and 500 goals.)

For the first time in years, training camp was held at Maple Leaf Gardens instead of Newmarket, and Burns was ready and waiting when the players arrived for their first-day medicals. He knew public expectations were high, but none was higher than his. He had never had a losing season in the NHL and he sure wasn't going to start now.

---

* A coach's contract resembles a player's more and more every day.

Lefebvre watches Mario Lemieux.
GRAIG ABEL

Winning was a matter of competing, of wanting to win and proving it. Pat Burns would get effort from his players or they would not play. One or the other. Those were his terms, his rules, his expectations. While everyone else was talking about points, goals, and statistics, Burns refused to fall into the prediction trap. He promised that his players would compete every night, and he wanted to make the playoffs. That was all he would say on the matter.

The Leafs had three big advantages heading into the '92–'93 season. First, they would play 16 games against expansion teams — nine with Tampa Bay, four with San Jose, three with Ottawa. Second, thanks to Fletcher, the Leafs' longest road trip would be just five days. Third, the team would start the season with seven of the first 10 games at home. These small but significant breaks in a long, arduous season gave the team all the assistance they could ever hope to get from the schedule. Now they had to go out and exploit it.

Burns knew he was inheriting a team that, after the Gilmour-Anderson duo, was entirely without scoring ability. Defence would be the order of the season, and Leaf immortal Hap Day's motto became sacrosanct: "If you score one goal, you should expect a tie. If you get two goals, you're entitled to a win." This suited Burns fine. In his four years in Montreal, his goalies won the Jennings trophy twice and finished runner-up the other two years. Refining a defensive system was nothing new to him, and as the season wore on the players grew fond of this system which produced many more wins than losses.

The early part of the schedule was critical. The Leafs could not afford a slow start and fall into that too familiar habit of "another losing season." One thing the Leafs, the bad Leafs of former years, were good at doing was building negative momentum. One loss became five without any difficulty, a bad week became a bad month, a bad month a bad year. A winning streak was much harder to come by, and seemed in the players' psychology more an aberration than the beginning of something positive. For this year, a quick start would immediately establish a new regime. The way the team responded to the positive end of the '91–'92 season was important in terms of character, and their reaction to — acceptance of — Burns would be critical. Burns' edict in camp was simple: "No one who doesn't want to compete will be playing for the Toronto Maple Leafs."

Gilmour again was expected to be the hero, and Clark was beginning the year in good health. Dougie promised to donate $93 to the Children's Wish Foundation for every assist he registered, and if he and Anderson could pick up from where they left off at the end of the '91–'92 season, the Foundation promised to be quite a bit wealthier in six months' time. Clark's new contract offered performance incentives that reflected how important it was to have him in the lineup. His basic salary of $600,000 would increase to $700,000 if he played 45 games, $775,000 after 55 games, and $825,000 after 65. As these two players went, so would go the Leaf offence.

By the end of camp, Burns was not particularly impressed with any of the newcomers. Rob Pearson, Kent Manderville, Joe Sacco, Guy Larose, Darryl Shannon, Dave Tomlinson, Mike Eastwood, and Dmitri Mironov were all given a fair shot at making the club, but none of them went out and positively won a place in the lineup. For most of the first half of the season, Burns kept as many as seven extra bodies in the press box each night, tinkering with his roster to see if anyone would shine. When opening night arrived, though, he had virtually the same lineup Watt had at the end of the previous year, with the exception of Nikolai Borschevsky, the 27-year-old Russian who was drafted 77th overall in the summer and who quickly proved he could skate and score.

For their home opener against Washington, the Leafs got away, far far away, from their defensive plans and lost 6–5. Burns was furious and Leaf fans leery. Their next two games were in Alberta. Sound

familiar? Was this going to be another 0–3 start? Another disheart-
ening trip out west to kill the entire year? Was Burns just like all
the others? Was this year like the last and the last before that?
Rick Wamsley had hurt his knee in training camp, so Felix Potvin
remained with the big club, his demotion to the Rock imminent but
suspended. He was given the start in Calgary, but the Leafs lost 3–2.
Close, yes, but not good enough for Burns. There would be no
10-game streak before he got upset, no lethargy behind the bench,
no "expected" losses, no "nice try; we did our best." The next night
in Edmonton, Burns scratched five young players — Sacco, Pearson,
Manderville, Mironov, and Lefebvre. In their place were added veterans
Gill, Foligno, and McRae and perhaps more eager newcomers,
Larose and Shannon. Two goals by Petr Klima and one by Bernie
Nicholls put the Oilers in command 3–0 by the early part of the
third, and all looked hopeless yet again for a strong start to the
season.

Then Dougie took over.

He scored at 4:50, then set up "old" rookie Nik Borschevsky at
13:25. With Fuhr on the bench, he assisted on Foligno's bang-in that
tied the game with just 42 seconds left. One point. It wasn't a win,
but it was a big, big moral victory that set the tone for the Leafs to
win five of their next six. Four of those wins were against expansion
teams, but this, too, was an important test. Former Leaf teams would
have *assumed* victory against these *lesser* opponents and would, in
turn, have lost. Burns' Leafs won the games they should have won,
easy games to look at on paper after the fact, but challenging at the
time. Toronto was proving early on that nothing would be taken for
granted, and that two points was always possible so long as you
competed for them every night.

Midway through this little streak, Fuhr strained his knee in practice badly enough to require surgery. With Wamsley still on the
sidelines, the Leafs were forced to make Potvin their number-one
goalie for a month until Fuhr recovered. Damian Rhodes was called
up from the Rock as the Cat's backup. Fletcher didn't want to use
the young Cat so much and risk hurting his confidence, but this
stretch of games was a good test for the kid. Fletcher made it clear
to Potvin that he was not being relied upon to take the Leafs to the
Cup, only to try his best under adverse circumstances until Fuhr got
healthy. He'd be back in St. John's as soon as the goalie situation
returned to normal.

The Leafs' first critical test of the season came at the end of
October, in a weekend home-and-home series with Detroit. They
were blown away at the Joe Louis Arena Friday night 7–1, and came
back to the Gardens more or less "having" to win. A lost weekend
to an established club after all the expansion wins would have been
a big blow to team morale. No one will know just how big a blow,
though. The Leafs played a flawless game and won 3–1 in a manner
much more convincing than the score would indicate. They proved

their ability to quell negative momentum early in the year, to take a bad loss on the chin but answer the bell next time out. Burns was establishing that rare and supreme quality — character — in the players, both individually and as a team. Hardly a coincidence, the Leafs were also tied for first place overall.

The so-called easy wins against new clubs had fostered greater team spirit, understanding of the Burns philosophy, team cohesion. They also helped pave the way for solid wins against the top-flight clubs: 4–2 against Pittsburgh, 4–1 in the Boston Garden, 3–2 over the Kings, 5–3 over the Red Wings. But inconsistency was the team's big problem early on, a shroud of years past. Too often a win wasn't treated with the respect it deserved. One win all of a sudden meant the team was the best and that next time out it would be so much easier to get two points. The new team still had to put the two points in perspective. Give yourself credit for a win, sure, but then forget about it because you have to start from scratch the next night. For every big game — always a hardworking, heavy-hitting, defensive-minded win by a goal or two — there was a game where most of the team didn't show up. Losses to L.A. 6–4, New Jersey 8–3, the Rangers 6–0, and Calgary 6–3 were clear indications of Burns' big worry. What would happen if Dougie had an off night or Potvin let in a soft goal? Was there the grit in the pits to pick up the slack? Apparently not. Not yet, anyway.

HOCKEY HALL OF FAME

After the first 20 games the standings reflected the obvious about the tough Norris Division: it was going to be a fight to the finish. Detroit and Minnesota were in first with 24 points, the Leafs and Chicago next with 23, Tampa Bay 20, and St. Louis 17. Burns and Fletcher had repeatedly stressed one goal for the team — make the playoffs. But in a six-team division with the top four qualifying, a spot was in no way to be taken for granted, no matter how well the team was playing. It looked as if 90 points at the very least would be required to get there and the Leafs had just 67 the year before. They were going to have to improve enormously to qualify for Cup competition this time around.

Fuhr returned from his injury, fully prepared to win back his job. In the 11 games he missed, Potvin played every minute and surrendered just 25 goals. Take out seven in the one game against Detroit, and in ten games he allowed only 18. Those were fightin' stats. The rumour mill started to turn: Fuhr was no longer needed in Toronto. Potvin, young as he was, proved beyond all doubt he was ready to play in the NHL *now*. The logical guess was that John Muckler, in his second year behind the Buffalo bench, would love to have the goalie he knew so well during their Edmonton Cup-winning days. Fuhr seemed to be on his way out.

In the first half of the season Fletcher made three deals, all

excellent attempts to fill the gaps without sacrificing team character or individual skill. He claimed Bob McGill on waivers from Tampa Bay as tough, defence insurance, and did the same with Bill Berg as a winger from the Islanders.

Berg, a big, pesky finish-your-check forward, developed the enviable reputation of "love to play with him, hate to play against him" in Toronto. Although he would never be relied upon to score, his less-Hollywood attributes would make him an invaluable addition to the Leafs. In November, Fletcher made his third and most significant deal, acquiring John Cullen from Hartford for a 2nd-rounder in '93.* This was a great move that promised to provide the perfect infusion of offence the Leafs were looking for. In Pittsburgh, Cullen had years of 92 and 110 points before being traded to Hartford for Ron Francis. He was a top-notch scorer, just about as fine a second-line centre as there was in the league. Hartford's willingness to trade such a talent was partly because of his incredible unpopularity in Hartford. Ron Francis was the city's most-loved Whaler, a fact that the fans constantly reminded Cullen of. When he didn't tear the league apart, he was hanged out to dry and as a result his play suffered. The move was also precipitated by Hartford's declining attendance and the resultant need to trim their payroll. Cullen was making $900,000, a sum that scared off many potentially interested teams, but not the Leafs. Fletcher was making one thing clear. If his club lost, it wasn't because he was too cheap to take the necessary risks or acquire the necessary talent.

Friday, December 11, 1992, was an historic night at the Gardens. It was the first time in the team's 65 years that the Leafs played a regular season game on a Friday! (It was also, unfortunately, the day Gary Bettman officially took office as the NHL's new Commissioner.) This was the result of Fletcher's schedule concerns of the previous year, and although the Leafs lost this one 6–3 to the Flames, the yearlong effect was positive. They played four Friday nights at the Gardens in '92–'93 with an excellent 3–1 record, but more impressively played only three Saturday night games all year after playing the night before (with a 2–0–1 record to boot). They also had only two road games on a Friday before a Saturday game and both times they won the second game. Their year-end Saturday-night-at-the-Gardens record was an almost unbeatable 12–3–3.

Compare this to the year before when they played 19 Saturday nights at the Gardens with a 9–9–1 record. On seven occasions they played Friday night on the road before playing at home on the Saturday. Their record in those Saturday games was just 2–5. The scheduling was just the kind of silent strategy Fletcher used to the

---

* Interestingly, the Whalers then traded this draft pick, as well as their 1st and 3rd, to San Jose for the Sharks 1st-round pick (#2 overall), who turned out to be Chris Pronger, one of the great prospects of the draft. San Jose used the 2nd-round pick to select Vlastimil Kroupa.

team's benefit. You won't see this manoeuvre in the record book, but it meant the difference of many vital points in the standings.

In December, the Leafs won only four of 14 games and were playing a kind of hockey that had Burns fuming. In Bloomington, the Stars scored three in the third to win 6–5. At the Aud in Buffalo, the Sabres scored four in the third to win 5–4. On Boxing Day, the Wings clobbered them 5–1 at the Gardens. Just like that they were 13 points back of first-place Chicago. During the month Fuhr missed four more games with yet another minor injury, this time to his shoulder, and Potvin and Wamsley had a tough time of it in his absence. The whole team was sagging.

The last game of 1992 was really the first game for Fletcher's new Leafs. They were playing in the Civic Arena in Pittsburgh, where they had been shelled 12–1 and 7–1 the season before. These, however, were pre-Burnsian occurrences. The New Year's Eve game proved to be a classic, a thrilling 3–3 tie that forced the Stanley Cup champion Penguins to battle back from 2–1 and 3–2 deficits to tie the score at 18:39 on a Kevin Stevens goal. The Leafs skated as though without equipment, and Fuhr splashed his body all over the place, facing 35 shots. The hitting was hard but clean and only six minors were called all night. It was vintage hockey, playoff hockey. Call it what you want, it sent shivers down your spine. When you swallowed, pride got caught in your throat and you gloried at the beauty of the game. God, if the Leafs could play like this all the time!

On January 9, Burns made his first visit to the Montreal Forum behind a Maple Leaf bench in what proved to be the emotional highlight of the year. No matter what kind of stone you like, you had to call this game a gem. The Leafs built up a 4–0 lead by the 17:00 mark of the second, playing Pittsburgh-perfect hockey from New Year's Eve, and then withstood a feverish Montreal attack in the third to win 5–4 (four games in six nights was starting to show). It was a win rooted and inspired by love. It had little to do with two points or a road win or moving up in the standings. This was a win for Pat Burns, a way of the players saying to their coach, you're the best. A sign of admiration and devotion and pride and support. A thank-you.

From that game to season's end, the Leafs had a record of 26–12–4, third best in the NHL.

After the Pittsburgh game, Potvin was sent to the minors again as promised, but again fate brought him back just two weeks later. The previously durable Fuhr was hurt again, in a game at the Stadium in Chicago, and although he missed only four more games Potvin was unbelievable as understudy, allowing only four goals. In that stretch Toronto played perhaps the most perfect post-'67 game in a 4–0 win over the Habs at the Gardens. The Cat stopped all 29 shots, the offence scored timely goals, and the defence stood up at the blueline all night long. Potvin never had to make a second stop, the net was clear in front, the corners and boards were dominated by the blue and white, everything was perfect.

Fuhr returned to play equally superbly in a 3–1 win over the Rangers a week later, but it was to be his last appearance in a Leaf uniform. Two days later Fletcher got the scorer he needed, trading Fuhr and the Leafs' 6th-round pick in '95 to the oft-rumoured Sabres for Dave Andreychuk, goalie Darren Puppa, and a first-round pick in '93 (Jonsson). Call it "The Trade, Part II," a sequel almost as one-sided as the original (with all due respect to Fuhr). For the Leafs it was a move whose time had come. Clearly Potvin would not gain from more seasoning in St. John's, but Fletcher was pressed — or, at least, encouraged — to make the deal for another reason: the Board of Governors of the NHL had agreed that for the upcoming expansion draft for the Mighty Ducks of Anaheim and Panthers of Florida existing teams could protect only one goalie. This was a Gary Bettman favour, intended to sweeten the pot for Anaheim's owner, the Disney Corporation, which apparently in the new Commissioner's eyes was doing the NHL a huge favour by deeming hockey worthy of its Mickey Mouseness. The previous year, the three expansion teams — Ottawa, San Jose, and Tampa Bay — were given no such perk. Established teams protected *two* goalies, so the new franchises had slim pickin's for goaltenders on draft day. Now, Anaheim and Florida were assured of getting a quality goaltender, and Toronto's roster looked the most desirable in the league with two of Fuhr, Potvin, Wamsley, and Rhodes available. Fletcher talked about circumventing the Bettman draft rule by making a deal with Anaheim and Florida to ensure they wouldn't select a Leaf goalie, but realistically he had to trade one.

Potvin's future was as secure with the Leafs as Fuhr's marketability was great, and Fletcher talked with a man near-desperate to get Fuhr. Muckler was under pressure to do something in Buffalo to ensure playoff success. Over the years the Sabres had always iced highly respectable teams but had not won a single round of the playoffs since 1983. Muckler believed post-season success rested on a "money" goalie, and who was more greenback in the NHL than Fuhr? The only problem was that Muckler traded too much to get him.

Andreychuk had averaged 34 goals a year over nine seasons with the Sabres but had already scored 29 in the first 52 games of the current season. Like Gilmour in Calgary, his play in Buffalo paled in comparison to how he performed in Toronto. He averaged nearly a goal a game for the rest of the year with the Leafs (25 in 31) and proved instrumental on the power play. His ability to withstand a gale of high-sticks and cross-checks in front of the net gave Dougie a much-needed power forward to feed in the slot. In Puppa the Leafs got an excellent backup to Potvin who could be let go in the upcoming draft if need be. The bonus was the Sabres' first-round draft choice, 12th overall in an excellent year, who turned out for the Leafs to be Kenny Jonsson. The most promising defenceman in Sweden, Jonsson helped his country win a gold medal at the '94 Olympics in Lillehammer and was named the best at his position at the World Junior Championships in 1993 and '94. He is being worked into the lineup this '95 season and will be a big force on the Leaf blueline for a long time to come. This trade has proven to be a huge steal for the Silver Fox (not to mention a gamble — had Potvin not continued his impressive play, giving up Fuhr could never have been justified).

While the Fuhr trade helped improve the team immeasurably, his contribution to the Leafs (primarily during the '91–'92 season) cannot be overstated. He brought a winning attitude to the dressing room and an ability to win to the ice. His determination, his utter hatred of losing, rubbed off on his teammates and was fully evident to Leaf fans. Although he wore the blue and white for only a year and a half, his presence as Fletcher's first big acquisition helped begin the renaissance of the Leafs.

That was all the refining Fletcher did to the roster until the expansion draft in June after the season. Andreychuk was the last piece in the puzzle and the team's performance exploded. The rest of the year provided nothing but happy events and record-breaking games. Dougie played in the first All-Star game of his 10-year career in Montreal in late January, and on February 13, at home to the North Stars, he registered six assists in a 6–1 win, tying Babe Pratt's club record set on January 8, 1944, against Boston in a 12–3 win. Valentine's night in Minnesota, the Leafs were trailing 5–2 but pulled out an amazing victory when Todd Gill scored his second goal of the game at 19:20 to win it 6–5 and move the team to within four points of the North Stars for third place.

Gill was by far the finest example of Burns' success as coach. With the team since 1984, Gill had seen many a coach and general manager come and go, somehow maintaining his tenuous position on the blueline despite the horrible team records and departure of everyone else. Undisciplined, weak in the corners, and an erratic playmaker, Gill was for years a terrible defenceman. He often lost the puck in front of his own net, made a lazy clearing pass up the middle, or tried to deke a man at his blueline with no one to back

SUCCESS IS OUR MOTTO
It Provides Great Fame!
It Pays Rich Dividends!!
WORK FOR IT EVERY DAY

GRAIG ABEL

him up. Burns fixed that. He gave Gill a specific job, primarily a defensive role, and emblazoned on Gill's forehead the virtues of *Defence 101*: take the man in front of the net; when in doubt, fire the puck along the boards; in the corners, take the body and forget about the puck. Gill responded. He became a solid player in his own end at the pleasant sacrifice of a few wild and crazy rushes that always ended prematurely. He was an integral part of the Leafs' climb to first in team defence after the All-Star game, and he became a reliable defenceman who could play in all situations. His improvement under Burns was remarkable, inconceivable.

The Leafs kept getting better and better and better. They went undefeated in 12 games at home and had one streak of six games undefeated on the road and another of 10 games without a loss. The club was fast approaching the team record of 41 wins in a season, set in 1950–51 and equalled in '77–'78. Dougie was quickly setting personal and team records, notably passing Sittler's 117-point season of '77–'78. Andreychuk approached 50 goals on the year; Cullen averaged a point a game; the team was inching toward first place and the Vezina Trophy. And Burns was grumbling. He knew that just as there was a yin for every yang, for every left a right, and every sneeze a "bless you," there was a losing streak for every winning streak. He kept confidence and enthusiasm from becoming overconfidence and arrogance, and up until the day the Leafs won a playoff spot swore that that was his only goal. It was always "if" we get into the playoffs, always "the team" had to do this or that. Discipline and success revolved around 20 guys, not one, and around one season, not one game or win streak.

As the schedule wound down, virtually every team was still in the hunt for a playoff spot or had the chance to move up in the standings. Thus, the final games were particularly tense and emotional. Before the Leafs' last trip out west for four games, Burns cautioned his players: "This is going to be a tough trip, very tough. If we play .500 hockey I'll be very, very happy." They beat Winnipeg 5–4, tied Minnesota 3–3, beat the Oilers, 6–2, and shut out the Flames 4–0.

They now had 92 points, just behind Detroit (93) and first-place Chicago (94) in the standings.

As a coach, Burns did not affect a frown 84 games long. He did everything possible to motivate the players and was tough when he had to be. But for every public tirade and scowl and curse and raving head-butt in the air there was always a word of encouragement, a pat on the shoulder, a day off after an important or exhausting win. He was hard-nosed, yes, but supremely fair. His public persona didn't hurt, either. In the city, he loved Harley-Davidsons. Away from the rink, he preferred an unshaven face and jamming with blues bands such as the Good Brothers. He had been an undercover cop for 17 years. He was a man's man, but without any artifice. Who could command more respect in the male world of the NHL? Players didn't ask what the "or else" was when he issued a threat. They didn't want to find out.

The Leafs ended the season on a bit of a low note, going 2–4 down the stretch and remaining in third place. The final standings looked as follows:

CLARENCE CAMPBELL CONFERENCE

Norris Division

	GP	W	L	T	GF	GA	PTS
Chicago	84	47	25	12	279	230	106
Detroit	84	47	28	9	369	280	103
Toronto	84	44	29	11	288	241	99
St. Louis	84	37	36	11	282	278	85
Minnesota	84	36	38	10	272	293	82
Tampa Bay	84	23	54	7	245	332	53

Smythe Division

	GP	W	L	T	GF	GA	PTS
Vancouver	84	46	29	9	346	278	101
Calgary	84	43	30	11	322	282	97
Los Angeles	84	39	35	10	338	340	88
Winnipeg	84	40	37	7	322	320	87
Edmonton	84	26	50	8	242	337	60
San Jose	84	11	71	2	218	414	24

PRINCE OF WALES CONFERENCE

Adams Division

	GP	W	L	T	GF	GA	PTS
Boston	84	51	26	7	332	268	109
Quebec	84	47	27	10	351	300	104
Montreal	84	48	30	6	326	280	102
Buffalo	84	38	36	10	335	297	86
Hartford	84	26	52	6	284	369	58
Ottawa	84	10	70	4	202	395	24

Patrick Division

	GP	W	L	T	GF	GA	PTS
Pittsburgh	84	56	21	7	367	268	119
Washington	84	43	34	7	325	286	93
NY Islanders	84	40	37	7	335	297	87
New Jersey	84	40	37	7	308	299	87
Philadelphia	84	36	37	11	319	319	83
NY Rangers	84	34	39	11	304	308	79

The Leafs would play Detroit in the first round, and the Red Wings would have home-ice advantage. The season had produced all kinds of team and personal records and established a new optimism and success that seemed real even to the greatest sceptic. Now was the time to put the regular season to the test, to see if what produced 99 points in 84 games could stand the rigours of the fiercest competition of them all.

The second season was about to begin.

XI

Run at the Cup:
The 1993 Playoffs

"I remember taking the streetcar to the Gardens and lining up for tickets. . . . When the Leafs were playing then, it seemed the city outside the Gardens was at a standstill. I'd love for it to be like that again."

— Steve Stavro

Befitting Fletcher's commitment to honouring excellence, the Leafs held many pre-game ceremonies during the '92–'93 season. In October, banners were raised to officially retire Ace Bailey's number 6 and Bill Barilko's number 5. Later that month the team presented an alumnus, Lorne Carr, with a replica of the 1942 Stanley Cup ring. A member of the Leafs' winning team that year, Carr, for one reason

King Clancy's Leaf jersey.
HOCKEY HALL OF FAME

or another, never got his finger furniture until half a century later. On another occasion, Glenn Anderson and his family were presented with gifts to acknowledge his 1,000th point. And at the last home game of the season, Dougie was honoured for his record-breaking achievements. He gave a brief speech which he ended by saying, "Thanks Toronto, the fans. We're going to do something for you yet, okay? Thank you."

The Stanley Cup has become more coveted as it has become harder to win. Players are aware how few chances there are to compete for it, and this has certainly produced fiercer playoff hockey. In the old days, with four of the only six teams in the league making the playoffs, you could be sure of having a grab at it just about every year. In the '90s, with 21, then 24, and now 26 teams, and with parity divvying up the talent more equally, each team has a slimmer chance of winning. One in 26, not one in six. The regular season, barely ended, is forgotten. The new season — the playoffs — consists of exactly seven games. To look beyond that guarantees looking back on the year sooner rather than later. The spirit of the games intensifies as qualifying teams are paired in a kind of passionate war no home-and-home series during the regular season can ever hope to approach in drama.

In the spring of 1993, there was only one sure bet. If Mario Lemieux remained healthy, the Penguins were certain to win the Cup. If he ran into back problems, there were 15 other teams equal to the challenge. Nothing made this clearer in the first-round match-ups than the 4–0 sweep the Blues handed Chicago. The Blackhawks finished third overall in the standings and 20 points ahead of the Blues in the Norris Division, but in the first round Curtis Joseph was unbeatable in the Blues' net, and in one week Chicago's great season was a thing of the past (remember 1967?). That's why Sather kept Ranford, why Muckler wanted Fuhr, why Fletcher had to be sure of Potvin. Goaltending could win a series for you.

In the other series, there was perhaps one more surprise, and even then it was not the outcome so much as its lopsidedness. Buffalo swept Boston 4–0 in a matchup that was dominated again by a goalie, the Leaf-cum-Sabre Grant Fuhr. Pittsburgh beat New Jersey in five games, while all the others but one went six: Montreal beat Quebec, the Islanders beat Washington, Vancouver beat Winnipeg, and Los Angeles beat the Flames.

And then there was Toronto and Detroit, the only matchup to go seven games, and by far the most dramatic of the eight series. Detroit was the definite favourite. Although they had finished only four points ahead of the Leafs in the standings, it was generally felt that Toronto had overachieved and Detroit under-. Detroit had home-ice advantage, and unquestionably the best one-two centre combination in the league with Steve Yzerman (137 points) and Sergei Fedorov (87) to go with their other stars, Dino Ciccarelli (97) and Paul Coffey (87). The Red Wings led the NHL in scoring, averaging more than a

goal a game more than the Leafs, and had the firepower to erase any 1–0 or 2–1 lead the Leafs might slowly gain.

For the first time this year, Toronto had a few injuries to worry about. Drake Berehowsky would miss the rest of the year after knee surgery; Bob McGill had a broken jaw and could no longer be used if the series got nasty; John Cullen, the Leafs' number two centre and the man the team desperately needed to have to take some of the scoring load off Gilmour, was out with a herniated disc in his neck. The teams entered the playoffs on opposite streaks, Detroit 9–1 in its last 10 games, the Leafs 2–4 to close out the season. They were, however, 3–3–1 in head-to-head meetings during the regular season, and the Wings were well aware of the Leafs' ability to raise their game an extra level for this ancient rivalry that had, in some ways, superseded the one with Montreal (this was the 23rd playoff series between the clubs, each having won 11 previously. In the '40s the great Leafs beat the Wings in the finals on four occasions; in the '50s the great Detroit teams beat Toronto in five semifinals).

If Detroit did have a weakness, it was Toronto's great strength: goal. Neither Tim Cheveldae nor Vincent Riendeau had proved they could pull a win from a seeming loss, an ability Potvin had amply demonstrated. Psychologically, the Wings were more intimidated by Potvin's abilities than the Leafs were by Cheveldae's or Riendeau's. Furthermore, Burns had had success behind the playoff bench while his adversary, Bryan Murray, had experienced McNamara-esque failure with the Capitals and Red Wings, winning only four rounds in his 11 years as coach in the NHL (never two in one year).

The wonderful, intense quality of a playoff series is that two teams must face each other night after night until one is eliminated. It's like bare-fisted, turn-of-the-century boxing, when a fight went on until one man was knocked out. There is no escape, no respite, no time to nurse wounds or play against someone else as a "bit of a change." It is not a time to dipsy-doodle and make pretty plays, gamble in front of your own net, or look for the breakaway. It is a time to play the most disciplined hockey you are capable of playing.

Skill is the most unvanquishable asset a team can possess. If its best players during the season are the best players in the playoffs, the team will win. But too often such does not occur. In the post-season, a regular season deke becomes a solid check, a pass to an open man in the slot becomes a deflection, a booming slap shot merely a glove save. If the regular season is tough, the playoffs are tougher. They require discipline and concentration, and an absolutely crystal-clear understanding of what it takes to win a game. Playoff success is determined by three elements: preparation, reaction, and execution.

Preparation is the simplest of the three because it is done before the series and between the seven games, during the calm daylight. It means reading notes and statistics and watching videos and listening to coaches and practising in the largeness of an empty arena. There

is no pressure yet. Preparation should build confidence because so far there has been no opposition. But anyone can nod his head when the coach has a whistle around his neck as he calmly provides instruction. When the nodding stops and the referee drops the puck for real and it's time to get the doing done, that's when desire reveals itself as a player's truth or a dreamer's lie. If preparation doesn't translate into execution, then the faceoff gives way to hand-shaking and the proverbial golf course.

Execution is made difficult since both teams want to do the same things. So an important part of the execution is how the team reacts, or fails to react, to the other team's strategy. Reaction is about correcting everything wrong with your own game and shutting down everything right about the other team's. If a centre is losing faceoffs, he has to do something differently or the coach has to use someone else for the draws. If the other team is taking cheap shots after the whistle, you can't be undisciplined. In the regular season you might drop the gloves; in the playoffs, you take a number and wait for next year. If the team is running your goalie, you have to prevent it or do the same. How you react becomes an important part of your execution. It's a constant battle because everything changes from one second to the next. Every pass, every check, every line change, alters the pace and direction of the game. The preparation gives way to the flow of the game itself and becomes reaction and execution, and the motivation for all these must not come from without — media, fans, coach — but within — heart, character, competitiveness.

The playoffs create a new league, a new level of skill, a new approach to the game. On a good team, each player is given a specific task and reminded not to go beyond that task. He is told that if that task is executed, and everyone performs his task properly, a win will be the result. Faith becomes the key motivating factor. Each player must believe that if all he does is keep the other team's power play scoreless, just shuts down the other team's big centre, covers the front of the net, keeps the puck low on power play point shots, checks the wingers on the boards, or takes a punch to the face without retaliating, his team will win the game. In the playoffs, how Mike Eastwood or Bill Berg executes becomes as important as how Dougie or Wendel executes. They have vastly different roles, but they all have to do their jobs if the team is to win night after night.

This is why Pat Burns took his team to Collingwood for three days before Game 1 in Detroit. Detroit had so much in its favour and was one of two or three teams that on some nights looked unbeatable. They were an offensive club that won many high-scoring games during the year: 10–5 and 9–7 over Tampa Bay, 11–6 over St. Louis, 8–0 over Pittsburgh. They had five 30-goal scorers and with home-ice advantage could match lines to keep their scorers away from Toronto's checkers. To control the attack, they had a fourth forward every other shift with Paul Coffey on the blueline. Sergei Fedorov, a great two-way centre, was given the job of shadowing Gilmour, the

Jacques Plante mask, 1969.
DOUG MACLELLAN / HOCKEY HALL OF FAME

Leafs' main threat. If he could hold Dougie in check, Toronto's offence would falter badly.

But the Leafs were hardly helpless victims waiting for Detroit to eliminate them. They had their own strengths that nullified those of Detroit perfectly, most notably great defence. They were used to winning games 1–0, 2–1, 3–2, and when they lost the scores were usually as low. While the Red Wings often won big, they also lost big: 9–6 to the Penguins, 10–7 to Buffalo, 9–3 to L.A. The Leafs didn't score nearly as often as the Wings, but Toronto was facing a vulnerable defence and suspect playoff goaltending (Cheveldae had won only six of 17 previous games). Shawn Burr of the Wings anticipated the series by calling it Hospital Hockey: "lots of patience." He was

fully aware of the Leafs' ability to play ultrasound defence, to make a goal hold up, to clog the middle, protect Potvin, win without scoring half a dozen goals. The season series reflected as much. The Leafs' wins were close (3–1, 5–3, 4–2), the Wings' minor blowouts (7–1, 5–1, 5–1). However, the Detroit approach, epitomized by Burr's remark, was too respectful of Toronto's game and not cocky enough about their own. Why should a team capable of scoring half a dozen goals or more a game talk about being patient? They should talk about exploding.

The series opened at the Joe Louis Arena and in Game 1 everything went according to Detroit's plans. After a 1–1 first period, they blew four by Felix in a fecund second and won easily 6–3. Of those four goals, two were on the power play and one short-handed. Dino Ciccarelli and Bob Probert crashed Potvin's net all game long and took the Cat's mind off the play by forcing him to worry about just seeing the ice. For the Leafs, Captain Clark was not up to snuff, as Probert boldly pointed out afterwards: "He [Clark] wasn't playing his game. You really couldn't find him out there on the ice."

The second game was a virtual reality of the first, except that if anything the Red Wings played even better and the Leafs even worse. Detroit won 6–2, as octopi rained on the ice in celebration of each Red Wing goal. Again it was Detroit's special teams — scoring two power-play goals and one short-handed — that were the Leafs' undoing, as well as another sloppy second period in which three of the Wings' six goals were scored. Potvin was again heavily screened, but at least the Leafs were much feistier and didn't lose in the alley. There were a number of scrums and post-whistle shoving matches to go along with the heavy hitting, and a mêlée broke out near the end of the game after a frustrated Potvin took his stick to Ciccarelli. Misconducts were given to Gilmour, Lefebvre, Ciccarelli, and Racine, and the closing minutes provided much speculation about the possibility of a violent series erupting when the matchup moved back to Toronto.

But the Wings made a huge mistake during the two games in Motown by taunting Clark with calls of "Wendy" whenever he skated by the bench. The old adage of letting a sleeping dog lie could not have been more appropriate here, and coach Murray would have done well to advise his players to leave Clark alone. The taunting continued unchecked, but these were the last games in the series Clark failed, in Probert's words, to "play his game."

The Leafs sustained a number of injuries during the two losses, most seriously to Nik Borschevsky who broke his cheekbone in a collision along the boards in Game 1 and looked to be lost for the series. Todd Gill left Game 2 because of back spasms, and Mark Osborne suffered a rib injury. Combined with the end-of-season hurts, the Leafs were returning to the Gardens a bruised and pained lot. But the spirit of the city helped lift the team out of the physical doldrums. Glenn Anderson wrote two playoff songs, "The Leafs Are

the Best" and "The Playoffs Are Here," that were recorded on a CD with the rest of the team and released in time for the Leafs' return. The fans were ecstatic just to be in the playoffs for the first time in three years, and the team's superb 25–11–6 home record during the year gave everyone confidence in Toronto's ability to tie the series at the Gardens. For Game 3, the fans gave the blue and white an unbelievable welcome, despite the two blowouts in Detroit, and a laser show provided further encouragement and a dramatic back-drop to the player introductions. Once the puck was dropped, the Leafs executed their game plan to perfection. They got on top of the Detroit defence quickly and forced turnovers in the Red Wing end. They checked tenaciously for 60 minutes, and they scored timely goals. Using last-change privileges of home ice, Burns put all his faith in Dougie and matched strength with strength, Gilmour against Yzerman, all night long. Yzerman was held pointless, but Gilmour set up Andreychuk twice in the early going. By 7:37 the Leafs had established a 2–0 lead.

Fedorov got a power play goal early in the second to make it 2–1, and then Potvin stoned the Wings, stopping 18 shots in the period as the Leafs stood around for a while admiring their lead. That is what great goaltending can do, and that is why the Cat was given the chance to replace Fuhr.

Before the game, Clark had been asked by a reporter whether he felt as captain he should be the spiritual leader of the club. Clark answered honestly and simply as he always did. "I'm not that deep. I'm a farmer, for God's sake." His job was to score and knock bodies around. He was rewarded in the third when he beat Cheveldae once and set up Pearson midway through the period to make it 4–1. The Leafs won a textbook Pat Burns game 4–2 and the series was close once again. Detroit players were no longer singing "Wendy" on the bench.

Game 4 was a carbon copy for the Leafs of their previous game, except *they* played even more perfectly. They were unrelenting in their checking, yet discipline was the order of the day, allowing the Wings only three power plays (no goals) while Detroit took two majors for boarding and high-sticking that cost them game miscon-ducts to Steve Chiasson in the first and Fedorov in the third. After a scoreless first period each team scored twice in the second. It was up to Dave Andreychuk, him of the 10-foot stick and 20-foot reach, to score on an incredible wraparound at 4:47 of the third for the winner. At the moment the puck crossed the goal line, his skates were behind the net, his body to the side of it, and his stick in the crease! Potvin was again rock solid, and just like that the overdog Red Wings were going home tied 2–2.

Two days later, back in Motown, the heat began to rise. This was going to be a long series, and the comfort of preparation had long ago taken a back seat to the pressure of execution. Yzerman had seemingly disappeared, going pointless in the last three games. Fedorov became the main Detroit threat, but Potvin, a rookie to

remember, was showing increasing poise and confidence. Gilmour was starting to look the romantic warrior/hockey player the playoffs will sometimes produce. He had a sore leg, a sprained wrist, facial cuts from being slammed into the boards by Chiasson, and no front teeth. If you couldn't get inspired by looking at him, let alone watching him play, you didn't deserve to speak the words Stanley Cup, let alone play for it.

Penalties were becoming less frequent as the players' determination to play hard and fair and avoid the cheap stuff allowed the referee to pocket his whistle and let the teams decide the outcome. The games were too important to get into a fight and risk an instigating minor, a major penalty, or an ejection. In Game 5, the Wings scored early and Andreychuk tied it up before Fedorov scored at 18:00 even to make it 2–1. Ray Sheppard and Ciccarelli scored early in the second and by 6:21 the Wings were up 4–1. Potvin looked a little soft, the fans were their wonderfully raucous Detroit selves and victory, if not a blowout, seemed assured. The Leafs reacted to this Detroit onslaught exactly the way they'd been taught — with patience and faith. There was still plenty of time left, and they knew they couldn't open up and watch the Wings whiz by and jack up the score. Their hopes were quickly raised when Ellett scored a dribbler at 9:12, and again with a more powerful slapper at 16:57 to bring them to within one before the second period was over. Detroit's confidence was eroding fast and their sit-on-the-lead strategy needed to be changed posthaste.

The third was more of the same for the Leafs. They continued to skate and create chances, but without gambling defensively. They needed only one goal in 20 minutes, so they didn't have to send two men deep to forecheck or force their defence to pinch in at the Detroit blueline. They simply had to work hard and do their jobs. Put simply, Toronto tried harder than Detroit and dominated both ends of the rink. When Clark scored at 11:38 it only served to answer the question "when," not "if." In the closing minutes Detroit still failed to find the form that had given them the early 4–1 lead. It was the Leafs who almost won in regulation, but the final buzzer sounded and overtime was a Zamboni ride away.

The Wings failed to get so much as a shot in OT. They played like a complacent team unwilling to believe that a lineup so talented could possibly lose in the first round of the playoffs. It was unimaginable. Until 2:05 anyway, when Mike Foligno jumped on a loose puck at the edge of the crease and put it through Cheveldae's legs. Down 4–1, the Leafs won 5–4 in overtime and were going home to wrap up the series.

This game confirmed a number of trends. Yzerman went pointless again; Potvin kept the team in the game in the second half while Cheveldae folded; the fewer power plays (just six in this game) meant less open ice and favoured Toronto. Most important, though, the Leafs had established a level of team determination far above

Detroit's. The fourth-line players were proving as effective in their roles as the first-line players were in theirs. For all their incredible individual talent, the Wings had no team chemistry, no sense of winning as a group. No teamwork.

Game 6. Maple Leaf Gardens. Fans coming out of College Station saw Maple Leaf history their every step. On the platform was Charlie Pachter's "Hockey Knights In Canada," accompanied nearby by two Leaf logos put up March 11, 1993, to augment the artwork.* As they went up the stairs or escalators they saw photographs of great Leafs past and present: Clancy, Armstrong, Sittler, Mahovlich, Gilmour, Potvin, Clark. Outside, the smell of roasted chestnuts wafted along Carlton Street. Vendors were selling big Leaf waving "hands" and pennants by the dozen, scalpers were hollering "Who's looking for a pair?" to anyone and everyone, the police under the marquee were talking, laughing, enjoying the enthusiasm of the crowd. "Leafsport" was packed, traffic crawled except for the cabs and limousines that roared up to the front doors. The celebration was in full swing, the parties planned, the bars staffed and stocked, the jubilant drunken march up Yonge Street as inevitable as the final siren.

Oh, how thin the thread that uses confident cloth to make an overconfident blanket. The Leafs covered themselves up in their great accomplishments of Game 5, abandoned the plan that produced three hard-earned wins in a row, and fell asleep. Again it was an awful second period that did them in. They actually led 2–1 after the first, but the Wings came out and played desperate hockey for the first time in the series. They scored five unanswered goals to go up 6–2 and put the game out of reach. The final score of 7–3 reflected the Red Wings' domination over the final 40 minutes. Detroit went 4-for-6 on the power play, scored two other goals short-handed, and kept the Leafs scoreless on their five power play chances. Once again, special teams were the deciding factor.

Now the momentum shifted. Fans' hearts sank back to reality. The Leafs had made a series of it. They had played their guts out, but now Detroit was going home to hammer the final nail in the coffin. Even die-hard Leaf fans felt the team had squandered its one chance to "steal" the series. Detroit would come out flying in Game 7 and the crowd would intimidate the Leafs into submission. It had been a great series, Fletcher and Burns were well on their way to erasing 20 years of "neglect," but the Leafs didn't have a hope in hell on enemy ice in a Game 7.

But players who are winners don't give up. Ever. And Doug Gilmour was a winner.

The last game of the series. Sure, there's a tomorrow. But will you be able to stomach it? Not if you lose. By this time the fatigue was

---

* In Pachter's murals the Leaf crest is on the players' jerseys, but not "Toronto Maple Leafs." Ballard refused to allow it.

palpable. Six games in 11 nights between two intense rivals playing fierce, hard-hitting hockey. Digging in the corners and one-on-one battles stretched the players' endurance as the shifts got shorter and the tension thicker. Burns made two lineup changes. Out were Krushelnyski and Mironov, back were Eastwood (for his digging) and Borschevsky, his broken face tender but protected by a visor. The Leafs were underdogs because of public perception, not because of inferior skill or lack of confidence. They were in Joe Louis to prove it.

Although the first period was dominated by the Red Wings, the score was 1–1 by the end. Potvin was superb, but the rest of the team was playing tentatively. Detroit looked loose and confident. The Leafs' attitude adjustment during the first-period intermission changed that. Maybe Detroit had the better *players*, but the Leafs weren't prepared to stop playing hockey just yet. In the second Detroit took a 3–2 lead on Dallas Drake's goal midway through, but that was the last the hometown fans saw of their team.

The Wings sat on their lead and allowed the Leafs to build confidence and momentum as the period wound down. As the third period began, Toronto began to dominate. Again, it seemed only a matter of time before the Leafs would tie the score, but the clock was ticking. You thought, maybe, just maybe, this time the Wings *would* hang on to win. Eight minutes to go, seven, six. . . . Finally the Wings had mastered defensive hockey. Victory was in sight and they weren't going to blow the game now. Five minutes, four minutes. The big sigh; the middle was too clogged up for Leaf forwards to gain momentum. They couldn't even get the puck in, let alone get a shot on goal.

Unbelievably, with less than three minutes to go, Clark wended his way down the left side along the boards into the Detroit corner. All of a sudden, he saw not one but two Leafs in the slot! Rouse was moving in from the point and Dougie from the right wing. They were both in the slot, wide, wide open. No Detroit defence to be found. Wendel drilled the puck to the opening and Dougie skated in front of Rouse, took the pass, and buried it. No chance for Cheveldae. The Leafs tied the game with just 2:43 left in the season! The Detroit bench melted. The series wasn't over yet.

In the dying minutes it was the Leafs who threw everything at Detroit, and a Zezel wraparound in the final minute rolled through the crease almost the winner. The Wings were lucky to make it to overtime. They crawled to their locker room, badly in need of regrouping. The Leafs danced off the ice; the game couldn't resume quickly enough. They had won a game in overtime in Joe Louis in Game 5, they had the momentum, the jump, the desire, the courage, the belief. Just as Detroit fans had shaken their heads after one period, wondering how the Leafs had hung in there, now they must have been surprised that their own team had somehow scraped into overtime. Outshot 23–11 in the final two periods, Detroit looked dead, beat.

When the fourth period began, it was as though 15 seconds, not 15 minutes, had elapsed. The Wings showed no signs of having recovered, and the Leafs went right back on the attack. Two and a half minutes into the overtime, Dougie got the puck inside the Detroit line at the left point and passed it over to Rouse who was open on the right. Rouse moved in a couple of strides and took a slap shot along the ice toward Tim Cheveldae who was moving way out to cut down the angle. Nikolai Borschevsky, crossing through the high slot with his stick at his waist and a defender at his side, jammed his stick down for a fraction of a second, a fraction long enough to redirect the puck into the net and lift Leaf fans everywhere into mid-air!

DOUG MACLELLAN / HOCKEY HALL OF FAME

Cliff Fletcher leaped from his press-box seat to hug those beside him. Bob Rouse, eyes closed, mouth open, tears of joy and beads of sweat over his face, looked heavenward as though tasting rainwater for the first time in a desert month. And Borschevsky, a shield on his helmet protecting the broken orbital bone under his eye, was the hero, scoring the most important Leaf goal since another battered, injured, masked hero, Lanny McDonald, beat Chico Resch to eliminate the Islanders in 1978! In his English, as broken as his cheekbone, Borschevsky's determination epitomized the guts of the team: "The doctors told me 10 days. But I say, I play today."

Dougie was in on all four goals and outplayed Yzerman and Fedorov both. His pasta diet was becoming famous, as was his toothless celebration smile, and his gaunt, ghost-like body. He was playing vintage Conn Smythe hockey in the tradition that gave the playoff trophy its honour.

And the playoffs were just beginning.

Round Two:
St. Louis

The St. Louis Blues had swept the first-place Blackhawks aside in four straight. They had a week's rest and watched the final three games of the Toronto/Detroit series from the comfort of their living rooms. Preparing for this series would be completely different from the first one for Pat Burns and his team. They were hurting and tired, and had just two days to recover before the first game of the second round. The one advantage they had was home ice. Their 4–0–3 record on the year against the Blues gave the Leafs confidence in knowing they could beat the Blues, but St. Louis, coming off such a huge and convincing series win, felt they, too, could win. The regular season meant nothing now.

At first the tension wasn't as great as it was against Detroit. There was less to hate about St. Louis, less history, less combativeness. Sure, the Blues had Brett Hull, but he almost certainly wouldn't be a factor. Pressure made him cower and wince. And there was Ron Caron, the gesticulating GM who made you want to cut off his arms and rip out his tongue. But that was as far as the hate went.

Yet the first game at the Gardens provided more than enough tension and drama. It boiled down to Gilmour versus "Cujo," the first two letters of Blues goalie Curtis Joseph's first and last names. Joseph had been sensational in the Chicago series, the reason they won, really, giving up only six goals in four games, and he proved to be just as intimidating against the Leafs. The game went into double overtime, and Toronto outshot St. Louis 64–34, a suitable indication of just how much the home team dominated. Without Joseph, this game would never have gone into overtime; it would never have even gone into the third period. That's how well the Leafs played and how poorly the Blues played around Joseph. In the first OT alone the Leafs had 19 shots, but it took the heroics of Dougie three minutes into the fifth period to decide the game. Behind the St. Louis net, he faked one way, then the other, then back, then back back, then twisted around on his backhand. While most people were still dizzy from his moves, he jammed the puck in the now-open side to give the Leafs an exhausting 2–1 win. If every game were going to be like this, the winning team would have to forfeit the next series due to exhaustion. Gilmour played an incredible 42 minutes on the night, enough to dehydrate most fans watching, and his emaciated form promptly underwent the rigorous pasta convalescence needed to prepare for the next game.

A team can get into all sorts of grooves and habits, and staying in them or getting out of them requires concentration and perseverance. Sometimes, *not* thinking is the best remedy. Even though they won Game 1, the Leafs were thinking too much about Joseph. Everyone knows of the heroics of goalies past, from Fuhr to Parent to Cheevers to Bower and back. Goalies can win games, you tell yourself, because you've *seen* them win games. It's as much a mind game and psych-out job as it is reflexes. Cujo almost stole one in Game 1. In Game 2, he did.

Conn Smythe never envisioned an 84-game schedule with 24 teams, a four-round best-of-seven playoffs, a Stanley Cup game in the spring. On this day in late May, the Gardens' ice began to fog. Another double overtime, another 2–1 win, another Toronto-dominated game that saw the rested St. Louis defence in tatters, an embarrassment that Joseph had to rescue every minute. The Leafs outshot St. Louis 58–40, but it was as though the Leafs had become mesmerized by Joseph's equipment. At times it seemed they were shooting to allow him to make the great save. They refused to "find" a way to win, to play that kind of desperate hockey they had played against Detroit. A goal by Jeff Brown at 3:03 in the fifth, after 83:03 minutes of play, gave the Blues a 2–1 win to tie the series. The Leafs were going to St. Louis, no longer with home-ice advantage. Like Detroit the series before, they knew they had a long, difficult fight on their hands.

Could have, should have, didn't. If Toronto had wanted to make this battle a little easier, Game 3 was the time, St. Louis the opportunity. Goals by Andreychuk, his seventh in 10 playoff games, and Ellett on the power play put the Leafs up 2–0 by 14:33 of the first, as Joseph looked merely great for the first time in the series. But the Leafs allowed the Blues to attack, something St. Louis hadn't done much of, and by the end of the second Toronto was trailing 3–2. In the third, the Leafs held the edge in play, but the Blues played textbook defence and won 4–3 to go up 2–1 in the series. One more loss would be crippling to Toronto. The next game became a must-win.

Just as the Leafs often fell back once they had reached lofty heights, so too did they rebound after falling. Burns took McLlwain, Pearson, and Cullen out of the lineup. Cullen had been ineffectual since returning early from his neck injury, and Pearson still lacked consistent spirit each game. In their place Burns put Mironov, Krushelnyski, and Eastwood, the latter two perfectly suited to a clutch-and-grab, check-and-dig game. Game 4 was a perfectly played match, grinding and rough, contested as much along the boards and in the corners as on open ice. Referee Mark Faucette called 24 penalties, but neither side could do much on the power play, Toronto going 1-for-8, St. Louis 1-for-7. But the Leafs played desperate and determined hockey for 60 minutes and won 4–1, outhustling and outplaying the Blues for the fourth straight game.

Yet the series was only tied 2–2. By this point, Leaf fans knew well the frustration that Detroit fans had felt, that "Why can't we just get rid of these guys?" feeling, and heading back to Maple Leaf Gardens it was the Leafs more than the Blues who were still burdened with having to win.

Toronto returned to Toronto and played exactly the same as the last game at the Arena. They also began to wear down the battered Cujo, who was facing more than 40 shots a game. This night he saw only 29 but allowed five. An off night, but no one else on coach Bob Berry's team was able to rescue the Blues. Only a Brett Hull power-play goal in the first beat Potvin, but Andreychuk and Rouse also scored on the power play to give the Leafs a 2–1 lead after one. Hard hitting, close checking, and unrelenting pressure created three more goals to give the Leafs a 5–1 win and a 3–2 series lead. They could wrap it up in Missouri, or try to do it the hard way again in Game 7 back home.

Winning in St. Louis was not vital in terms of the series outcome. There were seven games, after all, and the last would be at the Gardens. But the playoffs go four exhausting rounds and a rest at some point was crucial to success. Montreal had already advanced by sweeping the Sabres in four straight wins by the same 4–3 score, and the Kings eliminated Vancouver in six. The Islanders-Pittsburgh series was going to a seventh game, so a win in the Arena would have given the Leafs a four-day break, long enough to recuperate, not so long to get rusty. The beleaguered defence was the biggest worry. Burns had gone with his best five for most of the post-season: Gill, Lefebvre, Macoun, Rouse, and Ellett (Mironov played only the occasional shift). This was an exhausting task, now in its 13th game in 25 nights, but they had been incredibly reliable and had allowed only nine goals in five games with St. Louis. Besides, now was the time to wear your best players to the bone. They had all summer to revive.

The Leafs drew first blood early in Game 6 as Andreychuk scored on a power play at 1:53. But just as there is a fine line between confidence and overconfidence, so too is there a line between playing sound defensive hockey and sitting on a lead. The former demands discipline, hard work, quick shifts, dumping the puck in, getting on the defence, checking tenaciously, working hard. Defensive hockey begins in the offensive zone. Sitting on a lead means hanging on for dear life, letting the other team attack, getting sloppy and running around in your own end, giving up too many quality scoring chances, allowing the other team to sense the possibility of coming back. The Leafs crossed this line. For more than 41 minutes after the Andreychuk goal they sat and sat and sat until 3:33 of the third when Dave Lowry, inevitably, tied the game for the Blues. But still the Leafs hung on. On this night, they had forgotten how to attack. They were playing for overtime, it seemed, unable to muster the firepower needed to regain the lead. Less than five minutes later, Jeff Brown

scored for St. Louis on a power play and only then did the Leafs turn on the power. Too little, too late. St. Louis played sound defensive hockey in response and won 2–1. There would be a Game 7. For the second series in a row, the Leafs let the other team off the ropes and into the ring.

The last time a Game 7 was held at Maple Leaf Gardens was 1964. April 25 against Detroit, to be exact. Two days earlier Gordie Howe had nailed Bobby Baun with a slap shot in the third period, cracking a bone in his ankle. Baun was carried off on a stretcher, a fresh corpse from hockey's Vietnam, but arose for the overtime and scored the winning goal 4–3 to eke out a win in Detroit. That sent the series to the limit. The Leafs won 4–0 at the Gardens in Game 7 and kept the Stanley Cup. Fans have kept that memory ever since, no new ones to join or replace it.

May 15, 1993. The Leafs came out charging, shift after shift, wave after wave, period after period. For 60 minutes they didn't stop for breath. Andreychuk, Clark, Krushelnyski, and Clark again at 19:40 gave the Leafs a huge 4–0 lead after one period. Manderville and Gilmour made it 6–0 in the second, and the third was check, check, check to the chants of all the Leaf fans singing in the Gardens. Joseph was shelled again (36 shots) and the 6–0 clobbering put the Leafs in the semifinals for the first time since 1978. A shutout, just like in '64. A victorious Game 7.

There were many reasons the Leafs were able to beat the Blues, but primarily it was a matter of execution. Potvin allowed only 11 goals in seven games; the defence kept the Blues' only goal-scoring threat, Brett Hull, to just three goals; the Leafs got timely scoring from Gilmour (10 points) and Andreychuk (seven points); the checkers and bangers — Manderville, Foligno, Krushelnyski — provided superb checking and diligent work along the boards to outhustle the Blues.

St. Louis had only one weapon — Cujo. The defence, especially against the Leafs, proved consistently vulnerable and unreliable, and allowed the Leafs an average of 43 shots a game for the puck-weary Joseph to handle. Up front, the offence proved harmless. Yet St. Louis kept the series much closer than it ever should have been, and the Leafs failed once again to develop that killer instinct before desperation. They had to learn to develop that Game 7 mentality in Games 3, 4, 5, and 6 when a win could wrap up a series and give the team a much-needed rest. Instead, they let down their guard, and the other teams walked right back into the series. The St. Louis series was done like dinner. Now it was time to play for a place in the finest banquet of them all . . . the Stanley Cup finals.

Round Three:
Los Angeles

The Prince of Wales conference final was a huge surprise. The Islanders knocked off Pittsburgh right in the Civic Arena 4–3 in Game 7 to eliminate the two-time defending champion Penguins. New York would now play the well-rested Habs for one spot in the finals. In the Clarence Campbell conference final, the hugely anticipated cross-continental matchup featured the duet of Toronto and Los Angeles. This series was to become the most watched in the history of *Hockey Night in Canada* for two reasons. The first was that the Leafs were in it; the second was that Wayne Gretzky was "coming home."

The Kings had won both their series 4–2, so had a significant advantage of rest on their side. However, after the big win over St. Louis, the Leafs were sailing through the clouds on Phaeton's golden chariot, and with the series opening at the Gardens, adrenaline and excitement were more than enough to compensate for fatigue. Coach Barry Melrose, he of the ponytail and arrogance, was taking his Glamour Kings into the Gardens for the first semifinal game Los Angeles had played since the watered-down expansion series in 1969 against the Blues.

The Kings were very similar to the Red Wings. They had loads of scoring punch up front with Gretzky, Luc Robitaille (125 points), Jari Kurri (87), Tony Granato (82), and Jimmy Carson (73). Their main threats on defence were Rob Blake, Darryl Sydor, and Alexei Zhitnik, but they had a more solid defensive corps as well with Charlie Huddy and Marty McSorley, big men whose size would make it difficult for the Leaf forwards to penetrate the Kings' zone. Like Detroit, the Kings' goaltending was their Achilles' heel. Kelly Hrudey, he of the headband, was, is, and always will be sub-mediocrity personified. If the Kings' rough and tough defence could prevent him from having to face too many shots, the Kings had an excellent chance of winning. But if the Leafs could get the puck on net, from any angle, they would score enough goals to win.

Toronto was probably the better team, save one rather vital tangible: Wayne Gretzky. He had missed the first half of the season with a serious back injury as a result of degeneration in the vertebrae after years of cross-checks. He had only just returned in January '93, and then scored 65 points in 45 games. The timing was perfect: he was

now hitting mid-season form and was a step up on the Leafs who had played eight exhibition games, 84 in the regular season, and 14 more in the playoffs. And, he was coming to Toronto, his home away from playing home where he had never played a playoff game. His dad would be in the crowd; everyone, *a mare usque ad mari*, would be watching his every shift. Even during his days in Edmonton he didn't receive the scrutiny he did upon arriving at Pearson Airport to start this series, trying to do what even the great Dionne couldn't do: bring a Cup to the West Coast of the U.S., eh.

The way both teams played, the styles and personalities they brought to the rink, indicated this series would be decided by one matchup — Gilmour versus Gretzky. As those two went, so went their teams. They stood for the pride and honour of playing the game, for competing night after night, for winning. They just did it in two very different ways. Game 1 proved just how apposite the comparison was. The Leafs had control of much of the opening period, and Gilmour's goal on a pretty deflection at 17:19 gave them the lead. The second period saw a reversal of fortunes as the Kings took the play to Toronto and eventually tied the score on a goal by Pat Conacher with five minutes left.

Then Dougie blew the roof off the building.

In the middle six minutes of the third period he played a quality of hockey that could not be approached by mere mortals. From behind the Kings' net, he made a pithy pass to Anderson. Anderson, in the slot, deked Hrudey to make it 2–1 Leafs. A minute later Gilmour scored another himself from in tight, and shortly after set up Bill Berg. Dougie's four points on the night gave him 26 in the playoffs and moved him ahead of Gretzky (23) for top scorer. Final score: Leafs 4, Kings 1.

In the third period, the Leafs outshot L.A. 22–1, an incredible margin in such a tight game. For Toronto, fatigue was easily overcome by desire, and the sky-high emotions made this game feel more like Game 8 of the St. Louis series than Game 1 of this. Gilmour was far and away the best player on the ice and late in the game was at the centre of a mêlée. Coming over the L.A. line, he cut to the centre where Marty McSorley had lined him up. Dougie saw him just in the nick of time, so McSorley — in an effort to get a piece of him — threw his arms and elbows in Gilmour's face. Dougie fell hard to the ice and lay stunned for a few moments. That was all it took ("Kitty, bar the door"). Clark came in and gave McSorley a royal beating and the 15,720 fans went berserk with rage over the assault on Gilmour. Burns came within one police officer of beating the weasely weak Melrose to a pulp and after the game stressed the importance of the "team": "I feel I'm part of the team and if I can go out and help my players, I don't think I'd step on the ice to do it, but you want to do it sometimes because that's the type of coach I am, that's the kind of family I want, everybody pulling for everybody and everybody backing up everybody."

No one would ever have cheap-shotted Gretzky, the Leafs contended, and to have their star given the dirty treatment — especially when the game was won — was insult beyond measure. The incident seemed to overshadow much else of what good happened in the game and the frenzied media and fans discussed it endlessly over the next couple of days: Burns accusing Melrose of gooning his star; Gilmour's incredible determination and Gretzky's ineffectual play; getting back at McSorley directly or nailing Gretzky "an eye for an eye." The hype was outrageous and perhaps proved distracting and counterproductive to the Leafs, who had shown time and again their need to focus solely on the hockey game at hand.

With Game 2 both teams began to feel the drain of a third series. This round was always the most difficult. In the finals, no motivation

Glenn Anderson beats Kelly Hrudey.
GRAIG ABEL

would be necessary, but now it was critical to get ready mentally for games that made you physically tired just to think about. Gilmour in particular was looking as haggard as Gretzky was fresh, yet he was relentless in his leadership. He opened the scoring at 2:25 on a power play, and by the end of the period the Leafs were up 2–1. However, penalties proved costly in the second as the Leafs spent much of the time a man short. They gave the Kings nine power plays on the night and lost all the momentum they had established in Game 1. Tony Granato tied the game in the second and Tomas Sandstrom scored the winner midway through the third. L.A. won the game 3–2 and left Toronto with home-ice advantage in a 1–1 series. For the third time in a row, the Leafs lost a Game 2 and were once again making things as difficult as possible.

For Game 3 at the Great Western Forum, Burns made a few lineup changes, hoping that rested and more eager bodies could inject some spark into a weary Leaf team. Sent to the press box were Manderville, Foligno, and Eastwood; dressed were Pearson, Baumgartner, and McLlwain. Unfortunately, the Leafs lost two players early in the game. Peter Zezel fell heavily into the boards after a Zhitnik check behind the L.A. net and had to leave, while Andreychuk was given a high-sticking major and game misconduct. Gone were the Leafs' best face-off man and scorer, and by the middle of the game they were down 2–0 on goals by Blake and Kurri (the second short-handed).

As before, the Leafs proved capable of climbing out of a hole they had dug for themselves. Gilmour — again — and Baumgartner — of all — tied the score before the Kings scored yet another odd-man goal. Zhitnik scored on the power play at 18:18, but L.A. gave the Leafs a little opening when Robitaille was given a slashing penalty at 19:59. Toronto was down 3–2, but would have the man advantage to start the third.

Detroit's special teams almost killed the Leafs; Los Angeles' were threatening to do the same. The teams came out to start the final period, but for the sixth time this playoff year and the second in the game, the Leafs gave up a critical short-handed goal, this time at 1:26 to Dave Taylor. Toronto managed only five shots the rest of the way and lost handily 4–2. Once more they were behind the proverbial eight ball, having to win Game 4 in L.A. or come home to Toronto down 3–1.

Battle back they did, proving again their ability to win on the road in a pressure situation. Burns could not have been happier, especially since for once the superb 4–2 win was accomplished almost entirely without Gilmour. Four grinders — Rouse, Eastwood, Foligno, and Pearson — scored for the Leafs, who got two goals early to take the crowd out of the game (not a difficult task in LA LA land) and then checked the Kings into the ice the rest of the way. The series was even. The Leafs had regained home-ice advantage. This was going to be another long series. The drama was now just beginning.

Game 5 promised to be a classic, yet the Leafs came out in the first period as if this were their first exhibition game of the pre- season. Passes were ahead or behind the man and bounced over sticks; offsides resulted from sloppy stick-handling and lazy skating; giveaways came of mental errors. The team looked lousy. Yet after the first period the game was scoreless. Poorly as they had played, they had also recovered in time to at least play solid defence.

The second period was not much different except that L.A. scored twice, the second by Kurri with 5:45 to go, to put the Leafs in a deep hole. They looked frustrated. They knew they were having a terrible night; they just couldn't seem to do anything about it.

For years, whenever the Leafs played poorly they lost the game. They never got a break, never recovered quickly or got a fluky goal, never "created" something out of nothing. A poor start led to a poor game, a goal down meant a game lost, an early power play squandered meant a terrible night for special teams. Times, they have a-changed.

The Cat made a number of key saves to keep the score within reach while the rest of the team battled its bad luck and poor timing. Then they got a late power play chance and Krushelnyski cashed in at 16:11. It wasn't pretty, but it was a start. Down 2–1 going into the third didn't seem so bad given the way they had played. In fact, it provided a little inspiration: imagine what they could do if they got their act together.

The Kings came out for the final period content to sit on the lead, and the Leafs kept plugging away. Each shift produced a little more optimism, a sign of slightly greater life. Halfway through the period Hrudey let a shot by Sylvain Lefebvre slip by and suddenly the score was tied. This brought the Leafs to life, and but for some bad luck and missed chances the game might have ended in regulation. As it was, overtime beckoned. Things were getting tense. L.A. had their wake-up call, and the Leafs were playing excellent hockey again. Whoever won this game would be 3–2 up in the series and in a position to clinch two days later.

Toronto held the majority of play in the overtime, and although sound defensively they showed no signs of playing too tight or conservatively. They played to win. In the final minute of the fourth period Glenn Anderson batted his own rebound out of the air in the high slot and into the net. The Leafs got a very fortunate, breath-taking 3–2 victory and were now just one win away from playing in the finals for the first time since 1967.

Game 6. Los Angeles. Montreal had eliminated the weary Islanders in five games the night before, and the incredible, impossible dream of a Toronto-Montreal final was that close to becoming real enough to buy tickets for. It was an incredible fight. Glenn Anderson picked up from his overtime heroics of Game 5 to give the Leafs an early lead just 57 seconds into the game when his shot deflected off a skate past Hrudey. The rest of the period belonged mostly to L.A.,

GRAIG ABEL

and Granato tied the game halfway through. This got the Kings into gear and it was up to Potvin to withstand the onslaught of L.A. chances as the period ended.

The second, the great Leaf nemesis all playoffs long, was an unmitigated disaster. Clark gave the Leafs a 2–1 lead early but the Kings did what Detroit had done all series, taking control and scoring three times in just over eight minutes, all on the power play. Toronto was going into the third down 4–2. This was not a good way to get to the finals, but the Leafs always seemed to do things the hard way.

In the third they were positively relentless. Potvin was unbeatable, and the intense forechecking began to run down the wearying Kings' defence. Clark scored at 11:08 on a bullet wrist shot that would have killed Hrudey if he had been able to get in front of it. 4–3. The pressure continued, the clock ticked down. L.A. desperately tried to hold on. With almost two full minutes to go, Burns called Potvin to

the bench for a sixth attacker. The puck was in the Kings' zone, Dougie was in possession. He saw Wendel in the slot and another incredible wrist shot nailed the net with just 1:21 to go. The game was tied!

Overtime was inevitable as the time ran down, but referee Kerry Fraser, not wanting to be forgotten in this superb battle, called Glenn Anderson for boarding at 19:47. The Leafs had clawed back from the brink of disaster, but they'd have to kill a penalty first off to start the overtime.

The game lasted only another 101 seconds, but boy was there plenty to talk about afterwards. During the Los Angeles power play, with the puck in the Leafs' end, Gretzky accidentally high-sticked Gilmour in the face. Dougie went down, his face bloodied. Fraser saw the whole incident, yet play continued. Gilmour went off to receive eight stitches, the victim of Gretzky-rule hockey. Half a minute later Gretzky himself scored to give the Kings a 5–4 win and force one final game. Such a blatant, though wholly unintentional, foul was difficult to overlook, especially in light of Anderson's far lesser boarding penalty. It was an unfortunate finish that tarnished an otherwise excellent hockey game. But facts were facts. Toronto had to return to Maple Leaf Gardens for another Game 7, the only team ever to play three in a row in one season.

May 29, 1993. Toronto. This was the stuff dreams were made of. It had been a long year, full of joy and success, but it all boiled down to one game now. On this night the atmosphere in the city was beyond electric. It was nuclear. All day outside the Gardens cars pulled up, drivers talked to loiterers or friends, left. Some with tickets, some without. When the night slid over the day, noise filled the downtown and Yonge Street had more feet than wheels. Scalpers shouted "Who needs a pair?" to all passersby. Ticketholders made the privileged walk from Yonge Street to Church Street wearing Leaf paraphernalia, chanting "Go Leafs go! Go Leafs go!" and "Gretzky sucks! Gretzky sucks!" Gilmour and Clark shirts were everywhere and the call of "Bring on the Habs" filled the city. The entrance was plugged with television cameras and police and hangers-on who weren't able to get tickets to the game but wanted to be part of the excitement. The sound of passing streetcars that normally filled the air was inaudible above the din of Leaf fever. Tonight there would be a winner.

Inside the Gardens, the hawkers screamed "Get tonight's program!" as ushers ripped the historic tickets and hustled everyone through the turnstiles. Fans gravitated toward the souvenir stands to buy something, anything, by way of a good luck token and remembrance of something special for years to come. It was personal history as much as Leaf history in the making. The laser light show in the dark arena was mesmerizing and the excitement unreal. The Gardens seemed smaller than your dining room and people in the

HOCKEY HALL OF FAME

seats beside you became your next-door neighbour. Not a soul was rooting for L.A. on this night. No one in the Gardens, in the media booth, at home in their living room wanted to see the Kings win. This was the Leafs' return to glory, their moment of resurrection. The game hadn't started and already it felt like overtime. Double overtime. Triple. From the first faceoff and the first second there was no margin for error now, no second chance, no time to recover or make excuses about injury or fatigue. Steve Stavro had got his wish. It was time to play for the Stanley Cup.

On this night, truths would be told. Wendel Clark, who scored a hat trick in the last game, had to play just as well again tonight. He was the captain. He had to wear the "C" to the death. Dougie looked like a cross between a war-ravaged soldier and a Calcutta street person but had to fire up the juices one more time. Andreychuk, who scored a club record 12 times in the first two series, had yet to score in the six games against the Kings. He had to be big in the slot again and jam home a chance or two.

Before the game, Grant Fuhr dropped by the Gardens to visit Potvin and offer some Stanley Cup words of advice and encouragement. The Cat just had to be there or it would be over. Likewise, the four big bangers — Pearson and Manderville, the two Mikes, Foligno and Krushelnyski — had to get in on the L.A. defence and wear them down, *tear* them down, if need be. And they had to stop Gretzky. He had been silent, almost invisible in the series, scoring only twice and adding four assists. Only once, though, in overtime in Game 6, had his contribution been significant. If somehow he could disappear for one more game, the Leafs would be on their way to Montreal for the Classic Stanley Cup encounter, the one every Canadian boy dreamed of playing.

The player introductions were more exciting than most games. The more overrated the Kings player, the more hated, the louder the boos: loud for Hrudey, louder for McSorley, loudest for Gretzky. The Leaf introductions were obliterated by 15,720 scratchy Leaf screams.

The first period put to rest any idea the Leafs would storm the Kings and put them on the brink the way they had with St. Louis. Gretzky was one team leader who knew how to prepare for an important game and he wasn't going to come out flat. He scored a goal and assisted on Sandstrom's high shot at 17:30 to give the Kings an early 2–0 lead. This was going to be a fight. The fans clapped, the organ grinded, the tension built. The Leafs reached down deep and found more energy. They dominated the second and stormed back to tie the game. Clark got a quick goal on the power play at 1:25 and then a low shot by Anderson, after another incredible pass from Gilmour in the corner, slipped by Hrudey. But midway through the period Gretzky scored again, this time on a close-in slap shot after eluding a check from Manderville. The Leafs kept pressing, but the period ended 3–2 L.A.

Twenty minutes left in the season, 20 minutes to the Stanley Cup final. Wendel again tied the score just 1:25 into the third off another impossible behind-the-goal pass from Dougie, his fifth goal in two games and the finest two games of his career. The next 14 minutes were just plain scary. More than 4.2 million Canadians watched the game on the CBC, making this the most-watched playoff game in the history of the NHL.

The dream ended with less than four minutes to go. Coming in over the blueline on a simple three-on-three was Tony Granato. He fed the puck to Zhitnik who cut across the middle going left. The defence played the criss-cross perfectly. Zhitnik passed the puck back, but instead of going to the trailing man who was covered, it hit Rouse's skate and deflected to the front of the goal. Mike Donnelly, who was opposite to the side Potvin had moved toward to play the initial pass, had the half-empty net and made no mistake. Kings 4, Leafs 3. Less than a minute later Gretzky scored a fluke goal off Dave Ellett's skate (make no mistake, it was a fluke; luck at its sheerest), and then Ellett himself scored with 1:07 left to cut the

L.A. lead to 5–4. Potvin was pulled for the extra attacker, but the Leafs couldn't tie it. The Kings were going to Montreal. The season was over.

In the Kings dressing room after the game, Gretzky talked about the great personal satisfaction in winning: "I've taken the roses and I've taken the heat. But tonight I stood up and answered the bell. I don't think I've ever been more personally satisfied at winning a series. It's the sweetest moment of my career. I've played 14 years and I didn't want to be remembered as the guy who didn't play well in the semifinals versus Toronto." In the Leaf dressing room, Dougie talked about the team: "We fought back. . . . There is a lot of character on this team. Lots of guts and determination in here. At times on paper we're not as good as the other team, but we have a lot of determination. We've got a good coach who demands a lot and we want to win for him. We gave it a good run." He looked drained and vulnerable, a mere wisp of the ideal image of a hockey player, the knight in plastic armour. He looked like he needed a week in the hospital.

The season was over, but it wasn't lost on Mike Donnelly's goal so late in the seventh game against the Kings. It was lost much earlier, in Game 6 against Detroit when the Leafs had home ice and a 3–2 lead in games. It was lost again in Games 2 and 3 and 6 of the St. Louis series when again early victory would have provided much-needed rest for the banged-up defence and Dougie up front. It was lost when that killer instinct failed to materialize and help the team out in Games 2 and 6 of the L.A. series. The playoffs were simply too strenuous to play seven-game series each time. But the many memories of achievement will linger for a long, long time. For these '93 playoffs, Leaf fans expected to see five or six games — they got 21.

The season was over, but something remarkable happened. The excitement never stopped. The next day and all summer long people talked about how close it had been, about Gretzky's high-stick on Gilmour in Game 6 and his lucky goal in Game 7, about getting the next season started so they could get back to the semis and then to the finals this time. Cliff Fletcher was already talking of change, adding speed and offence to a lineup that needed to help reduce the reliance on Gilmour, a second centre to replace John Cullen, a winger with Anderson's speed. He had arranged for the team to hold a mini-camp in London, England, in September, and to play two games with the Rangers at Wembley Arena. The season was over, but hockey had become fun again.

It had been a long time since a Leaf won a major trophy. Salming was the runner-up for the Norris in 1977 and 1980, Keon runner-up for the Lady Byng in 1971, Horton for the Norris in '69, and Bower and Gamble for the '68 Vezina. But at the awards ceremony in June 1993 the Leafs had a winner for the first time since Dave Keon won the Conn Smythe back in Cup year 1967. Gilmour was nominated

for both the Hart and Selke, but when Lemieux returned successfully after his battle with Hodgkin's disease to win the scoring title
he was also given the Hart. As Hart "runner-up" (unofficially, of
course), Dougie won the Frank J. Selke Trophy. Felix Potvin, who
led the league in goals against and save percentage in his rookie year,
was a Calder Trophy finalist, but lost to high-scoring Finn Teemu
Selanne. And for the second time in his young NHL career, Pat Burns
was awarded the Jack Adams Trophy for improving the Leafs by an
astounding 32 points in one year. It was a wonderful season for
players and fans, and the awards confirmed the return of the Toronto
Maple Leafs to their prestigious place in hockey. Yes, the season was
over, but the game was just beginning anew.

GRAIG ABEL

RECORDS SET IN 1992–1993

Regular Season

Team Records
Most wins, season: 44
Most points, season: 99
Most home wins, season: 25

Individual Records
Most points, season: 127, Doug Gilmour
Most assists, season: 95, Doug Gilmour
Most points, centre, season: 127, Doug Gilmour
Most points, first-year player: 74, Nikolai Borschevsky
Most goals, first-year player: 34 (tied with one other), Nikolai Borschevsky
Most assists, game: 6 (tied with one other), Doug Gilmour versus Minnesota, February 13, 1993, at the Gardens. Toronto won 6–1.

Playoffs

Team Records
Most playoff victories, season: 11
Most playoff games, season: 21
Most 7-Game series, season: 3
Most shots, playoff game: 64, Game 1 versus St. Louis, May 5, 1993, at the Gardens. Toronto won 2–1.
Fewest shots allowed, period: 1, Game 1 versus Los Angeles, 3rd period, May 17, 1993, at the Gardens. Toronto won 4–1.

Individual Records
Most playoff points, season: 35, Doug Gilmour
Most playoff points, centre, season: 35, Doug Gilmour
Most playoff points, left wing, season: 20, Wendel Clark
Most playoff points, right wing, season: 18, Glenn Anderson
Most playoff goals, season: 12, Dave Andreychuk
Most playoff goals, left wing, season: 12, Dave Andreychuk
Most playoff goals, centre, season: 10, Doug Gilmour
Most playoff assists, season: 25, Doug Gilmour
Most playoff assists, centre, season: 25, Doug Gilmour
Most playoff assists, right wing, season: 11, Glenn Anderson
Most playoff penalty minutes, right wing, season: 42, Mike Foligno

DOUG MACLELLAN / HOCKEY HALL OF FAME

XII

The New Order

"The first goal for a rebuilding club is to become respectable and competitive, and we've done that. The next step is to prove you belong with the top seven or eight teams on a consistent basis. That's the next challenge."

— Cliff Fletcher

The 1993 playoffs were an enormous bonus for Fletcher and Leaf fans. Thanks to "The Trade" with Calgary and Fuhr's injuries (which allowed Potvin the opportunity to prove his talent and the Leafs to acquire Andreychuk), the team went further than anyone had expected. Fletcher's plans to bring the Cup to Toronto moved up a few years and created two not necessarily compatible considerations. He wanted to establish a farm system and player-development program that would see a new generation of young Leafs compete for the Cup sometime down the line, say five to seven years. At the same time, the players he had been able to acquire gave the Leafs an unexpected chance to "steal" a Cup in the immediate future. Gilmour, Anderson, Andreychuk, Ellett, Macoun, and Rouse were all 30 or older, and the next three years would be their last chance to play at the peak of their abilities. After that, a new crop of young players — Potvin, Lefebvre, Manderville, and Pearson — would have to develop and take over.

Fletcher had been able to bridge the interminable gap between present chaos and future success by trading for players who were capable of winning the Cup now. It was an incredible accomplishment and allowed the growing pains of the redevelopment of the whole organization to be less harshly felt. Even today the true value of Fletcher's drafting isn't known, and it won't be for quite some time. The roster that played in Game 7 against Los Angeles was put together almost entirely by trades. The only Leaf draft choices to play that night were Potvin, Clark, Gill, Borschevsky, Mironov, and Pearson. The only other draft choice to play at all in the '93 playoffs was Eastwood. The rest of the team was acquired by Fletcher's trading acumen.

Fletcher was in a strange betwixt-and-between position. The current team was so close to winning the Cup that he had to try to take that extra step to get the team to the finals. Yet his original plan called for patience and devotion to young players and the system of development. He wanted to help Gilmour by getting a second centre,

and to improve team speed, but he would never trade Potvin or his great young prospects or future high-draft choices to do so. To make matters more complicated, many other teams were similarly close to the Stanley Cup and were trying to get the same kinds of players as Fletcher. What team didn't need a second centre or a rushing defenceman? To improve the team immediately, Fletcher would have to give up more than what he'd get in return, and decided not to do too much with the roster over the summer. He bought out the contract of Bob McGill, released Darryl Shannon outright, and signed three young players — Alexei Kudashov, Chris Snell, and goalie Bruce Racine.

His next order of business was the expansion draft on June 24 for the new Florida and Anaheim franchises. To this end, he had to submit a "protected" list, exposing all but 15 eligible players in the Leaf system under contract:

Protected	Unprotected
Felix Potvin	Darren Puppa
Todd Gill	Rick Wamsley
Dave Ellett	Damian Rhodes
Sylvain Lefebvre	Dmitri Mironov
Jamie Macoun	Ted Crowley
Bob Rouse	Jerome Dupont
Kent Manderville	Curtis Hunt
Rob Pearson	Guy Lehoux
Peter Zezel	Brad Miller
Glenn Anderson	Rob Cimetta
Dave Andreychuk	Greg Johnston
Ken Baumgartner	John Cullen
Wendel Clark	Mike Foligno
Mike Eastwood	Mike Krushelnyski
Doug Gilmour	Guy Larose
	Dave McLlwain
	Mark Osborne
	Joe Sacco
	Ken McRae
	Kevin McLelland
	Yanic Perreault
	Jeff Perry

No team could lose more than one goalie and one defenceman, or two players in total, and two is exactly what the Leafs lost. To no one's surprise, Florida took Darren Puppa, and later in the draft the Mighty Ducks took Joe Sacco. No great damage had been done. Two

days later at the 1993 entry draft at the Colisée in Quebec City it was the Leafs' turn to make the selections.

Toronto picked 12th overall courtesy of the Sabres and the Grant Fuhr trade. Head scout Pierre Dorion selected Swedish defenceman Kenny Jonsson, a player highly favoured by the Leafs' European scout Anders Hedberg. Jonsson was the first Swede of significance to join the Leafs since Salming and Hammarstrom 20 years earlier and was the result of the kind of overseas scouting the Leafs should have had in place in 1974. Dorion was also very optimistic about his next two picks, Landon Wilson (19th) and Zdenek Nedved (123rd), but these were players who would need three or four years to develop. Fletcher hoped that Jonsson, with his size, international experience, and maturity, could play in a year's time if need be.

The only real "move" Fletcher made involved solidifying the Leafs' goaltending future. After his brilliant rookie season, Felix Potvin entered the option year of his $145,000 contract thinking he deserved a raise. Fletcher agreed, but he and the Cat's agent, Gilles Lupien, were a little out of synch as to what "raise" translated to financially. Lupien demanded $2 million a year. Fletcher, outraged, countered with what he thought was a more realistic figure — $700,000. Lupien waged a war of words most of the summer with the happy cooperation of the press, and while this soap opera played out Fletcher signed other players also entering their option years. Clark became the Leafs' second million-dollar-a-year man, while Gill signed for three years at $675,000, $725,000, and $750,000. Berehowsky agreed to a year and an option at $350,000, and Rouse decided to play out the year and test the free agent market the following spring. Osborne and Berg signed new deals and later Ellett became a millionaire with a three-year, $3.2 million deal. The great defensive defenceman Lefebvre was given a fresh four-year, $2.6 million deal, and even Burns reaped the benefits from the late spring harvest, upping his salary to $450,000.

Meanwhile, Lupien continued to publicly threaten Fletcher that his Cat client would play out his option and sign as a free agent if $2 million were not forthcoming. For comparison, he cited Alexandre Daigle's inane five-year, $12.5 million deal in Ottawa, Patrick Roy's $2 million, and Kelly Kisio's $1 million contract as a free agent signing by the Flames. From this point of view — taking the high

end of the entire league — Lupien made some sense. Fletcher argued that within the pay scale of the club, $2 million was simply unworkable. Neither Gilmour nor Clark, many years senior and proven consistent, made that much. To grant Potvin such a contract would mean restructuring the whole team's pay scale.

Potvin was caught in the middle. He sought peace, not greed, and in mid-September agreed to a three-year, $4 million contract, relieved that a settlement had been reached before Leaf fans turned on him for being big-headed and money-grubbing. Besides, settling for $1,300,000 a year — a 900% salary increase — wasn't so bad.

In his first summer as NHL Commissioner, Gary Bettman made three disruptive changes to the league. First, as part of the realignment to work the newcomers Anaheim and Florida into the standings, Tampa Bay was moved out of the Norris Division and into the Patrick Division. In its place, Winnipeg came to Toronto's division. Second, the names of the divisions were scrapped. Gone were Norris, Patrick, Smythe, and Adams, names that paid tribute to hockey's founding fathers in the same tradition as the trophy names (Hart, Calder, Vezina, Smythe *et al.*). These names were deemed by Bettman to be too confusing for (American) fans. Giving the league geographic names for the divisions would make the NHL easier (for Americans) to follow and increase popularity (in the U.S.). Here's how the old and new set-ups compare:

1992–93	1993–94
CLARENCE CAMPBELL CONFERENCE	WESTERN CONFERENCE
Norris Division	*Central Division*
Toronto	Toronto
Detroit	Detroit
Chicago	Chicago
St. Louis	St. Louis
Minnesota	Dallas
Tampa Bay	Winnipeg
Smythe Division	*Pacific Division*
Vancouver	Vancouver
Calgary	Calgary
Edmonton	Edmonton
Los Angeles	Los Angeles
San Jose	San Jose
Winnipeg	Anaheim

PRINCE OF WALES CONFERENCE	EASTERN CONFERENCE
Adams Division	*Northeast Division*
Ottawa	Ottawa
Boston	Boston
Buffalo	Buffalo
Quebec	Quebec
Hartford	Hartford
Montreal	Montreal
	Pittsburgh
Patrick Division	*Pacific Division*
N.Y. Rangers	N.Y. Rangers
N.Y. Islanders	N.Y. Islanders
New Jersey	New Jersey
Philadelphia	Philadelphia
Washington	Washington
Pittsburgh	Tampa Bay
	Florida

A major change to the playoff format was also made. The playoff matchups would be determined by *conference*, not division. The top eight from each would qualify for the playoffs, with the two division champions being ranked 1 and 2. Then, in the first round, number 1 would play number 8, 2 would play 7, 3 and 6, 4 and 5. For each succeeding round the remaining teams would always be ordered according to their regular season rankings to determine their next opponent. It rendered division standings virtually useless, but Americans no doubt found this format easier to follow. Had this set-up been used for the '93 playoffs, here's what would have happened:

Norris		*Smythe*		*Adams*		*Patrick*	
Chicago	106	Vancouver	101	Boston	109	Pittsburgh	119
Detroit	103	Calgary	97	Quebec	104	Washington	93
Toronto	99	Los Angeles	88	Montreal	102	New Jersey	87
St. Louis	85	Winnipeg	87	Buffalo	86	Islanders	87
Minnesota	82	Edmonton	60	Hartford	58	Flyers	83
Tampa Bay	53	San Jose	24	Ottawa	24	Rangers	79

These division alignments meant nothing except for the four first-place finishers. To determine first-round opponents, they would be

ranked 1 and 2, and the other six in order of points. The top four would have home-ice advantage:

Chicago	106	Pittsburgh	119
Vancouver	101	Boston	109
Detroit	103	Quebec	104
Toronto	99	Montreal	102
Calgary	97	Washington	93
Los Angeles	88	New Jersey	87
Winnipeg	87	Islanders	87
St. Louis	85	Buffalo	86

Vancouver, by virtue of first place in their division, is placed ahead of Detroit which had more points but were second in the Norris. The matchups would then be: Chicago and St. Louis; Vancouver and Winnipeg; Detroit and L.A.; Toronto and Calgary; Pittsburgh and Buffalo; Boston and the Islanders; Quebec and New Jersey; Montreal and Washington. The top four in each conference would have home-ice advantage and the winners would be re-ranked after each round. If Chicago, L.A., Vancouver, and Toronto won their series, for instance, the next matchups would be determined by regular season finish again:

Chicago	106
Vancouver	101
Toronto	99
Los Angeles	88

This would mean the Blackhawks and Canucks would have home-ice advantage and play the Kings and Leafs respectively. Simple.

Pat Burns was an honest and straightforward man. He didn't worry about contracts or newspapers or ticket sales or any other aspect of the hockey organization. He was the coach. He worried about how his players played the game. In his first year, he improved the Leafs by 32 points, and for the new season expectations were, as the song goes, high high high. Nothing could have augured better for the Leafs than to see Burns begin camp in a surly mood. He had this damn trip to England to disrupt the team; the Potvin dispute was a distraction for everyone; and the Leafs' schedule was awful and

included five road trips out west. That meant 15 fewer practice days than last year. They would again play 16 games against expansion teams (Anaheim four, San Jose four, Tampa Bay three, Florida three, Ottawa two) but also play six times against new division rivals Winnipeg, a much tougher opponent than Tampa Bay. While most fans were singing "Bring on the Cup," Burns was hoping only to have his team play in the same key of consistency this year as last.

Then there was the question of roster. Over the summer the Leafs had lost only four players — Puppa, Sacco, Shannon, McGill — none of whom had figured prominently in the Leafs' success.* They had added only young and inexperienced players to the team, thus setting up the two-edged argument of whether the club was stable or stale. Burns invited a slew of kids to camp, and hoped that they might augment the "stable" while preventing the "stale": "These guys want to wear a Maple Leaf uniform? Well, I want them to prove to me that they deserve it. I'll be disappointed if someone doesn't take someone else's job. Really disappointed." While competition for jobs during training camp was healthy and motivating, the list of rookies who failed to impress was as long as Burns was disappointed. Yanic Perreault, David Sacco, Alexei Kudashov, Matt Martin, Chris Snell, Patrick Augusta, Eric Lacroix, David Harlock, Chris Govedaris, and Ken McRae were all given ample opportunity to crack the lineup. None succeeded. The lack of depth on the big team and within the organization was there for all to see. Fletcher had to keep signing and developing the kids, while hoping to make a surprise trade, but come opening day Burns had to make do with the status quo.

What Burns was primarily worried about was the kind of complacency the Leafs showed in London, losing to the Rangers 5–3 and 3–1 with veteran rosters. The players skated like they knew they had a lock on their positions and that Burns didn't have anyone better to replace them with. This attitude, needless to say, infuriated the coach as much for its truth as its unhealthiness. The resulting worries, however, proved to be unfounded.

On October 3, between training camp and opening night, the Leafs held a special team dinner at the Royal York Hotel to present the Bickell Cup for the first time in 14 years. Last won in 1979 by Mike Palmateer, this Leaf award is given at the discretion of the Board of Directors who this year felt Doug Gilmour deserved the honour for his incredible first full season with the team. Ted Kennedy had been the first recipient in 1953, but like so much else at the Gardens the prestigious trophy was all but abandoned during the you-know-who era.

Conn Smythe had inaugurated the trophy in honour of J.P. (John) Bickell, a financier and part owner of the St. Pats** who arranged

---

* Early in the season they also lost Dave McLlwain to Ottawa in the waiver draft.

** Along with Charles Querrie, N.L. Nathanson, and Paul Ciceri.

Gilmour and Clark with their rings and the Bickell Cup.
GRAIG ABEL

Conn's bank loan* to build Maple Leaf Gardens in 1931 at the height
of the Great Depression. Bickell became the first president of Maple
Leaf Gardens and then served as chairman of the board until his
death on August 22, 1951. Without him, Smythe used to say proudly,
the Gardens never would have been built. The gold Bickell Cup is
kept in a special glass case in the Board of Directors lounge at the
Gardens and is every bit as beautiful as it is unknown.

The presentation to Gilmour was made by Dr. Hugh Smythe, the
special guest host was Bobby Baun, and the tables were full of
Alumni. That same night Steve Stavro also presented the entire team
with Championship rings** to honour their magnificent playoff run
in the spring. It was a generous gesture — perhaps overly so — that
set the tone of celebration and success for the season and gave the

---

* Using his influence with friend Sir John Aird, president of the Canadian Bank
of Commerce.

** As winners of the Norris Division.

players a tempting taste of the treats they would receive if they won the Cup.

The season began in earnest with a bang and a streak. Once the 48th Highlanders left the ice after their 63rd home opener appearance, the Leafs beat Dallas 6–3. The game featured the best of everything: four goals in the third, three assists by Gilmour, two goals by Andreychuk, and superb goaltending from Potvin. Rob Pearson scored once and banged along the boards and in the corners all night long, finally giving hope that here was one young player ready to join the ranks of the seasoned pros. The Leafs followed up two nights later with a 2–1 win over the Blackhawks with Clark scoring the winner midway through the third. This was a tough, physical, defensive game that showed the team at its checking best and gave them a quick 2–0 start to the year.

Momentum was building, confidence bubbling, and Leaf luck turning all blue and white. In a seesaw game at the Spectrum that saw the Leafs down 2–0 and then up 4–2 and then tied 4–4, John Cullen scored the winner with just 1:51 left on a spectacular diving goal. An early 3–0 record and the Leafs were picking up from where they left off. Those 99 points the year before were no fluke. That was no Cinderella playoff run. Hard work and faith was all.

Game 4 at the Gardens was more of the same. In a pre-game ceremony, the Leafs established a new tradition unique in the NHL called "honoured" numbers, in this case Syl Apps' 9 and Ted Kennedy's 10. "Honoured numbers" would not be retired, but banners would be raised to the rafters to commemorate great Leafs. The jersey would be kept in circulation, and a patch to signify the merit of the number would be sewn onto the current player's sleeve (Anderson's 9 and Berg's 10). It was a great innovation that both addressed the problem of ignoring great Leafs of the past and of retiring every number from 1 to 30 as in the Montreal tradition. Once the numbers were raised and the blue Leaf carpet rolled up and removed, Toronto went out and shelled the Caps 7–1, Pearson getting two more goals and looking like the kind of winger/banger/scorer the Leafs so desperately needed.

Game 5 began a back-to-back showdown with the Motown Red Wings, those of OT elimination on Borschevsky's goal the previous spring. The first game at the Gardens featured the heart and hands of the team. Dougie had three goals and two assists and the Cat nabbed 40 of 43 shots in a great 6–3 performance. The next night in Detroit, the Cat was again superlative. The Leafs were outshot 33–17, outplayed badly, and staved off three separate five-on-three situations to win 2–1.

Whoa! 6–0!! A positive start to the year was now looking awfully early like Stanley Cup play. Everything the team did turned to victory. But the second win over Detroit had a price. Wendel hurt his knee, Zezel's back acted up, and Rouse was suspended for four games for a stick incident with Bob Probert in the Toronto end of

the series. However, any negative repercussions weren't in evidence in their next game, a 7–2 thrashing of the fast-sinking Hartford Whalers. Seven wins, no losses.

Game 8, their first against the new Florida Panthers at a joint called the Miami Arena. A 3–3 tie sent the game into overtime, but Pearson on a great playoffian effort scored at 2:17 to give the Leafs their eighth win in a row and tie an NHL mark for victories from the start of a season (set by the '34–'35 Leafs and equalled by the '75–'76 Sabres).

On to the Thunder Dome to play the other farcical Florida franchise, the Tampa Bay Lightning. A pair of rare-as-an-emu goals by Mark Osborne and a Potvin goose egg gave the Leafs a 2–0 win and a new NHL record of 9–0. It seemed to happen so easily, the number on the left increasing with consistency, the number on the right remaining constant, yet it was an achievement that had never been accomplished in 76 previous NHL seasons. Burns, as always, was cautious in praise: "The main thing is, we've picked up 18 points that no one can take away from us. That cushion will come in handy when we go down into the dumps for a while."

The dumps seemed at hand. Wendel and Zezel were still out, and Pearson, who had six goals and 10 points, hurt his knee in the Tampa game and was lost to the team indefinitely. The Leafs were at the start of a stretch that had just four home games in 39 days. Game 10 was in Chicago, where they had lost 13 in a row including one five-game stretch in which they scored just *one* goal. After giving up an early one to Darin Kimble, Toronto scored three in the second and won 4–2. Potvin stopped 46 shots; the jinx was over. The Leafs had outscored the opposition 45–20 in the new season and after 10 games had a perfect record, a new league record, and enough confidence to fly through the rest of the season.

But all good things must come to an end, and two days later at the Forum Vincent Damphousse scored three and the Habs beat the Leafs 5–2. The streak was over, the record a blemished 10–1. The year could now resume in the peace and quiet of consistent play. Consistency, though, was going to be difficult. Two games later Borschevsky suffered a ruptured spleen after an innocent check by Bill Lindsay of the Panthers, and Todd Gill suffered what proved to be a serious groin injury. Pearson, Zezel, and Clark were a long way from returning, so the team was now without five regulars. The lineup was further depleted when Fletcher traded Mike Foligno to Florida for future considerations, a testament to his qualities as a GM and the Leafs' new "class." Foligno was in the final year of his contract and was not being used much by Burns, watching most of the games from the press box or the end of the bench while the rookies were given a chance to impress. The trade was Fletcher's way of getting Foligno to a team that could use him right away (and probably the following year) and allow him to reach 1,000 career games. It was a generous move appreciated by both Foligno and the

rest of the team, and was markedly dissimilar to Punch's treatment of Red Kelly at the '67 expansion draft and Ron Ellis during the '80–'81 season.

Meanwhile, Commissioner Gary Bettman was grinding the NHL to a standstill. An officials' strike became imminent when he refused to bargain in good faith with the referees and linesmen. His legal counsel, Jeff Pash, threatened the officials in one letter by saying, "In the event of a strike . . . there can be no assurance that you will be re-employed," and further commented: "The reality is that anytime there's a strike, some replacement workers inevitably end up taking the place of the striking workers. It happens in many industries. It's not so much a threat as it is a reality." Hardly the way to inspire confidence in the bargaining process or give referees due recognition as the best, most qualified in the world. Bettman's position also provided a wealth of insight for hockey lovers in Canada, who were ignorant of the fact that the NHL was an "industry" and the refs "striking workers" who should be governed accordingly. Air traffic controllers, referees and linesmen: same thing.

Although the strike lasted only 10 days, it shook the hockey world into sober realization of just how out-of-touch Bettman was with the NHL. The officials were just about the most docile union in North America (which was one of the reasons they were so greatly under-paid), yet even *they* were riled enough to unlace the blades. Bett-man's heavy suit-and-tie methods were not the way to resolve the problem. He failed miserably to see not how difficult but how *easy* they were to bargain with. While the replacement referees did an adequate enough job in the interim, the resentment Bettman engen-dered within the league was far more damaging than any dollar figure the NHL ceded in the end. That, too, Bettman had yet to realize, as the owners' 1994–95 lockout only too clearly indicated.

Another Bettman implementation involved using a computer to arrange the league schedule. Prior to '93–'94 and his involvement in the NHL, the games were always scheduled by hand to help provide a little balance and sanity to an otherwise insane 84-game season. No longer could the scheduler allow teams special accommodations and reasonable road trips whenever possible. All 26 teams and 700 players were hurt by inhuman travel obligations, as evidenced by the Leafs' five games in eight nights on a west coast trip in mid-November. Incredibly, they won the first four — 4–3 in Anaheim, 3–2 in L.A. and again 3–2 in Edmonton, and 5–2 in Vancouver — before losing to Calgary. At the Saddledome, the Leafs went up 3–1 in the first on Clark's league-leading 22nd goal, scored on a penalty shot. But the Flames got one in the second and by the third Toronto had run out of energy. Three unanswered goals gave Calgary a 5–3 win.

The injuries kept coming. Berg was hurt before the L.A. game and Ellett was gone for a month after a rib-cage wound. Burns was forced to use more of his rookies than he cared to, and none was able to

contribute to such a degree as to threaten the injured player's job. To ease the burden, Burns even tried Clark on the power play point, but that experiment quickly went the way of a broken test tube. As a result, December, just like the previous year, was not a good month. In one stretch the Leafs won just two of 14 games and although Gill and Borschevsky returned to the fold, Mironov was sidelined with a bad charley-horse.

For the first time in his young NHL career, Potvin was also struggling. Burns, the personification of patience, had to pull the Cat three times in a span of seven games, the third time after giving up seven goals through half a game with the Kings. Rhodes came in for three impressive starts (a win, a tie, a loss, seven goals allowed) to spot the Cat, who spent all his time practising with Wamsley on angles and body discipline to cure his woes. Despite the struggling, though, Toronto finished the calendar year with a record of 50–25–12,* best in the NHL, and in the current standings they were second overall with 49 points (behind the Rangers with 55).

Just after the New Year, the Leafs found the Stanley Cup gear they had been playing in at the start of the season. They beat Ottawa 6–3 and Vancouver 5–3 to get on track, and Potvin's strong showing in the Canucks game proved he had returned to form. The team then went into Boston and played a perfect game, shutting out the Bruins in the Garden for the first time since Johnny Bower did it on March 12, 1961. It was 5–0 then. Stanley, Olmstead, Nevin, Duff, and Pulford scored. It was 3–0 now. Andreychuk twice, and Anderson scored. Another streak was under way, and again the Leafs began to win games in improbable ways and times. Down 3–1 to Dallas in the third, Andreychuk and Eastwood scored midway through to tie it. Then, in the dying moments of overtime, Anderson drove to the net and converted Gilmour's pass for the winner at 4:47.

Zezel's back was strong enough for him to return, and Clark's injury had taken him from the NHL's goal-scoring lead by the time he returned. The number-one honcho in the league now was Andreychuk, who scored his 38th in a 3–3 tie with the Ducks in only the Leafs' 49th game of the year. The team had slipped a bit, going from great to merely mortal, but they were still battling the Rangers for the President's Trophy, a position they held jointly with 63 points at the All-Star break. As soon as the league schedule began again, so too did the odd combination of wins and injuries. The Leafs lost Cullen for six weeks with a badly sprained ankle and Rouse for 20 games when he tore cartilage in his right knee and required surgery. But the Burnsian philosophy — the desire to compete — overcame the apparent lack of depth from which the Leafs suffered. When they scored two in the last four minutes to tie the Blues 4–4 on February 1, Burns' team tied Joe Primeau's '50–'51 Leafs by going 11 in a row

---

* The second half of '92–'93 and the first half of '93–'94.

without a loss. But just as Primeau's team had the streak snapped by the Red Wings, so too did these new Leafs, although it was now by a 4–3 score, not 3–1, and the winner was scored by Sergei Fedorov, not Metro Prystai.

Toronto played "just" .500 hockey the rest of the season, going 15–15–1, while revealing the same weaknesses they had shown in last year's playoffs. Andreychuk scored but eight goals in the final 24 games, and as he faded so did the team. Fletcher noticed why — anyone could score with Gilmour as his centre; no one could score without him. Clark started the year as Gilmour's left-winger and was on a record-setting course until he got hurt. In his absence, Andreychuk took Dougie's left side and lit the NHL, but when Clark got back, he resumed his spot with Dougie and again scored in fabulous bunches.* Andreychuk's well ran dry when Burns gave him another centre.

All along, Glenn Anderson had given up the ghost on Dougie's right side. One of the reasons he agreed to sign with the Leafs for the season was Fletcher's promise to release him in January to play for Canada's Olympic team. Fletcher was more than willing, but the plan hit a snag. Anderson would have to clear waivers before he could play outside the NHL, but of course as the playoffs drew near many teams would certainly want to claim him. The Leafs weren't just going to give him away! Fletcher then appealed to Bettman for a courtesy waiver-clearing, explaining the simple, honourable, well-intentioned plan. Bettman said no. By the 73rd game, Anderson was floating along with just 17 goals and 35 points, totals not nearly good enough for a "scoring" winger pulling in a million bucks.

And so, at 2:55 EST on March 21, 1994, five minutes before the trading deadline, Fletcher made his move. He sent Anderson, Scott Malone, and a 4th-round pick in '94 (Alexander Korobolin) to the Rangers for Mike Gartner, the fifth-leading scorer in the history of the NHL.** Gartner was all Anderson wasn't. He had incredible speed, and hadn't lost a step the way Anderson had. He had that breakaway stride, low to the ice, straight as the crow flies, that was more enduring than Anderson's move to the outside which was highly checkable without the blistering speed of yesteryear. Although Gartner was 34, he still had two or three years left, and if nothing else was an unparalleled model of consistency in both goal production and avoiding injury. He also never hurt his club by taking those high-sticking major/game misconduct penalties Anderson was only too prone to getting.

---

* Including back-to-back hat tricks against Ottawa and Detroit to become only the third Leaf to do so. Charlie Conacher turned the hat trick double in 1931 against Chicago and Ottawa, and Darryl Sittler, incredibly, did it *twice* in 1980, first against Detroit and Pittsburgh, then L.A. and Vancouver.

** And five days later in his third game with the Leafs, the only man to score 30 goals for an incredible 15 straight years.

GARTNER, MIKE TOR.

Right wing. Shoots right. 6', 190 lbs. Born, Ottawa, Ont., October 29, 1959.
(Washington's 1st choice, 4th overall, in 1979 Entry Draft).

Season	Club	Lea	Regular Season					Playoffs				
			GP	G	A	TP	PIM	GP	G	A	TP	PIM
1976-77	Niagara Falls	OHA	62	33	42	75	125	....				
1977-78a	Niagara Falls	OHA	64	41	49	90	56	....				
1978-79	Cincinnati	WHA	78	27	25	52	123	3	0	2	2	2
1979-80	Washington	NHL	77	36	32	68	66	....				
1980-81	Washington	NHL	80	48	46	94	100	....				
1981-82	Washington	NHL	80	35	45	80	121	....				
1982-83	Washington	NHL	73	38	38	76	54	4	0	0	0	4
1983-84	Washington	NHL	80	40	45	85	90	8	3	7	10	16
1984-85	Washington	NHL	80	50	52	102	71	5	4	3	7	9
1985-86	Washington	NHL	74	35	40	75	63	9	2	10	12	4
1986-87	Washington	NHL	78	41	32	73	61	7	4	3	7	14
1987-88	Washington	NHL	80	48	33	81	73	14	3	4	7	14
1988-89	Washington	NHL	56	26	29	55	71	....				
	Minnesota	NHL	13	7	7	14	2	5	0	0	0	6
1989-90	Minnesota	NHL	67	34	36	70	32	....				
	NY Rangers	NHL	12	11	5	16	6	10	5	3	8	12
1990-91	NY Rangers	NHL	79	49	20	69	53	6	1	1	2	0
1991-92	NY Rangers	NHL	76	40	41	81	55	13	8	8	16	4
1992-93	NY Rangers	NHL	84	45	23	68	59	....				
1993-94	NY Rangers	NHL	71	28	24	52	58	....				
	Toronto	NHL	10	6	6	12	4	18	5	6	11	14
NHL Totals			1170	617	554	1171	1039	99	35	45	80	97

a OHA First All-Star Team (1978)

Played in NHL All-Star Game (1980, 1985, 1986, 1988, 1990, 1993)

Traded to **Minnesota** by **Washington** with Larry Murphy for Dino Ciccarelli and Bob Rouse, March 7, 1989. Traded to **NY Rangers** by **Minnesota** for Ulf Dahlen, Los Angeles' fourth round choice (previously acquired by NY Rangers — Minnesota selected Cal McGowan) in 1990 Entry Draft and future considerations, March 6, 1990. Traded to **Toronto** by **NY Rangers** for Glenn Anderson, the rights to Scott Malone and Toronto's fourth round choice (Alexander Korobolin) in 1994 Entry Draft, March 21, 1994.

Oh, how the injuries were hurting the club. Borschevsky returned from his serious spleen injury only to suffer a separated shoulder when he collided with Rumble in Ottawa, and Baumgartner required surgery on his left wrist after a fight with Dennis Vial in the same game. Over the course of the year, the number of man-games lost was staggering: Zezel 43, Gill and Borschevsky 39, Cullen 31, Rouse 21, Clark and Baumgartner 20, Pearson 17, Ellet 16, Mironov 8. Even on a team with loads of depth, these losses would have been difficult to overcome. With the Leafs, all the more pressure was transferred to Gilmour, Potvin, and the core of the team.

But a new standard of achievement had been set and these Leafs were eager to be judged by it. Troubles be damned. Mediocrity was not acceptable; injuries were not an excuse. Results were the point of the game. Although the Leafs had a dreadful one win-four loss road trip in March, the final game of the season April 14 in Chicago set an important tone for the playoffs. They went into the Stadium without Gilmour, Gartner, and Potvin, and through guts and grit and four power-play goals won 6–4. They finished the year with 98 points, one fewer than the year before, and 43 wins, also one fewer. But their 99 points in '92–'93 was only eighth overall, whereas the 98 this year placed them fifth, indicating a better performance in a more even and competitive NHL. Ironically, their record against the expansion teams dropped sharply (to 6–6–4), but the divisional realignment that saw them face Winnipeg six times was in fact a help (4–1–1 against the Jets). The final standings looked like this:

WESTERN CONFERENCE
Central Division

	GP	W	L	T	GF	GA	PTS
Detroit	84	46	30	8	356	275	100
Toronto	84	43	29	12	280	243	98
Dallas	84	42	29	13	286	265	97
St. Louis	84	40	33	11	270	283	91
Chicago	84	39	36	9	254	240	87
Winnipeg	84	24	51	9	245	344	57

Pacific Division

	GP	W	L	T	GF	GA	PTS
Calgary	84	42	29	13	302	256	97
Vancouver	84	41	40	3	279	276	85
San Jose	84	33	35	16	252	265	82
Anaheim	84	33	46	5	229	251	71
Los Angeles	84	27	45	12	294	322	66
Edmonton	84	25	45	14	261	305	64

EASTERN CONFERENCE
Northeast Division

	GP	W	L	T	GF	GA	PTS
Pittsburgh	84	44	27	13	299	285	101
Boston	84	42	29	13	289	252	97
Montreal	84	41	29	14	283	248	96
Buffalo	84	43	32	9	282	218	95
Quebec	84	34	42	8	277	292	76
Hartford	84	27	48	9	227	288	63
Ottawa	84	14	61	9	201	397	37

Atlantic Division

	GP	W	L	T	GF	GA	PTS
NY Rangers	84	52	24	8	299	231	112
New Jersey	84	47	25	12	306	220	106
Washington	84	39	35	10	277	263	88
NY Islanders	84	36	36	12	282	264	84
Florida	84	33	34	17	233	233	83
Philadelphia	84	35	39	10	294	314	80
Tampa Bay	84	30	43	11	224	251	71

As a result of the new playoff format, the divisions gave way to the
conference standings:

Western Conference		Eastern Conference	
Detroit	100	N.Y. Rangers	112
Calgary	97*	Pittsburgh	101*
Toronto	98	New Jersey	106
Dallas	97	Boston	97
St. Louis	91	Montreal	96
Chicago	87	Buffalo	95
Vancouver	85	Washington	88
San Jose	82	N.Y. Islanders	84

* Division champions

The matchups were as follows: San Jose at Detroit, Vancouver at Calgary, Chicago at Toronto, the Islanders at the Rangers, Washington at Pittsburgh, Buffalo at New Jersey, Montreal at Boston.

The '93–'94 year had been just as good, and in some ways better than the year before, but the element of surprise was missing as these playoffs approached. No one bought into Burns' "I just hope we can make the playoffs" underscoring anymore. He was too good a coach, had too good a team, and had come too close the year before to be so easily satisfied. The mood now was different, the naïve excitement tempered by expectation. The Leafs were now fortune's slaves. The playoffs were about to begin and already the finals were being talked about with confidence. The injuries during the year hadn't affected the club's performance in terms of points or goals scored, but it was achieved at the cost of wearing down the core four or five players who absorbed the pressures of a whole team's season while the rookie replacements struggled. Dougie now had three great scorers to pass to — Andreychuk (53 goals), Clark (46 in just 64 games), and Gartner (34 between the Rangers and Leafs) — but still there was no second centre to spell him. He couldn't pass to all three at once or play three shifts in a row all playoffs. Like last year, the offensive load was still his to carry.

XIII

Second Time 'Round:
The 1994 Playoffs

"It's not the skill any more. It's the will."
— Pat Burns

The '93–'94 NHL season saw a dramatic shift to defence, thanks mostly to the emergence of a number of remarkable goalies. The

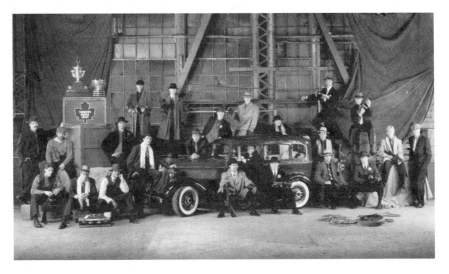

SYLVIA PECOTA / ABALENE PROMOTIONS

previous season Felix Potvin led the league with an average of 2.50. This year, his excellent 2.89 average was 16th,* indicating an under 3.00 GAA had become easier to achieve. By comparison, only three

---

* Behind Dominik Hasek (Buffalo) 1.95, Martin Brodeur (New Jersey) 2.40, Patrick Roy (Montreal) 2.50, John Vanbiesbrouck (Florida) 2.53, Mike Richter (Rangers) 2.57, Darcy Wakaluk (Dallas) 2.64, Darren Puppa (Tampa Bay) 2.71, Chris Terreri (New Jersey) 2.72, Mark Fitzpatrick (Florida) 2.73, Mike Vernon (Calgary) 2.81, Guy Hébert (Anaheim) 2.83, Don Beaupre (Washington) 2.84, Arturs Irbe (San Jose) 2.84, Chris Osgood (Detroit) 2.86, and Jon Casey (Boston) 2.88.

goalies were under 3.00 in the '83–'84 season during the height of the Edmonton goal-scoring dynasty. In 1992–93, an incredible 13 players scored 50 goals and 21 got 100 points. This season, only seven scored 50 and eight got 100 points, and the number of 20-goal scorers went from 125 (with 24 teams or 5.2 a team) down to 120 (with 26 teams or 4.6 a team). Furthermore, the Montreal approach to team defence was spreading through the league like wildfire, credit going to coaches such as Roger Neilson, Scotty Bowman, Bob Gainey, Jacques Lemaire, and of course Burns.

Gilmour's 117 points and Andreychuk's 53 goals, totals that were comparable to the year before, were all the more impressive given this league-wide attention to defence. Add to that Clark's semi-healthy, career-high 46 goals, and it seemed that the Leafs had maintained their ability to keep the puck out of their own net while becoming better at putting it in at the other end.

The main fact was that Burns' boys were back in the playoffs, but unlike the year before everyone from coast to coast now expected the team to go far. Los Angeles, meanwhile, led by the less-arrogant Melrose (oh, what losing does to an ego!) failed to qualify for the post-season by 16 points. For the Leafs, Chicago would be the first-round opponent, and this time Toronto was the favourite. The Blackhawks finished just three games above .500, and fifth in their division. The year before they would have missed the playoffs, but their record was better than four other teams in the Western Conference and this time around that was plenty good enough to make it.

The Leafs' role as favourites was easily tempered by a number of hard cold facts. Last year Chicago had been the overwhelming favourite but were blown away in the first round. This time they hadn't used up all their energy to finish first overall, and so perhaps had enough left to be the upsetters. There was also the fact that Chicago had three stars of its own: Ed Belfour in goal could easily win a game by himself, as his seven regular season shutouts attested; Chris Chelios, the defenceman everyone but his wife loved to hate, would play half of each game and on a given night was capable of shutting down Gilmour *et al.*; and Jeremy Roenick had 107 points and was to his team what Dougie was to Toronto.

While the Leafs had home-ice advantage, their record in the Stadium over the last few years had been so bad nothing could be taken for granted. And as this was the last year the Blackhawks would play in the Stadium before moving into their spiffy new digs across the street, sentiment might provide Chicago with a little extra inspiration. The Leafs were favourites only because everyone expected them to raise their game to a level Chicago wouldn't be able to match.

There were two big questions that would more than likely decide the winner of the series. Would Potvin or Belfour be the better goalie? Would Dougie or Roenick be more dominant? The Leafs had certain

advantages that could contribute to determining these answers. Mired by injury all year, Toronto was entering the playoffs reasonably healthy. Their Big Six defencemen — Lefebvre, Macoun, Gill, Rouse, Mironov, and Ellett — had rarely played at the same time but had an awesome 14–3–4 record when they did. They were all healthy and ready now. The Leafs' left-wing duo of Clark and Andreychuk combined for 99 goals during the year, by far the highest total in the league for that position. They each had 21 power-play goals, so if the Leafs could get Chicago to play undisciplined hockey, and use the special teams to their advantage, the offence was capable of being the difference in the series. A case in point was the final game of the regular season when they scored four goals with the man advantage against the Hawks. But these two guys would have to produce consistently if this advantage were to hold true.

If the Leafs had learned anything from the success of the year before, it was that they couldn't keep going to seven games. They had to go for the jugular from the opening faceoff of Game 1 and not let go until they had won four games. The sooner the series ended, the sooner they could recuperate and prepare for the next round. Second, they couldn't look to number 93 to pull out a victory night after night. Clark and Andreychuk had to create chances by themselves, and others had to learn to set these guys up. Gilmour couldn't log the ice time game after game as he had the year before. If he did, the finals would definitely be out of the question.

In the first game at the Gardens the Leafs played textbook everything. Just 2:33 into the first period Clark ripped a shot past a lax Belfour from outside the blueline to give the Leafs a 1–0 lead. The crowd taunted him with shouts of "Ed-eee, Ed-eee" for the remainder of the series. Chicago never got on track after that goal, and by the midway point of the game Gilmour (on a power play), Manderville (short-handed), Macoun, and Andreychuk (on another power play) had the Leafs up five zip. Only a Chelios shot in the third beat Potvin, and the final was as convincing on the ice as the score looked on the clock above it.

In Game 2 Potvin played just as well, but Belfour rebounded to play superbly at the Blackhawk end. The first was all Chicago — they outshot the Leafs 16–8 — as the Leafs seemed determined to keep their "lose Game 2" streak alive. But the Cat was superb, and made one of the most memorable saves in the history of the playoffs. He was snug to the right post when the puck came quickly across to Paul Ysebaert at the left side. Ysebaert had the empty net, and one-timed the pass quickly and accurately, but Potvin stretched across and got his glove on the puck. The fans went wild, the team was inspired, and the score remained 0–0. The rest of the game saw the Leafs get stronger and stronger, but it was Belfour who saved the day time and again for Chicago. Only six minors were called all night, and after 60 minutes the game was still without a goal. For only the third time

since 1954, a scoreless tie was going to have to be decided in overtime.*

It didn't take long. At 2:15 a Todd Gill slapshot from the blueline slid under Belfour's pads and the Leafs won 1–0. Belfour had been distracted by the imminent arrival of Clark in the crease, and afterwards ranted about goalie interference (although it looked awfully like goalie lack-of-concentration). The replay didn't support his tirade, the win stood, and the Leafs looked to be doing what they had to do — win fast. They were going to the Windy City for two games and, if they could win one, they'd be able to end the series in T.O. and rest up.

For the first game at the Stadium, Burns made two lineup changes. Borschevsky and tough guy Ken McRae were scratched; Krushelnyski and, of all people, Cullen, were dressed. McRae had become redundant because Burns didn't anticipate the series getting dirty or rough, and Nikolai simply hadn't been scoring (just 10 goals since January). Cullen had cleared waivers toward the end of the season and seemed to be through with the Leafs; he simply never rediscovered his scoring touch. But Burns, desperate to find a second centre, thought the playoff opportunity might inspire Cullen. Perhaps he would seize the day and sprinkle the scoresheet with a needed goal or assist.

Conn Smythe Trophy.
HOCKEY HALL OF FAME

By the eight-minute mark of the game, all hell had broken loose. Two goals by Tony Amonte and another by Joe Murphy put the noisy crowd in the Stadium game and the Blackhawks up 3–0. Ellett and Berg made it 3–2 before the end of the period, and at 1:00 even of the second Mironov tied the score. But the night belonged to Amonte, who scored two more goals in a 5–4 win. At 3–3, there were still 39 minutes left in the game, yet once they had tied the score, the Leafs played like victors, when in fact all they had done was atone for an atrocious start. Excellent saves by Belfour and the lack of production from the Leafs' big guns spelled the end. Three goals by the defence and one by Berg would not win many playoff series. The big forwards had to be tenacious for 60 minutes and had to score.

Toronto almost corrected their game for Game 4. Almost. Borschevsky was back

* The Islanders beat Chicago 1–0 in 1979 and Detroit beat Minnesota 1–0 in '92. The last time the Leafs were 0–0 was April 9, 1950, when Leo Reise scored at 8:39 to give Detroit a 1–0 win in Game 7 of the semifinals.

and Krushelnyski out, but two goals by Gary Suter had the Hawks up 2–0 after 14 minutes. Again the Leafs rallied, via the power play. Dougie late in the first and Andreychuk at 14:40 of the second made it 2–2. This time, though, the Leafs kept coming, and three minutes into the third were rewarded. Dougie made a great pass from behind Belfour's net (Gretzky's office? Forget it. More like Dougie's desk) out to Pearson in front, and a quick shot later Toronto was up 3–2. Now, if they could just play solid defensive hockey, they would go back to the Gardens with the chance to clinch.

A cross-checking penalty to Todd Gill midway through the period changed that. Suter scored his third goal of the game on the ensuing power play, and a cautious end sent the game into overtime for the second time in the series. Just like Gill's goal in Game 2, Roenick's game winner came quickly, 1:23 quickly to be exact, on a low shot in the slot. The Leafs had squandered their hopes of ending the series in five, and headed back to Toronto desperately needing to win. It was now a best-of-three series, and any brief Chicago break would put the Leafs on the brink. Goals couldn't be missed, power plays couldn't be fudged, and desire couldn't be compromised. Chicago no longer looked like underdogs.

The two stars in Game 5 were at opposite ends of the ice. Belfour was sensational and busy at one end, Potvin tested less frequently but equally skilfully at the other. The Leafs outshot the Blackhawks 37–17, setting a new club record for fewest shots allowed in a playoff game. There were only two differences on the night, a Mike East-wood power-play goal at 10:07 of the third, and a miraculous glove save by the Cat on Joe Murphy a few minutes later. The slimmest of margins, the smallest of differences. But another 1–0 win put the Leafs up three games to two going back to the Stadium. Perhaps the biggest difference of all, though, was Dougie. In the third period he fell awkwardly while battling Suter for a loose puck and was helped off the ice with an ankle injury. His status wavered between day-to-day and doubtful as Game 6 approached, so as a safeguard the Leafs called up 21-year-old rookie Darby Hendrickson from the Rock to take Dougie's place in the event the ankle was too badly damaged.

Mere mortals would have scratched and rested in the press box. Dougie put on his blue-and-white, war-ravaged tunic and played a full shift most of the night in Chicago. A Dave Ellett point shot on the power play bounced off Mike Gartner's thigh and into the net at 14:49 of the first. The Leafs played perfect, flawless, defensive hockey the rest of the way, holding Chicago to only three shots in the third and making Gartner's thigh goal stand up. A tough, fair, clean, grinding game, another 1–0 win, a third shutout in the series for Potvin.* An early elimination of the Hawks.

---

* Tying the NHL record for shutouts in a series established by the Leafs' Frank McCool in the 1945 finals versus Detroit.

DOUG MACLELLAN / HOCKEY HALL OF FAME

The Leafs had finally given themselves a break, and the very last game at the now "old" Chicago Stadium was a classic Original Six contest, an historic ending to one of the venerable arenas of the 20th century. The "new" Chicago Stadium, crassly called the United Centre, would never hold the maniacal hollerings of Chicagoans with anywhere near the same feeling of excitement. An era had passed. It was Chicago that beat the Leafs 2–1 in 1931 in the very first game at Maple Leaf Gardens, and now, 63 years later, the Leafs had beaten the Hawks 1–0 in the last game at the Stadium. It was a true rivalry between two great hockey cities. Sadly, sickeningly, the 66-year-old Madhouse on Madison was razed to make a *parking lot* for the new arena just across the street.

Because of the new playoff format, the Leafs had no idea who they were going to play in the next round the night they eliminated the Blackhawks. The way the other matchups were going gave an even clearer indication of just how close so many teams were to winning the Cup. Only the Rangers stuck out as odds-on favourites. They destroyed the Islanders in four embarrassing games — 6–0, 6–0, 5–1, 5–2 — where the only excitement was to see if the Islanders would ever score at all. And in ancient biblical tradition, St. Louis had done unto them what they had done unto Chicago the year before; the Dallas (a.k.a. Minnesota North) Stars swept them in four straight. Washington eliminated the Penguins, who had a very wobbly Mario in the lineup, 4–2, while the other series, full of interesting sidebars, went the full seven games: New Jersey beat Buffalo in a matchup that saw both teams score a *total* of just 28 goals. Boston eliminated Montreal yet again, despite the fact that Burns was not there to lose road games, the series, and his job on purpose. Vancouver won three

consecutive overtime games, two in the Saddledome, to eliminate Calgary after being down 3–1. And the expansion San Jose Sharks drove the loyal Detroit fans to jeers by winning the final game 3–2 right in the Joe Louis Arena, the second time in as many years the Wings lost a Game 7 at home in the first round, and a far more embarrassing loss than the year before.

After the smoke had cleared and the dust had settled and the computers put to work, the Leafs found themselves the number one team among the survivors in the Western Conference:

Western Conference		Eastern Conference	
Toronto	98	N.Y. Rangers	112
Dallas	97	New Jersey	106
Vancouver	85	Boston	97
San Jose	82	Washington	88

Toronto would now play San Jose, Dallas Vancouver, the Rangers Washington, and New Jersey Boston.

San Jose? The Sharks? Mail the Leafs the series and let's get on with it. Where is that Stanley Cup, anyway?

Nothing, no number of statistics or warnings or threats could dissuade the fans and the Leafs from letting up and loosening that tight grip on concentration, at the prospect of facing a professional NHL team called the Sharks. It was psychologically impossible not to let down. But the Sharks had just eliminated the same Red Wings club the Leafs had the year before (despite being outscored 27–21) and their regular season record was no fluke. They started the season 0–8–1 but improved immensely as the year continued. In the second half, they earned 49 points, the same as the Leafs, the Flames, and the Habs. Excellence over 40 games was not fluky. Nor was the "ov" line of Makarov, Larionov, and Garpenlov, or the coach Kevin Constantine[*] anything to take for granted. The very fact the Leafs had managed only two ties and eight goals against San Jose in four regular season meetings should also have been warning enough that the series would have to be earned.

Because the Sharks played on the West Coast, the playoff format actually favoured them. The first two games would be at the Gardens, then the next three at the Arena, before the final two in Toronto. If the Sharks could win a game in Toronto, they could clinch the series at home without ever having to head back east. Not that anyone but them thought that was possible, but the reality was that it could

---

[*] The youngest in the NHL at 35 and the only one U.S. born.

happen. The Sharks were new and unknown, impossible to hate, but they were a hockey team to take seriously. The Leafs had eliminated Chicago in six games but had not won convincingly. They scored only 15 goals, and although Potvin was superb in giving up only ten (seven of those to just two players, Amonte and Suter), Gilmour's bad ankle and the team's weak offence were serious causes for concern.

Clark opened Game 1 with another early goal at 2:31, but when the Leafs had a two-man advantage for 37 seconds a little after, they didn't even get a shot on net. Half a minute later Larionov tied the score. In the second, Osborne and Falloon exchanged goals and then, with just 2:16 left in regulation, Garpenlov converted a perfect Larionov pass to give the beer line their second goal and the Sharks a 3–2 win. All of a sudden things didn't look so hot. The Leaf power play went 0-for-5; Andreychuk and Gartner were invisible yet again; Gilmour was hobbling on a terrible ankle that had to be frozen before each game. And to make matters worse, Manderville suffered a wrist injury and Baumgartner a shoulder wound. Home ice had now turned to San Jose's advantage. Because of the 2–3–2 format, to lose the next game would be disastrous for the Leafs.

The danger with San Jose, from the Leafs' point of view, was that they were a supremely quiet team. There was nothing about them to loathe or despise. They didn't have goons, they didn't crash the goalie or use their sticks or take stupid penalties or play dirty or in-your-face hockey or instigate or retaliate or Watergate. They didn't have superstars, just "washed-up" thirty-something Europeans. They did nothing to make it easy for the other team to get motivated the way the Hawks or Habs or Wings did. They were like the basketball teams the Harlem Globetrotters always played, except that the Sharks won.

The Leafs had plenty of will for Game 2 and did everything right that they had done wrong in the opener. They outshot San Jose 38–20, went 3-for-7 on the power play, scored one short-handed goal, and held the Sharks scoreless on their six-man advantage chances. Gartner, Gilmour, and Clark all scored, and only a third-period goal by Gaetan Duchesne beat Potvin. The final score was 5–1 and the attitude after the game seemed to be that while it had taken the Leafs a game to get on track, the series would now be over quickly. Sayonara San Jose.

Such was not to be the case. Just as the Leafs had been mesmerized by one player in consecutive games in the Chicago series (first Amonte, then Suter), so too did Ulf Dahlen turn the (hat) trick in Game 3 in Californ-I-A. His first goal made it 3–1 at 1:58 of the second and sent Potvin to the bench in favour of Rhodes who surrendered two more to Dahlen before the game had ended. The 5–2 Shark win proved they could bounce back from a bad loss, but this too should have come as no surprise. Just a week earlier, in the Detroit series, they were blown away 7–1 in Game 6 only to win the deciding, eliminating game. During the regular season, the Sharks

followed up every bad loss with victory. A 10–3 loss to the Red Wings in January was answered with a four-game unbeaten streak. After an 8–3 loss to the Rangers they went on to a 6–2–1 record in their next nine games. A 5–2 loss to Calgary produced a 3–1 win over the Canucks. These guys had to be taken seriously. That, or the Leafs had to get their act together. They trailed two games to one.

Toronto rebounded by trouncing San Jose 8–3. All the big guns were firing. Dougie had a goal and four assists;[*] Andreychuk two goals, one assist; Wendel and Gartner one and one. They chased Irbe from the net after building up a 6–1 lead by the end of the second, and Potvin was great early on, stopping Todd Elik on a breakaway before the Leafs had a shot on goal. Shortly after, Wendel reduced Jeff Norton to two dimensions right at the San Jose bench to set the tone, and that was all she wrote.

DOUG MACLELLAN /
HOCKEY HALL OF FAME

Again Toronto had a great opportunity. If they could use their performance in Game 4 to come up with a great effort for the last game at the Arena, they could wrap the series up at home in Game 6. But reality proved more complicated. Potvin let in five of the first 17 shots he faced and Makarov, pointless in the series to date, had two goals and two assists. The Sharks won it going away and coming home, 5–2. The Leafs would now have to win two in a row at the Gardens if they were going to move on to the semifinals. They'd have to endure another seven-game series at a time when fans had expected a sweep. They were finding out that it was far easier to exceed small expectations than to meet great ones.

Now the tension was real, the pressure was cooking. The Leafs were down 3–2 in games and faced elimination. It was time to get serious, really serious. Wendel was feeling a little mean but, whatever he did, the Sharks responded in kind. He scored at 5:26 of the first; Larionov tied it three minutes later. He scored at 5:32 in the third; Norton tied it up two minutes later. Overtime. Elimination. Dead serious. The margin of error thing? Down to zero.

Sometimes a team has to be lucky to be good, and the Leafs were awfully good in the overtime. John Garpenlov rang a shot off the cross bar in the second minute and a few minutes later Sandis Ozolinsh had Potvin dead to rights in the slot but decided to pass instead of score.

Mike Gartner made no such error. At 8:53 he took yet another great pass from Dougie behind the net and shot quickly. It may have been going wide, it may not have. It didn't matter; the puck hit Irbe's skate and went in. The Gardens crowd rose in unison, the Leafs'

---

[*] Tying Ian Turnbull's record for assists in a playoff game, set against Philadelphia on April 22, 1976, at the Gardens.

bench emptied, and coach Burns heaved an enormous sigh of relief on his short walk from the bench to the dressing room. One down, one to go.

By now, the Leafs and Sharks were the only game in the NHL. The Rangers had ripped through the Capitals 4–1, as did Vancouver with Dallas, and Jersey beat Boston 4–2. The Rangers and Devils would play in one conference final, which meant the Canucks were resting, feet up, for the Leafs/Sharks winner to emerge for the right to crawl, limp, into *their* conference final.

Another Game 7. Experience favoured the Leafs, but Dougie was still on the limp. This Game 7 had to be like midnight in Algonquin Park: the stars had to come out. Wendel's shone brightest. He took a shot off the cheekbone early in the game but opened the scoring at 8:58 with a wrist shot so hard it frightened fans in the Greys. Midway through the second he scored on a rebound to make it 2–0 and the Leafs never looked back. The Cat was cool and quick. Before each Clark goal he made big saves and I-couldn't-score-if-my-life-depended-on-it Osborne somehow made it 3–0 early in the third. Clearly, Fate was on the Leafs' side. Referee Terry Gregson let them play, calling only two minors against each team, and Toronto advanced with a 4–2 win. The series was over. You could hear the fear in the players' silent satisfaction afterward. The excitement of advancing had been tempered by the closeness of the call. Two days later the puck would drop and the Canucks would be the opposition. Thankfully. Anything but the Sharks.

The Canucks were unlike any other team the new Leafs had faced in the playoffs. They were a big, strong, physical team with a complete roster. Kirk McLean was a superb goalie; the defence had size, speed, and offence; they had Trevor Linden and Pavel Bure up front; and Sergio Momesso and Cliff Ronning were movers and shakers of the first order. Vancouver was a team to take seriously, and they had the away-ice advantage with the 2–3–2 format in use again.

This was the first time the clubs had ever met in the playoffs, but the anticipation was much greater than the Leafs–Sharks series. *This* was playoff hockey. Good old Canadian teams going coast to coast, two known quantities that had the skill and that *je ne sais quoi* that goes with fighting to get to the finals. Both teams won two games in head-to-head meetings during the year (Toronto won 5–2 and 5–3; Vancouver won 3–2 [in OT] and 4–1). This was sure to have everything: good goaltending, hard hitting, and fast skating.

All this expectation caused more than a little trepidation early on, accounting for a scoreless opening period in Game 1. Andreychuk scored the series' first goal on the power play at 4:26 of the second, but Dave Babych tied it up just four minutes later. Zezel scored 38 seconds into the third to make it 2–1, and then the defence was on. The Leafs' Big Six played superbly, but then Mike Gartner got a holding penalty with just 1:42 to play to give the Canucks one last

chance. Coach Pat Quinn pulled McLean for the sixth attacker and, sure enough, Linden tied the game at 19:30. Another costly, unlucky late penalty. Another overtime.

The Canucks weren't playing for a break. They came out flying in the extra time and could have (should have?) won the game twice, once when Momesso hit the crossbar à la Garpenlov, twice when Potvin stoned Bure on a breakaway. Then came the winner, near the end of the period, on a harmless looking play. As the puck rolled in behind the Canuck goal, McLean came out and beat Berg to the puck. He cleared it off the boards, but Zezel knocked the puck down in midair at the faceoff circle and one-timed it before McLean could get back. The Leafs won it 3–2.

They were up 1–0 in the series and had the upper hand. Because of the playoff setup, the Canucks more or less had to win Game 2. If they did, they could end the series at home, where the next three games would be played. If they didn't, the Leafs could lose the next three and still have home-ice advantage. Psychologically, it was the turning point in the series.

In Game 2 the Canucks benefitted again from a late power play. In a 3–3 game Jamie Macoun was given a holding penalty by referee Don Koharski at 14:49 of the third for pulling down Cliff Ronning. Less than a minute later, Jyrki Lumme scored on a quick spin-around in the slot. The Canucks won 4–3 to tie the series 1–1 under pressure. The Leafs went 3-for-4 with the man advantage (Vancouver 2-for-4) but failed to score at even strength. To make matters worse, Mironov had two and Ellett the other, leaving the forwards' contribution glaringly empty on the night. The scoring drought that began in the Chicago series and was relieved with only sporadic sprinklings against San Jose in the second round was again hurting the Leafs' chances of victory against the Canucks. They now had to go to Vancouver and win at least one of three games at the Pacific Coliseum. If they had any hope of doing that, though, the scorers had to start scoring.

The Leafs had a two-man advantage for 89 seconds in the first period in Game 3 — had five shots on goal — but couldn't score. An unlucky 13 seconds after the Canucks came back to full strength, Bure beat Potvin to make it 1–0. He scored another, to go with goals by Adams and Gelinas, and a convincing 4–0 win put Vancouver in control of the series and the Leafs desperate for a scorer. The Canucks' defence seemed as impenetrable as the Leafs' offence was impotent.

By this point in the season, Vancouver was that much the stronger team. They were a bigger team, and they knew that Gilmour was the key to the Leaf attack, whether on one leg or two. They hit him hard and often all series long and, with his ankle in no great shape, successfully limited his effectiveness. No other Leaf came to the fore. With three minutes to go and Game 3 clearly won, Tim Hunter nailed Dougie behind the Vancouver net, and Pearson came to his defence in a flash. The ensuing fracas resulted in four game misconducts and

created bad blood that, unfortunately, the Leafs couldn't use to their advantage. Baumgartner and Manderville were injured, and the other players were simply too tired or weak to match or endure Vancouver's toughness. Their power play, 4-for-9 in the first two games, went 0-for-4. For the first three games, Gilmour, Clark, Andreychuk, and Gartner had combined for *one goal*. The stars were naught.

For Leaf fans, it was a kind of slow torture. You knew what was going to happen, but you didn't want to admit it. Besides, some little thing like the Zezel goal might happen to make things better. It sure didn't happen in Game 4, as the Chicago-style goalless fest lasted for the first 57 minutes of the game. Incredibly, another 0–0 overtime seemed inevitable. Vancouver had only seven shots in the first and were held shotless for the first 13 minutes of the second. The Leafs outplayed the Canucks, should have scored but couldn't, and Gilmour was being checked into the ice by Linden, a man double Dougie's size. A give-and-go between Ronning and Momesso gave the Canucks the goal they needed with just 2:25 left in regulation. Bure scored into an empty net — his most favourite play in the whole wide world — to make it 2–0, and McLean now had a shutout streak 135 minutes long. The Canucks were up 3–1 in the series and could clinch in 48 hours' time.

Now the Leafs were desperate. The season's end was straight ahead, rabbit-in-the-headlights style, but the feeling was different from last year with Los Angeles. The drama of a Game 7 was missing, the feeling that *both* teams were in a position to win, *both* in a position to lose. The sense that the series was even-steven, attack, counter-attack, goal at one end, goal at the other, was certainly missing. The Pacific Coliseum, in the middle of a fairgrounds in the middle of sterile Vancouver, couldn't possibly provide the same stage for high drama as the Act v of *Hamlet* of Maple Leaf Gardens. There was no tension between stars, no Dougie/Wayner matchup, no fierce hatred for the Canucks, no Montreal waiting in the wings for the finals. There was just Bure, a non-Canadian who skated with the carefree abandon of someone who doesn't take the Stanley Cup seriously enough, who would play the same way on an outdoor shinny rink on a Saturday morning as in a Game 7 for the Cup. His frivolous skill was not the stuff of Stanley Cup heroics that Canadians loved. He didn't hobble or limp or play along the boards, defend his mates, muck around, dig loose pucks free, backcheck. He swirled and twirled and fancied his way to personal success. The team followed.

This was Toronto's 39th playoff game in the last two years, more than any other team in that time and as many as the Leafs played from 1980 to 1989. Borschevsky was back, Burns hoping for more heroics from *his* Russian skate-meister who had sat out the last two games and who had only two goals and three points this playoff year. Maybe he was due; maybe the well was dry. The way Game 5 started, the series seemed to take another turn, move up another notch in hockey lore. The Leafs bolted to a 3–0 lead after one, on goals by

Eastwood, Dougie, and Wendel. They were flying, hitting, finally scoring. It looked as if 40 more minutes of this domination would come naturally, on the wings of desire. They couldn't blow this lead; Game 6 was inevitable.

The Canucks, however, knew what coming from behind was all about. They had done it big-time against Dave King's Flames, so 3–0 down in a game with two periods left in it was by no means impossible. And besides, they were entering the Leafs' greatest nemesis, the second period. The period in which Toronto should have been pulling away always turned out to be the one they relaxed in and let the other team get back in the game. Sure enough, Quinn's team took advantage of Leaf complacence. Craven, LaFayette, and Adams (at 17:57) tied the game, and a tense, tight, checking third produced another overtime. Elimination was that close, but so was Game 6. The difference between the two was only one shot, a shot that even the fourth period failed to provide. The winning goal came unexpectedly and innocently. On the first play of the second overtime Potvin made a great pad save on Dave Babych, but the Leafs were slow coming back on the rush and the rebound came right to Adams who was staring at an empty net.

There was no glove save by the Cat on this one, no glorious cheers from the hometown fans of a goal denied, no spectacular save or horrible miss to keep the puck out, the series alive. No, Adams didn't miss. Just 14 seconds into the fifth period, the game was over. 4–3 Vancouver in the game, 4–1 in the series. The players were shaking hands at centre ice while Leaf fans shook their heads in dismay. The series was over before the Leafs had a chance to make one of it.

The season was over, but the only thing you could think about, really, was how sorry you felt for Dougie. Night after night he had done the impossible. What more was he supposed to do? On one leg he had done more than anyone else in the league on two. The Leafs scored only 50 goals in their 18 playoff games; Gilmour was in on 28 of them. It was not until two weeks later, midway through the Rangers-Canucks finals, that Brian Leetch got his 28th point to tie Gilmour in playoff scoring. If ever a player from the playoffs *not* in the finals were to win the Conn Smythe, Dougie would have been the player, 1994 the season (or perhaps '93 even).

At the other end of the spectrum were Andreychuk and Gartner. When they were acquired by Fletcher, about a year apart, their common weakness was thought to be their inability to do in the playoffs what they were supreme masters of during the regular season — score. While Gartner had an incredible 617 goals in 15 years, he had only 35 in 99 career playoff games. Before Andreychuk arrived, he had but 12 in 41. At first, Andreychuk shook this reputation by scoring 12 goals in the first 14 games of the Leafs' '93 playoff run. A new team with a new attitude seemed to cure him of his playoff woes. But then he went goalless in the seven-game L.A. series (when even *one* might have been the difference between the Leafs'

winning and losing) and had only five in this 18-game playoffs. Gartner, too, had just five, and this lack of production seemed to indicate a lack of focus and intensity. It's a two-edged argument: the opposition checkers did a great job; the scorers were unable to break free.

Andreychuk almost never scored on a wrist shot from the top of the circle, or on an end-to-end rush. He had to stand on the edge of the crease, bum-to-mask with the goalie, two defencemen all over him, and deflect a shot, knock in a loose puck, or free his stick for a nanosecond to convert a pass from behind the net. In the regular season, no one in the league was better at this. In the playoffs he was too easily checked. The intensity of the defencemen was greater than his own. The deflection went wide, the loose pucks were covered up or cleared, and the referees were more willing to allow a holding or cross-check penalty go uncalled during the playoffs, giving the defenders the edge.

Gartner's game was much different. He relied on skating full speed down the wing and along the boards, letting rip inside the blueline or cutting to open ice for the pass. If he could get into position he had the advantage. But "position" was more difficult to get into in the playoffs. The boards were less kind, the rink somehow smaller, the open ice now player-clogged. The Leafs' own superb defence was the key to much of the team's success. This was the faith Burns had preached, that if a fourth-line centre or sixth defenceman just did his job, just did *one* thing (check the other team's scorer, for instance), his team would probably win. In these playoffs, it was the Leafs' scorers who were stopped by the other team. Potvin was excellent in goal, but he can't win games 0–0.

One thing was clear. The team had given Leaf fans a second superb season and proved they could indeed compete with the best on a regular basis. They were the only semifinalists from the previous year. Many league and team records were tied or broken again, many memorable nights of excitement provided. But the players Burns had used had been stretched to the limit. Nine goals in five games against Vancouver had proved that this team, this roster, could go no further.

Changes had to be made.

DOUG MACLELLAN / HOCKEY HALL OF FAME

RECORDS SET IN 1993–1994

Regular Season

Team Records

Longest winning steak from start of season — 10, October 7 –
    October 28, 1993*

Longest unbeaten streak — 11 (tied with one other), January 6 –
    February 1, 1994 (7 wins, 4 ties)

Least shots by opponent, one period — 1 (tied with 4 others), 1st
    period, January 11, 1994, at Washington. Toronto won 2–1.

Individual Records

Most goals, left wing — 53, Dave Andreychuk

Most points, left wing — 99, Dave Andreychuk

Playoffs

Team Records

Most goals, 7-game series — 26, versus San Jose. Toronto won 4–3.

Least shots, opponent, one game — 17, versus Chicago, Game 5,
    April 26, 1994, at the Gardens. Toronto won 1–0.

Least shots, Leafs, one period — 3, versus San Jose, 2nd period,
    Game 6, May 12, 1994, at the Gardens. Toronto won 3–2.

Most short-handed goals, one period — 2 (tied with many others),
    at the Arena in San Jose, 3rd period, Game 4, May 8, 1994.
    Toronto won 8–3.*

Most short-handed goals, both teams, one period — 3, versus San
    Jose, 3rd period, Game 4, May 8, 1994. Toronto scored 2, San
    Jose 1. Toronto won 8–3.*

Individual Records

Most playoff points, season, defence — 18, Dave Ellett

Most playoff assists, season, defence — 15, Dave Ellett

Most playoff goals, season, defence — 6 (tied with one other), Dmitri
    Mironov

Most playoff penalty minutes, season, centre — 42 (tied with one
    other), Doug Gilmour

Most assists, one game — 4 (tied with one other), Doug Gilmour, at
    the Arena in San Jose, Game 4, May 8, 1994. Toronto won 8–3.

Most power-play goals, one player, one period — 2 (tied with two
    others), Dmitri Mironov at the Gardens, 2nd period, Game 2,
    May 18, 1994. Vancouver won 4–3.

*NHL record

DOUG MACLELLAN / HOCKEY HALL OF FAME

XIV

Change

Cliff Fletcher had made a number of big deals during his three years in Toronto. He made the biggest trade in NHL history to get Dougie (10 players in all), and acquiring Fuhr and then Andreychuk were major reasons the team improved so much so soon. But by the spring, the team had levelled off, and without a Stanley Cup Fletcher could not take satisfaction in the strides the club had made. Draft day 1994 changed everything.

The draft was held at the Civic Centre in Hartford on June 28 and promised to be anticlimactic for the Leafs. Three days earlier their chief scout, Pierre Dorion, had died of a heart attack at his home in Orléans, outside Ottawa. He was just 49. That same day Fletcher had signed Dorion's pride and joy of the '93 draft, Kenny Jonsson, to a lucrative but cautious contract. Worth $2.8 million over three years, it consisted of a $1.3 million signing bonus and a $500,000 base salary that was contingent upon him making the team. If Burns cut him, Jonsson would make 20% of that — $100,000 — playing in St. John's.

Dorion's death stunned the Leaf organization, but as he was a master of preparation the draft work had all been seen to. The Leafs were set to pick 22nd overall, but a series of trades, including the biggest Leaf departure since Darryl Sittler went to Philadelphia in 1982, changed all that. Fletcher gambled big-time: he traded Captain Clark, the heart and soul of the Leafs for the last nine years, to an enemy team. He was going to Quebec with Sylvain Lefebvre and prospect Landon Wilson for Mats Sundin, Garth Butcher, and young Todd Warriner. As part of the deal they also swapped draft choices, the Nordiques getting the Leafs' 22nd, Toronto moving up into Quebec's 10th-place slot. This last part was not a meaningless footnote to the deal. Fletcher wanted to acquire Brett Lindros and hoped 10th would give him that chance.

There was a neat little catch, though. Quebec also held the number 9 choice. Fletcher knew this, but try as he might he couldn't pry the 9th from Nordiques' GM Pierre Lacroix. This didn't faze Fletcher because he knew Quebec wouldn't draft Lindros II who, like Eric the original, long ago announced his intention never to play for the Nordiques. What Fletcher didn't count on was Lacroix trading the 9th selection to someone else, which he did, to the Islanders,

Pierre Dorion and
his wife, Margot.
GRAIG ABEL

along with Ron Sutter, for Uwe Krupp and the Islanders' first-round draft choice (number 12 overall, which Quebec used to select Wade Belak). When it was time to make that 9th selection, the Islanders — surprise, surprise — drafted Brett Lindros.

The Lindros family claimed the Nordiques made the trade because the club was bent on revenge for Eric's shabby treatment of Quebec four years earlier. According to Mr. and Mrs. Lindros, the club knew Brett wanted to play for the Leafs and was intent on doing everything they could to prevent that from happening. Lacroix denied such petty-mindedness on his club's part, and Fletcher claimed he wasn't *that* interested in Brett. Hopefully, this was true, because Brett was as massively over-rated as he was big in the shoulders and, like his big brother Eric, will find intimidating NHL opponents doesn't work so well when you're injured. Unlike Eric's, Brett's value was minimal: if you could use a draft pick to get him, he was worth it. To trade for him? Forget it. The bottom line was that the Nordiques gave up very little and got a big, solid defenceman — Krupp — in return.

As a result of this turn of the screw, Fletcher turned around to the Capitals' table and traded his number 10 pick along with Rob Pearson to Washington for their 16th selection and centre Mike Ridley (Gartner's centre for so many excellent years in the District of Columbia). The Leafs then used that pick to draft Eric Fichaud, a goalie with virtually the identical background to Felix Potvin and, incidentally, another player Dorion had coveted. Fletcher's busiest day as a Leaf transformed the starting lineup every bit as much as the Calgary Trade had two and a half years earlier:

In	*Out*
Mats Sundin	Wendel Clark
Garth Butcher	Sylvain Lefebvre
Todd Warriner	Landon Wilson
Mike Ridley	Rob Pearson
Eric Fichaud (16th)	Nolan Baumgartner (10th)

Only Fletcher could have traded Clark and lived to hold the press conference. While Clark wasn't awesome in the '94 playoffs the way he had been in 1993, he certainly wasn't the most culpable for the loss to Vancouver. If anything, it was the prolonged scoring drought

of Andreychuk and Gartner that led to the elimination. If changes were going to be made, it would have made more sense to trade one of those two, who put plenty of points on the board but who weren't part of the Leafs' central nervous system as was Clark. Wendel was as popular a Leaf as any to ever wear the jersey. He made the whole team tough; Sundin — bigger, younger, more skilled — would never do that. Wendel was brought up on the Prairies and thought Heaven was in the shape of Lord Stanley's bowl; Sundin's childhood dreams were different. Wendel brought that pride, that nine-year commitment that had no name but whose value had no ceiling, to a Leaf team so close to the Cup. Although Fletcher improved the skill of the team with the trade, he also altered its chemistry.

But Fletcher had to do something and Clark was coming off his best season ever. Taking the heart out of the matter, what were the chances Wendel would play 65 games again? Score 46 goals again?* Wendel was at the height of his trading value and Fletcher did now what Jim Gregory and Roger Neilson should have been allowed to do with Ian Turnbull in 1978 after his great playoffs. Sundin certainly wasn't the leader Clark was, but he was easily a 100-point-a-year-man who was only going to get better. It might be argued that Clark's greatest attribute was his huge popularity with the fans, but even that became an eminently tradeable quality when Dougie arrived and the Cat emerged from the minors. Furthermore, Sundin arrived in Toronto inheriting Salming's Swedish connection, so his popularity had a well-grounded base for expanding if he played well. Fletcher never would have made the Sundin deal in August 1991 when he first arrived in Leafland, but he could afford to now.

What Wendel did during the dark days of the late '80s was incalculable: keeping the organization from falling apart completely, maintaining pride in the Leaf jersey at a time when it was *de rigeur* to ridicule it. On ice, a scowl from Wendel was as good as a hip check from any other player, but in his nine years he averaged only 52 games a season. Too often the scowl was in sick bay, where its effect was minimal. Wendel wore the "C" hard and he wore it long. He wore it to breakfast and wore it to bed, and most important he wore it in the heart of every Leaf fan.

With Jonsson signed and set to play and Sundin in a Leaf jersey, Fletcher was shouting his confidence in Hedberg's scouting and the desirability of an international lineup. Fletcher was the first GM in the NHL to sign a Soviet national team member to a contract when he acquired Sergei Priakin for his Calgary Flames in March 1989.

---

* In fact, at training camp in September 1994, Clark suffered a serious concussion after slamming into the boards. Even if the season had started on time, he certainly would have missed the first half. Then, after playing the first 26 games of the shortened season, he suffered a hamstring injury that caused him to miss the next 12 games. He will never change: fierce, dominant, indomitable, injured. Forever Wendel.

DOUG MACLELLAN / HOCKEY HALL OF FAME

With the Leafs, he and scout Anders Hedberg orchestrated the acquisition of Dmitri Mironov in late 1991, and a few months later another Russian, Borschevsky, was selected in the '92 entry draft. Since arriving in Toronto, Fletcher has used 11 of his 29 draft picks for Europeans,* perhaps becoming too fascinated with a foreign pool

---

* In 1992: Borschevsky from Spartak, 77th; Janne Gronvall, Lukko, 101st; Mikail Hakansson, Nacka, 125th; Patrik Augusta, Dukla Jihlava, 149th; Sergei Simonov, Kristall Saratov, 221st. In 1993: Jonsson, Rogle, 12th; Zdenek Nedved, Sudbury, 123rd; Mikhail Lapin, Western Michigan, 279th. In 1994: Fredrik Modin, Sundsvall, 64th; Tommi Rajamaki, Assat Jr., 178th; Sergei Berezin, Khimik, 256th.

of talent of very unproven quality. League-wide, the '90s has become to Russia what the '70s were to the Swedes and the '80s to the Czechs. When Fletcher got Ridley, the Leafs went from needing someone to help Gilmour up the middle to perhaps the best centred team in the NHL on paper (Gilmour, Sundin, and Ridley). Fletcher gambled that the loss of Lefebvre in the trade and the departure of free agent Bob Rouse* would be balanced by the emergence of Jonsson, the maturity of Berehowsky, and Butcher's proven commitment to team defence. Therein lay the risk. It was the kind of trade

DOUG MACLELLAN / HOCKEY HALL OF FAME

you'd shake your head at a million times, but try as you might to convince yourself it was stupid and bad for the team to trade Wendel, you had to admit that it made sense. Sundin's youth and proven ability at centre were just what the Leafs needed. (The loss of Lefebvre and Rouse was another matter.)

Over the summer, the Leafs also lost three veterans whose playoff performances had made them expendable. The Red Wings signed Mike Krushelnyski, a free agent without compensation, to a one-year deal, the Penguins re-acquired John Cullen, and the Rangers seriously hurt their chances to repeat as Cup champs when they signed

---

* Who signed with Detroit for $4 million over four years.

Mark Osborne. Fletcher also signed two more young prospects, Mark Kolesar, a Brandon left-winger, and Trent Kull, a defenceman with the Kingston Canadiens.

Fletcher also dipped into the risky stall at the free agent market, the one that requires compensation. He signed Mike Craig of Dallas to a four-year, $2.4 million deal and then had to prepare an arbitration case to determine who the Leafs would lose to the Stars as "equal value" compensation. It was an oftentimes unfair business, but he felt Craig was just the kind of under-rated talent the Leafs could use. Toronto offered Peter Zezel and Grant Marshall, thinking the combination of youth and age, proven skill and future promise, would be an impressive combination. The Stars countered by asking for Kenny Jonsson and a 2nd-round pick in '95, a proposal that suffered from two weaknesses: greed and stupidity. Jonsson was one of the top prospects in the NHL (Craig hadn't proved he was *that* good), and the Leafs didn't have a 2nd-round pick in '95. The arbitrator sided with Toronto's more reasonable, not to mention more logical, offer, but again skill was acquired at the expense of character. Zezel, like Clark, Rouse, and Lefebvre had proved his ability to raise his game another level for the playoffs. He would be missed more than one might have thought.

The final piece of the roster puzzle was the least surprising and took place at the Hockey Hall of Fame on August 18, 1994. In attendance were former Leaf captains Red Horner, George Armstrong, Bob Davidson, Sid Smith, Rob Ramage, and Darryl Sittler to present Doug Gilmour with the new '93 "C" to confirm the most obvious unofficial fact in the hockey world. Dougie was now the leader of the Toronto Maple Leafs. The new Leaf roster was one that had a decent blend of youth and experience, still a little heavy on the latter, but vastly improved over the team that went to the semifinals two years in a row. Now they just needed time to play together and to see if their stats on paper translated to winning team chemistry.

The final in-house preparations for the 1994–95 season were many. Dave Andreychuk signed a mega-monster deal for five years at $2.32 million a year plus performance clauses; Sundin agreed to a renegotiated contract for $10 million over five years;* Gartner signed for three years at $1.5 million per season; Manderville agreed to three years, the first for $425,000, the next two at $450,000, plus performance bonuses. Nick Beverley, the L.A. GM fired in May 1994, was

---

* Sundin's contract contains a very peculiar performance clause that could see his salary jump from $2 million to $3 million *or* the average of the top 10 salaries in the NHL (whichever is greater) provided he meets the following criteria: he leads the team in scoring; he is one of the top three plus/minus players on the team; the Leafs win the first round of the playoffs. Should he be first or second in plus/minus on the team, his salary could be the average of the top *five* NHL salaries.

hired to replace Dorion as the Leafs' head scout. Mike Murphy left the team to assume assistant coaching duties in the Big Apple and was replaced full-time by Wamsley. Paul Dennis maintained his almost clandestine job as the man who prepared videos for Burns and the team to study during intermissions. On the Rock, Tom Watt became the new St. John's coach when Marc Crawford left to become the Nordiques' head coach, and in Watt's place Fletcher brought in the recently fired Quebec general manager Pierre Pagé as a part-time scout.

At the 1994 training camp everyone seemed to have a good idea of his place with the Leafs. Each spot was carefully chosen, with the lineup set by Fletcher's incredible trading more than Pat Burns' decision-making during the workouts. The competition for spots was fierce, not by quantity but quality, and although there was the sense the lineup was pretty much set *before* camp, Burns couldn't have been happier with the level of skill:

Goal	Defence	
Felix Potvin	Todd Gill	Kenny Jonsson
Damian Rhodes	Jamie Macoun	Dmitri Mironov
Pat Jablonski	Garth Butcher	Dave Ellett
Eric Fichaud	Drake Berehowsky	Matt Martin
	David Harlock	Chris Snell
	Janne Gronvall	

Left Wing	Centre	Right Wing
Dave Andreychuk	Doug Gilmour	Mike Gartner
Kent Manderville	Mats Sundin	Nik Borschevsky
Bill Berg	Mike Ridley	Mike Craig
Ken Baumgartner	Mike Eastwood	Patrik Augusta
Todd Warriner	Alexei Kudashov	Zdenek Nedved
Chris Govedaris	Brandon Convery	Shayne Stevenson
Eric Lacroix	David Sacco	
Stewart Gavin	Darby Hendrickson	

In goal, Fichaud, who was only 18 years old, was at camp for the experience. He was definitely going to be sent back to his junior team in Chicoutimi in the Quebec Major Junior Hockey League after camp. That left Rhodes to fight Jablonski for the number two spot until Fletcher could trade one of them. It was a tricky business, for coach Burns would never want to go with three goalies, but GM Fletcher wanted a third in case of injury. Rhodes, if traded, would be the steal of the year for the team that got him. He had proved himself a superb goalie when he spotted Potvin for 22 games in

HOCKEY HALL OF FAME

'93–'94 (with a great 2.62 GAA), and could be a starter for most other teams in the league. Jablonski's trading value wasn't as great, but he could be a capable backup to Potvin none-theless.

On defence, there were seven good bets fighting for six jobs, with Berehowsky and Mironov as the ones to really watch out for. The Leafs expected both to develop and be a force on the blueline; if one didn't show prom-ise, though, he'd be quickly replaced. Logi-cally, in the end, Berehowsky deserved the extra chance. He represented the future and Mironov's weak defensive abilities would be highlighted all the more by the absence of Lefebvre and Rouse (Gill, Macoun, Butcher, Ellett, and Jonsson were virtual certainties).

On the right side, Gartner and Craig were certain to play, but Borschevsky's place was more tenuous. He had become prone to injury and had proved checkable in the playoffs, faults the Leafs could do without if something better came along. On the left, Andreychuk, Manderville, Berg, and Baumgartner were in. The only complication was that Manderville's wrist (the one he hurt during the previous playoffs) was taking eons to heal. Centre, too, was a sure bet for the first three places — Gilmour, Sundin, and Ridley — and East-wood certainly had earned a chance to play fourth-line checker and penalty-killer.*

The problem in camp was that Fletcher had made so many trades the team's draft choices were going to have an almost impossible time squeezing in. Although many of the young players were former Leaf picks still in the system — Martin, Kudashov, and Hendrick-son — they were supposed to represent the near future. Instead, they showed little ability to compete with the older, more experienced Leafs Fletcher had traded for. To this end, he made a series of minor moves. He sent Lacroix, Snell, and a 4th pick in '96 to L.A. for Dixon Ward, Guy Levesque, Shayne Toporowski, and Kelly Fairchild. The key player in the deal was Ward, who scored 22 goals in Vancouver before falling

---

* Gilmour spent most of training camp discomforted by very sore feet after having calcium deposits removed from both in July.

to just 12 in 67 games last year with the Canucks and Kings, and who would definitely be given a chance to play right wing (Borschevsky's job just got a little less secure). With Anaheim, Fletcher traded one for one: David Sacco for Terry Yake, the Ducks' leading scorer in their first, and so far only, full year. Why the Ducks would ditch their best scorer was beyond comprehension, but Yake, too, would certainly play on the right side, further bolstering that position (Borschevsky's job just got even *less* secure).

Burns cut Harlock, Gronvall, Govedaris, Convery, Augusta, Kudashov, and Gavin, and by the end of camp there weren't too many stragglers aboard. In fact, Fletcher could easily have afforded to wait a full season to see what this group was capable of doing, and to see what happened in the playoffs, before making another significant move. On paper, this was a Stanley Cup finals team and was entirely different from the one Fletcher inherited in July 1991, only five of whose players he was not responsible for acquiring:

May 1991	*September 1994*
Brian Bradley	Dave Andreychuk (Fletcher trade)
Aaron Broten	Ken Baumgartner (Fletcher trade)
Wendel Clark	Drake Berehowsky (pre-Fletcher draft)
Vincent Damphousse	Bill Berg (waivers by Fletcher)
Lucien Deblois	Nik Borschevsky (Fletcher draft)
Dave Ellett	Garth Butcher (Fletcher trade)
Mike Foligno	Mike Craig (free agent by Fletcher)
Dave Hannan	Mike Eastwood (pre-Fletcher draft)
Todd Gill	Dave Ellett (trade before Fletcher)
Mike Krushelnyski	Mike Gartner (Fletcher trade)
Gary Leeman	Todd Gill (pre-Fletcher draft)
Claude Loiselle	Doug Gilmour (Fletcher trade)
Kevin Maguire	Kenny Jonsson (Fletcher draft)
Daniel Marois	Jamie Macoun (Fletcher trade)
Michel Petit	Kent Manderville (Fletcher trade)
Dave Reid	Dmitri Mironov (Fletcher draft)
Luke Richardson	Felix Potvin (pre-Fletcher draft)
Bob Rouse	Damian Rhodes (pre-Fletcher draft)
Peter Zezel	Mike Ridley (Fletcher trade)
Peter Ing	Mats Sundin (Fletcher trade)
Jeff Reese	Dixon Ward (Fletcher trade)
Damian Rhodes*	Terry Yake (Fletcher trade)
Drake Berehowsky	
Rob Ramage	
Joe Sacco	
Darryl Shannon	

*Played one game so he could be exposed in the draft.

Although on-ice preparations were going smoothly, the off-ice changes from the fans' point of view were less successful. Beside the

ticket booths in the lobby of the Gardens was built "Memory Lane," a stand-up bar and restaurant that pays homage to the past. As the sign at the entrance explains: "These walls honour the 11 Toronto Maple Leaf Stanley Cup winning teams. Remember them with pride. They showed the way. They built the tradition we strive to uphold and build on today." Wonderful intention, but sadly the 11 teams are represented by tacky cardboard cutouts of the superb team photographs that used to greet you in the main lobby. The original, beautifully framed team pictures now lie out of the public's eye in the newly-built Champions' Room.

The Leafs have also been using Ticketmaster as the sole outlet for buying Leaf tickets, another grave mistake that belies the Garden's proud past. The one-day lineup for tickets that used to swirl around the enormous Gardens block each September stirred magical memories that gave answer to the dreams of those in line. Half the fun of buying Leaf tickets is to go to the Gardens and stand in the lobby, smell the ice and stands and the hockey, hope to see a player or coach. The prized reward of colour tickets worth more in pride and joy than any dollar value could calculate has been replaced by busy signals, credit cards,

HOCKEY HALL OF FAME

and dingy record store outlets. Ticketmaster prints cheap, generic computer stubs that don't differentiate between the Leafs and any other event. They add an enormous surcharge to *every* ticket ($3.25), which makes the cheap seats not so cheap. Greys are advertised as costing $22, but if the only place you can buy them is Ticketmaster, the real cost is $25.25. If the fans have to pay that extra money, why doesn't the Gardens sell the tickets and keep the extra profits themselves? The building looks deserted now and Ticketmaster's system is unfair and expensive. It's a rip-off.

On August 8, 1994, Commissioner Gary Bettman issued an ultimatum to the players on behalf of the 26 NHL owners. If a collective bargaining agreement were not in place by opening day (October 1) the season would not begin. Despite the fact that the last agreement had expired the previous September 15, it had taken the new com-

missioner 327 days to initiate serious negotiations. In a supposed effort to motivate these negotiations, he instituted a series of roll-backs on player expenses intended to save the owners $20 million during the bargaining process and the pre-season. These included:

- making two-way contracts mandatory (i.e., an NHL salary and a minor league salary)
- eliminating salary arbitration
- eliminating guaranteed contracts and buyout provisions
- reducing the players' playoff and awards funds from $9 million to $2 million
- eliminating ALL per diem allowances
- reducing the player roster from 18 skaters and two goalies to 17 and two
- reducing the major league roster to 22 players
- forcing players to pay the first $750 of medical costs
- forcing players earning more than $350,000 to pay their own life insurance, health care, and disability premiums
- eliminating the senior player benefit of a $250,000 lump-sum payment at age 55 for every player who plays 400 games or more in the NHL
- forcing players earning more than $350,000 to pay 50% of annual pension contributions
- compulsory currency conversion (if a player is traded across the border, he doesn't receive the same amount in American dollars as he was in Canadian funds, i.e., his $300,000 Canadian salary would become $216,000 U.S.)
- forcing players to pay for travel to training camp and return home after camp
- increasing discipline fining authority from $500 to $50,000 and designating game suspensions as costing players 1/84 of annual salary per game
- requiring players to wear NHL-approved apparel on and off ice
- unilaterally determining the length of training camp and exhibition schedule as well as veteran and rookie mini-camps
- eliminating housing allowance for traded players and reducing lease obligations to a maximum of two months
- making public appearances mandatory

It was hard to fathom the time and effort that went into crafting these demeaning and counterproductive sanctions. Yet all along Bettman claimed that his justification for implementing them was that they would *encourage* bargaining. In good faith, the players abided by these rules and played through training camp. The owners reaped all gate receipt profits; the players incurred virtually all the expenses.

On September 22, Bettman reiterated his threat in even simpler terms: "We are not prepared to open a season that could be lost prior

to its conclusion." He went on to assume that "there is every likelihood that the Players' Association would strike at some point during this season as it did in 1992, threatening the Stanley Cup playoffs." The "we" indicated Bettman's mandate. He didn't have the good of the league in mind, only the will of the owners. That was why he was called "commissioner" instead of "president." The omnipotence of the latter term had been tempered by the subservience of the former. That was why he had a job.

By issuing his ultimatum, Bettman made a mockery of the pre-season games: players stopped checking and began shaking hands after the final siren in a show of "solidarity." After a 5–3–1 pre-season, Burns took his Leafs to Teen Ranch in Caledon Hills to train and relax for a few days before the home opener. When they returned to the Gardens, the team photo session was cancelled and the doors were locked. Bettman "postponed" the start of the season for two weeks, but an agreement was nowhere in sight. For more than 100 days it remained nowhere in sight. The NHLPA placed a notice in newspapers across the continent explaining its situation:

NATIONAL HOCKEY LEAGUE PLAYERS' ASSOCIATION

To the fans of the National Hockey League:
When we showed up to play last night, the doors were locked and the lights were out. Yesterday, the NHL slammed the door shut on 700 hockey players and millions of fans around the world. It is difficult to understand the logic behind this decision.

Consider how well the NHL has done over the last year:

- The 1993–94 season produced one of the finest years in league history, capped by the New York Rangers' first Stanley Cup championship in 54 years;
- Strong new franchises in Anaheim and Miami played to sellout crowds;
- New arenas in St. Louis and Chicago have opened, creating increased revenue opportunities;
- Three weeks ago, the NHL announced new television deals worth approximately $200 million;
- This week, the NHL announced that merchandise sales last year surpassed the one billion dollar mark.

We have worked very hard to achieve a new agreement with the NHL. As you know, we played all last season, the playoffs, and this pre-season without a contract.

We believe a lockout is not in the best interest of our game. We would much prefer to be playing the game we love before all of our fans.

We appreciate your support for us and our great game. We are committed to the continued growth of hockey in North America and internationally. Unfortunately, the NHL's decision to deprive

the players and fans of the game does not show the same appreciation and commitment.

Sincerely,

The 700 members of the National Hockey League
Players' Association

October 2, 1994.

If that weren't enough to distract fans from the more simple pleasures in hockey life such as passing and skating and watching *Hockey Night in Canada*, there was the new problem of ownership of Maple Leaf Gardens. Steve Stavro was all set to reverse what Major Conn Smythe had done almost 70 years ago — make MLGL a private company. Ontario law stipulated that 90% ownership would allow a majority owner to force the remaining small shareholders to sell their holdings, in this case to a company called MLG Ventures. It was owned by two groups, the Ontario Teachers Pension Plan Board (49%) and MLG Holdings Limited. MLG Holdings was operated by the Toronto-Dominion Bank (20%), and Stavro Investments Limited (80%).

MLG Ventures
Ontario Teachers Pension Plan Board 49%
MLG Holdings Ltd. 51%

MLG Holdings Ltd.
Stavro Investments Limited 80%
TD Bank 20%

Stavro was the chairman of the board, president, secretary, and director of Ventures, so clearly the company (and the Leafs) marched to his tune.

On April 2, 1994, Ventures exercised the "Stavro Option" of September 23, 1993, which allowed for the sale of Molson's 19.99% stake in Maple Leaf Gardens to Knob Hill Farms Limited. The chunk of shares was sold for $29 each or $21,331,675, and as part of the deal Stavro agreed with the estate (which he controlled) to buy its 60.28% for $34 a share ($75,373,920 in total). Stavro now had a controlling interest in 91.27% of the Leaf empire and offered to buy any of the public's shares for $34 each. But by August 4, 1994, only 9,553 of these shares had been tendered, leaving more than 320,000 still in public hands. Under the Business Corporation Act of Ontario he could now legally force all 2,500 shareholders, only 260 of whom owned more than 100 shares, to sell their holdings for $34 each.* However, before Stavro's scheduled meeting to take the Gardens

---

* $33.80 + $.20 dividend.

OFFER TO PURCHASE FOR CASH

all of the outstanding Common Shares of

MAPLE LEAF GARDENS, LIMITED

at

$34.00 per Common Share

by

MLG VENTURES LIMITED

This Offer is open for acceptance until 5:00 o'clock p.m. (Toronto time) on Monday, May 2, 1994, unless this Offer is extended or withdrawn.

MLG Ventures Limited currently owns, indirectly, 19.99% of the outstanding Common Shares of Maple Leaf Gardens, Limited. MLG Ventures has entered into an irrevocable lock-up agreement with the Estate of Harold E. Ballard whereby MLG Ventures will acquire the Estate's direct and indirect 60.3% holding of Common Shares at a price equal to $34.00 per Common Share. See "Agreements with Largest Holders of Common Shares" in the Offering Circular.

The conditions of this Offer are fully described in the Offer to Purchase under Section 5, "Conditions of this Offer".

To accept this Offer, a holder of Common Shares must, prior to the expiry of this Offer, either (i) deposit the certificates representing such Common Shares in proper form for transfer, together with the accompanying blue Letter of Acceptance and Transmittal or a facsimile thereof properly completed and duly executed in accordance with the instructions in the Letter of Acceptance and Transmittal and any other documents required by the Letter of Acceptance and Transmittal, at the office of The R-M Trust Company specified therein, or (ii) follow the guaranteed delivery procedures set out in the Offer to Purchase under Section 3, "Manner and Time of Acceptance — Guaranteed Delivery Procedures". A holder of Common Shares whose certificates are registered in the name of an investment dealer, stockbroker, bank, trust company or other nominee should immediately contact such nominee in order to take the necessary steps to be able to deposit such Common Shares under this Offer.

Questions and requests for assistance may be directed to, and additional copies of this Offer and the accompanying blue Letter of Acceptance and Transmittal may be obtained without charge on request from Midland Walwyn Capital Inc. or from The R-M Trust Company at the office specified on the last page of this Offer.

The Dealer Manager for this Offer is:

MIDLAND WALWYN CAPITAL INC.

April 8, 1994

private on August 9 at the Sheraton Centre in Toronto, Mr. Justice Sidney Lederman blocked Stavro, citing evidence that the shares might be worth more than $34 and that while the takeover might be legal, Stavro should have to shoulder the responsibility of proving that legality in a court of law.

The public objections to Stavro's moves were initiated entirely by Harry Ornest, former owner of the Argos and now vice-chairman of Hollywood Parks Inc., an L.A. racetrack; and Jim Devellano, the Red Wings' senior vice-president. They owned the majority of the public's shares, small potatoes by Stavro's standards but substantial nonetheless. (By this time, Ventures controlled 3,357,052 of 3,677,400 shares. Of the 320,348 shares in the public domain, Devellano and Ornest owned 164,350 [51.3%] of them.) They petitioned the Public Trustee's office, which in turn acted on behalf of the charities that would eventually receive the money from the sale of the estate. The machinations were complex in the extreme:

Plaintiffs — The Public Trustee

Defendants — Steve Stavro, Donald Crump, Terence Kelly, Knob Hill Farms Limited, MLG Ventures Limited, Maple Leaf Gardens Limited

Intervenors — Harry Ornest, Ruth Ornest, Cindy Ornest, Laura Ornest, Michael Ornest, Maury Ornest, the Ornest Family Partnership, Jim Devellano

Stavro was one of the trustees of Ballard's estate, and as such his "fiduciary" (i.e., financial) obligation was to the charities first and foremost. At the same time, the courts had permitted him to acquire the rights to purchase Molson's 80.27% first option in the Gardens, supporting the idea that one of the trustees could in fact take control of the Leafs. Stavro appeared to be doing everything by the book in his takeover bid. But the $34 was the sticking point for Ornest and Devellano. Ballard's will stated that trustees could purchase estate property at "fair market value, supported by two independent appraisals" without court authorization. Stavro got the requisite appraisals through the estate, and paid $150,000 for each of them. In their report dated October 15, 1993, Burns Fry Limited concluded that fair market value of the estate's interest was between $25.83 and $29.91 a share. Another report dated October 1, 1993, produced by RBC Dominion Securities Inc., quoted $27 to $34 a share. Stavro took the highest of the figures. The Public Trustee was informed and allowed Stavro to continue; all looked to be in perfect order.

But Ornest and Devellano argued that the only way to determine fair market value was to put the shares up for public auction. This would have maximized the profits for the charities, and because of Stavro's first option on the holdings, he could have matched the offer and taken control. Certainly one reason Stavro didn't exercise the auction option was because it might have cost him tens of millions of dollars had someone bid, say, $50 or $60 a share. The 60.28% that he wanted to acquire was in the form of 2,216,880 shares, so every dollar increase would, in fact, cost more than $2.2 million.

Furthermore, the estate did not *have* to sell the shares. The trustees — Stavro, Crump, and Kelly* — could refuse to sell by virtue of the will: "The Trustees are authorized to pay, at their discretion, any portion of the income of the Trust to designated beneficiaries and to transfer the capital of the Trust to the Foundation on Division Day, namely, either 21 years after the death of the settlor [Ballard] or at any earlier time selected by the Trustees." In truth, they had 21 years to sell the estate's shares of the Gardens. In the event they chose not to sell, though, they would get a clear idea through auction

---

* Kelly was appointed by Stavro and Crump when Giffin died, as stipulated in the will. Both he and Crump were close friends of Stavro.

of the high-end value of the stock. The apparent necessity to sell now was based on Stavro's desire to own Maple Leaf Gardens rather than the estate's need to obtain the cash or relinquish ownership.

Ornest and Devellano argued that the two appraisals by Burns Fry and RBC Dominion were "stale-dated" by five-and-a-half months. But they, and the Public Trustee, failed to acknowledge that Stavro, through *his* ownership, had improved the price of the shares in the interim through his strong and silent control, the hockey team's great play, the playoff revenue *et al*. Without his huge financial investments* such stability on ice would not have been possible and would have translated into an even more unstable, fluctuating market value.

Stavro stabilized ownership by not getting in Fletcher's way of running the hockey team. Right after he took control, in fact, the price of MLGL shares dropped, but then slowly and steadily rose as the team took off. Also, the week before he positioned himself to take MLGL private, in April '94, shares jumped from $36 to $47.50. Revenue for the Leafs' fiscal year ending May 31, 1993, was $56.2 million, up 31% from the $43.1 million in 1992. The increase was due to four factors: playoffs ($7 million more than '92); increased ticket prices ($4 million); new private boxes ($1.2 million); wine and beer sales ($.9 million). All these profits were attributable to Stavro and Fletcher and were the prime reasons for the increase in the value of the shares.

If the Gardens were open to public bidding to determine such a price, an artificially high value for the shares might be created, especially now that the team was so successful on ice and at the bank. Was Stavro to be punished for establishing, creating, that success? If the stale-dating were bad at the low end, wasn't auctioning unfair at the high end?

After Stavro's attempt to make the Gardens private became publicly known, no fewer than three groups came forward to claim that they had previously enquired about buying the MLGL stock. David Peterson, the former premier of Ontario and chair of the Raptors basketball club, declared his team would have been very interested in buying the Leafs and having the two franchises play out of the same new arena to be built in the next couple of years for the NBA. Ornest claimed to have enquired about buying the Leafs with a group of investors, and ditto for Frank Mahovlich. All three claimed Stavro had told them in no uncertain terms the Leafs were not for sale. In a sworn affidavit of August 8, 1994, Peterson said: "At no time were we informed that the shares of the Estate were for sale. Had there been a solicitation for bids, the Raptors basketball club would have been prepared to make an initial bid which was

---

* He had also personally guaranteed $4.5 million of the $21 million loan from the Toronto-Dominion to buy out Bill Ballard, another important part of stabilizing the ownership.

significantly higher than the $34 a share that was paid to the Estate by MLG Ventures Limited."

Peterson's claim was supported by at least one irrefutable fact. On November 11, 1993, Fletcher presented his "New Arena Feasibility Report" to the board of directors at the Gardens, favouring a joint venture project with the Palestra Group to build a new NHL-NBA arena for hockey and basketball. While this move might have increased the price of MLGL shares and the value of the hockey team in dollars and cents, it would have grossly compromised the integrity and tradition of the Toronto Maple Leafs established by Conn Smythe in 1927. The arena would not have been called Maple Leaf Gardens; the prime tenants would not have been the Leafs; the hallowed halls would not have been devoted to the glory of the blue and white; the location wouldn't have been as historically significant. However, the none-too-subtle implication put forth by the Public Trustee was that if there were *any* reason to believe that the shares of MLGL would increase if a new arena were jointly purchased, it must be done to fulfil the fiduciary duties to the charities.

But Fletcher's report was hastily planned. To speculate about the profitability of a "joint venture complex" was as negligent on Peterson's, Fletcher's, and the Public Trustee's part as anything Stavro had done. The NBA demanded that the Raptors have 12,500 season tickets sold by December 31, 1994, or the franchise would be revoked. Was Stavro supposed to enter into such a gamble in 1993 or '94 based on an assumption the goal would be met? On January 7, 1995, the Raptors took out a full page ad in the *Toronto Star* to announce their total of 15,287 season seats sold. However, the number was reached only because of Shoppers Drug Mart, which bought 4,250 tickets for promotional purposes, and without which the franchise would have been revoked. The seats were in the lowest price range and purchased only for the two years the team would play at SkyDome. In two years' time, the Raptors might well be on the verge of bankruptcy. Hardly a risk the venerable Toronto Maple Leaf hockey club should have ventured into.

Furthermore, if Conn can build the Gardens in 155 days at the height of the worst depression in the industrial age, so too can Stavro and Fletcher with a thriving team in a modern, affluent city. In 1971, W. Sefton and Associates drafted a design to expand the Gardens to seat 23,400 by raising the roof and adding "White" and "Black" seats above the Greys.* In 1989, Ballard had Angelo del Zotto of Tridel Corporation make designs for another expansion, but while the plans never came to fruition, the modern construction know-how is there to do something similar in 1995 and beyond. Under no circumstances should the Leafs *ever* have to share a building or play out of some corporate advertisement like the Air Canada Centre (as

---

* They also designed some of the mid-'80s corporate boxes.

the Raptors' new stadium will be called) when they can indeed have the best of both worlds: a bigger arena but at the original, gorgeous Maple Leaf Gardens.

Thankfully, it would seem the team isn't going anywhere soon. The Leafs purchased the Warner Brothers building across the street, on the northeast corner of Carlton and Church, and plan to move the marketing department there (which presently occupies Ballard's former apartment) to enable them to expand restaurant/concession services inside the Gardens. The Leafs have also researched the possibility of installing air conditioning and a huge new JumboTron scoreboard, together requiring a $13 million investment. If these plans go ahead, the Leafs will be staying put for a very long time to come.

During the initial takeover negotiations shortly after Ballard's death, Stavro reluctantly accepted Molson's offer to extend their loan deadline of December 31, 1990, until March 1, 1991, and then refused a further 60-day extension to allow the estate to listen to parties interested in acquiring MLGL to come forward. As the Public Trustee charged: "No attempt was made by either the Executors or the Valuators to have meaningful discussions with any potential purchasers or to otherwise test the market by exposing the shares to the market place. No financial advisors were retained to advise on the best way to solicit the market place in order to ensure that the best possible price was obtained for the shares." Ornest and Devellano contended that Stavro's sale to himself was done unilaterally and without any possible competitor's knowledge. But the truth was that anyone who read a newspaper had been aware of the general situation at the Gardens and could have pressed for details considerably sooner. Stavro's lawyer Brian Bellmore (also on the Board of Directors) argued that no one showed any interest in buying the Gardens. This, said Justice Lederman, was no excuse: "Executors cannot avoid their obligation to maximize the value of the Estate assets by taking a passive stance, essentially saying, 'If other potential purchasers are out there, they know where they can find me.' "

Further details of the "Stavro Option" on Molson's shares also shed light on the ambiguity of the acquisition. One thing everyone was in agreement on was that a settlement of the option was necessary and in the best interests of the club, charities, and ownership (interest charges were mounting daily). On February 14, 1991, Stavro offered Molson's fair terms for the payback of the money the estate owed in exchange for the option to buy Molson's shares: a two-year loan at prime rate plus five-eighths of 1% interest. Giffin disagreed with the ethical implications of Stavro's bid and favoured Bill Ballard's bid of a few days later because it was financially better and was without conflict of interest: a four-year loan at 5% for the first two years, prime plus one-half of 1% for the balance. But then on February 26, Stavro countered with another offer that was significantly better than the one he had made on Valentine's Day, a

loan of $19,892,975.98 over four years, with interest of 5% for two years and five-eighths of 1% thereafter. Molson's accepted. The option had to be exercised on at least 50% of Molson's shares and be completed by April 15, 1994, with the price determined by the daily average of the previous 20 days of trading. The Public Trustee argued that in two weeks, competition between just two parties — Stavro and Bill Ballard — saved the estate $2 million. Imagine the savings that might have occurred had the process been open to even more bidding.

But you-know-who had made it very clear before his death that he didn't want his children to have anything to do with HEBL, MLGL, or any other letters connected with the Leafs. While Stavro might have been in the wrong legally, he was being loyal to the terms of the will. He and the executors had an obligation to turn down Bill Ballard's offer. They were made executors because the dead guy knew they would follow his wishes, not because he wanted them to make money for charities.

Because Harold had not objected to one of his trustees owning the team, and so implicitly endorsed such an ownership, where did Stavro's allegiance have to lie? To the will or the textbook legal interpretation of the law? By the former, he had done no wrong; by the latter, possibly. In one way it was a classic case of conflict of interest. Yet Stavro was supported by Ballard's will and the courts who allowed him to go ahead with purchasing the MLGL shares. These facts are what the Public Trustee's office used to state its case:

> Stavro, as an Executor of the Estate, Trustee of the Trust, Officer and Director of MLGL and beneficiary of the Stavro Option and the acquisition of the shares held by the Estate, was in a conflict of interest. He was intimately involved in the obtaining of the Valuations and as Chief Executive Officer of MLGL controlled the information made available to the valuators. Stavro breached his fiduciary duties as Executor and Trustee by putting his own interests before those of the Estate and the Trust. Further, Stavro exercised his powers as a Director and Officer of MLGL in a manner that was oppressive, unfairly prejudicial to or that unfairly disregarded the interests of security holders, including the Estate.

Justice Lederman agreed:

> Stavro is caught in a conflict of interest between his fiduciary obligation to maximize the value of the estate's interest in MLGL and his personal interest in minimizing that value. His paramount obligation, however, is to the estate and he must be scrupulous in satisfying that duty. The evidence before me raises some questions about that.

Perhaps what Stavro did was wrong, but he was abetted by the Public Trustee at every step of the way. On November 26, 1993, it was given copies of the two valuation reports commissioned by the estate, yet

saw no reason then to challenge the veracity or fairness of the figures. It was also aware of Giffin's dissent to the "Stavro Option." Giffin apprised the Public Trustee of his misgivings, of Bill Ballard's offer, and the interest expressed by I.H. Asper, president of CanWest Global Communication Corporation, in buying HEBL shares.*

In November 1994, Stavro filed a countersuit against the Public Trustee, arguing that because it originally saw no wrongdoing in his bid, his actions were both justified and supported by the law. He argued that the Public Trustee took an inordinate length of time — three months — to act on his suddenly inappropriate takeover and was doing so only because of the loud outcry from disgruntled and powerful minority shareholders (Ornest and Devellano). Stavro also argued that the claim was not in support of the charities but rather the self-serving interests of Ornest and Devellano, who simply were trying to get more money for their shares.

DOUG MACLELLAN / HOCKEY HALL OF FAME

Stavro faced legal action from both the Public Trustee and Ornest and Devellano. The private suit was for breach of fiduciary duty to shareholders; the Public Trustee's was for the same breach to the charities. Because of the common ground, Mr. Justice John Ground allowed the two suits to be heard at the same time, but on January 20, 1995, a third figure entered the fray. Gwen Maxwell of Etobicoke, owner of 4,000 MLGL shares, filed a $13.6 million lawsuit on behalf of all Gardens shareholders, alleging that the information in a

---

* These inquiries occurred during the February 14–25, 1991, finagling between Stavro and Bill Ballard to acquire the Molson Option.

circular that was sent by MLG Ventures to shareholders induced them to sell their stock by misrepresenting or omitting salient facts. It was now up to the courts to interpret the justness of Stavro's actions.

The uncertainty of Stavro's ownership also posed another question. What consideration should the hockey club receive in all this? If the shares were sold to another party, and that new owner fired Fletcher and Burns and traded Gilmour and Potvin, would justice have been done? As the case goes to court, the future of the hockey team has not been given any consideration, a sad irony since it is the company's main asset.

Lastly, is Harold Ballard not to blame for this whole mess? He left HEBL with such huge debts* that the charities might never get a penny. If he really wanted them to profit, he could have sold MLGL just before his death, when the shares were going through the Toronto Stock Exchange roof. He seemed to be as happy creating this enormous legal wrangle as he was to help the charities by spiting his family and keeping his name alive. Even in his dying days, the good of the Leafs was last on his mind. The charities weren't being cheated by Stavro; they were being used by the dead guy.** Now that he couldn't be held to account for his actions, perhaps the Public Trustee itself should be held accountable since it allowed the situation to become so tangled and complex. Had it been more thorough earlier on, or had it dismissed Ornest and Devellano's claim out of hand, none of this legal mess might have occurred.

While the courts decide this case, a few simple truths can be decided outside the justice system. Ornest and Devellano may be right about their allegations regarding Stavro, but certainly not on any moral or ethical level. They didn't care about the execution of the will or the health of the charities or the fortunes of the hockey team. They were looking for one thing: money. Furthermore, if Ornest had expressed interest in buying the Gardens, was he also not in a conflict of interest, simply trying to force the Gardens onto the market so he could buy it? And how does Devellano, as senior employee for the Red Wings, have the ethical nerve to even own Leafs shares in the first place? This was as real a conflict of interest as Stavro's.

Whether Stavro had committed any legal wrong was for the courts to decide, but the team was winning and his quiet ownership was largely responsible. The turmoil that would ensue should Stavro be forced out of control could only hurt the Leafs. Stavro was, first and

---

* More than $60 million to acquire his children's shares: a $20 million loan from Molson's for Mary Elizabeth's; $20 million from the Toronto-Dominion Bank for Harold Jr.'s; $21 million for Bill's.

** In exactly the same way Ballard had requested the executors donate anything they saw fit to the Hockey Hall of Fame. Ballard destroyed everything to do with the Leafs, and had virtually nothing to give! The gesture sounded generous but was in fact as empty as a desert sky.

foremost, a Leaf fan, and was interested primarily in giving the city a winning hockey team and a Stanley Cup. Ornest, Devellano, the Public Trustee, and David Peterson couldn't care less about the welfare of the hockey club. Just the dollars and cents.

Where should Leaf-lubbers' allegiance lie? Steve Stavro.

POSTPONED

Column 1 (left, partially cut off)

...er

...1
  7:30 PM
...ers 7:30 PM
...sey 7:30 PM
...phia 7:30 PM
...nto 7:00 PM
  7:00 PM
...ary 8:30 PM
...n Jose
...ct. 2
...go 6:00 PM
...nton
Oct. 3
...gers 7:30 PM
...a Bay 7:30 PM
...Florida 7:30 PM
...nto 7:30 PM
...s
...ay, Oct. 5
...burgh 7:30 PM
...Ottawa 7:30 PM
...innipeg 7:30 PM
...imonton 7:30 PM
...ancouver 7:30 PM
...ngles
...ay, Oct. 6
...ston 7:30 PM
...at Rangers 7:30 PM
...at Chicago 7:30 PM
...Florida
...ay, Oct. 7
...Buffalo 7:30 PM
...landers 7:30 PM
...at Washington 8:00 PM
...Tampa Bay 7:30 PM
...at Winnipeg 7:30 PM
...Vancouver 6:00 PM
...San Jose
...urday, Oct. 8
...Boston 7:30 PM
...Hartford 7:00 PM
...Montreal 7:30 PM
...New Jersey 7:30 PM
...ay at Philadelphia 7:30 PM
...s at Washington 1:00 PM
...at Florida 7:00 PM
...Dallas 7:30 PM
...at Los Angeles
Sunday, Oct. 9
...ton at Chicago 7:30 PM
...ver at San Jose 2:00 PM
...y at Anaheim 5:00 PM
Monday, Oct. 10
...at Boston 1:30 PM
...o at Buffalo 7:00 PM
Tuesday, Oct. 11
...urgh at Quebec 7:30 PM
...a Bay at Rangers 7:30 PM
...wa at Toronto 7:30 PM
...ago at St. Louis 7:30 PM
...niped at Dallas 7:30 PM
...Jose at Los Angeles 7:30 PM
Wednesday, Oct. 12
...da at Hartford 7:00 PM
...shington at Pittsburgh 7:30 PM
...nders at New Jersey 7:30 PM
...iladelphia at New Jersey 7:30
...ffalo at Detroit
...lgary at Edmonton
...ston at San Jose
...ncouver at Anaheim
Thursday, Oct. 13
...uebec at Toronto
...Winnipeg at Chicago
...angers at Los A...
...ancouver at Los A...
Friday, O...
...Hartford at Buff...
...Montreal at D...
...Florida at De...peg
...Philadelphi...
...San Jose...
...Boston a...
Satu...
...Rangers at Harti...
7. Montreal at Pittsburgh
8. Chicago at Quebec
9. Detroit at Islanders
0. Buffalo at Washington
.. New Jersey at Toronto 7:30 PM
2. St. Louis at Toronto 7:30 PM
3. Ottawa at Dallas 7:00 PM
84. Edmonton at Vancouver 7:30 PM
85. Boston at Los Angeles
Sunday, Oct. 16
86. New Jersey at Florida 6:00 PM
87. Tampa Bay at St. Louis 6:00 PM
88. San Jose at Winnipeg 6:30 PM
89. Philadelphia at Calgary 6:00 PM
Monday, Oct. 17
90. Chicago at Montreal 7:30 PM
91. Dallas at Detroit 7:30 PM
92. Philadelphia at Vancouver 7:30 PM
93. Edmonton at Anaheim 7:30 PM
Tuesday, Oct. 18

Column 2

Wednesday, Oct. 19
99. Ottawa at Hartford 7:00 PM
100. Washington at New Jersey 7:30 PM
101. Toronto at Florida 7:30 PM
102. Montreal at Detroit 7:30 PM
103. Dallas at Winnipeg 7:30 PM
104. Anaheim at Vancouver 7:30 PM
105. Boston at Edmonton 7:30 PM
Thursday, Oct. 20
106. Los Angeles at Rangers 7:30 PM
107. Quebec at Philadelphia 7:30 PM
108. Toronto at Tampa Bay 7:30 PM
109. San Jose at Chicago 7:30 PM
110. Anaheim at Calgary 7:30 PM
Friday, Oct. 21
111. Florida at Buffalo 7:30 PM
112. Hartford at Washington 8:00 PM
113. Pittsburgh at Detroit 7:30 PM
114. Vancouver at Dallas 7:30 PM
115. Boston at Edmonton 7:30 PM
Saturday, Oct. 22
116. Washington at Hartford 7:00 PM
117. Los Angeles at Pittsburgh 7:30 PM
118. Rangers at Montreal 7:00 PM
119. Detroit at Quebec 7:00 PM
120. Florida at Islanders 1:00 PM
121. San Jose at New Jersey 1:00 PM
122. Ottawa at St. Louis 5:30 PM
123. Toronto at Winnipeg 6:30 PM
124. Chicago at Winnipeg 8:30 PM
125. Boston at Calgary
Sunday, Oct. 23
126. Quebec at Buffalo 1:30 PM
127. Tampa Bay at Ottawa 7:30 PM
128. San Jose at Rangers 7:30 PM
129. Los Angeles at Chicago 6:00 PM
130. Vancouver at St. Louis 12:00 PM
131. Edmonton at Dallas 3:00 PM
132. Anaheim at Winnipeg
Monday, Oct. 24
133. New Jersey at Montreal 7:30 PM
134. Calgary at Toronto 7:30 PM
Tuesday, Oct. 25
135. Dallas at Pittsburgh 7:30 PM
136. Edmonton at Quebec 7:30 PM
137. Vancouver at Islanders 7:30 PM
138. Los Angeles at Florida 7:30 PM
139. Anaheim at Detroit 7:30 PM
140. Washington at St. Louis 7:30 PM
Wednesday, Oct. 26
141. Pittsburgh at Ottawa 7:30 PM
142. Edmonton at Montreal 7:30 PM
143. Dallas at Rangers 7:30 PM
144. Calgary at New Jersey 7:30 PM
145. Los Angeles at Tampa Bay 7:30 PM
Thursday, Oct. 27
146. Montreal at Boston 7:30 PM
147. Quebec at Hartford 7:00 PM
148. Vancouver at Philadelphia 7:30 PM
149. Buffalo at Florida 7:30 PM
150. Anaheim at Chicago 7:30 PM
151. Washington at St. Louis 7:30 PM
Friday, Oct. 28
152. Calgary at Rangers 7:30 PM
153. Edmonton at Toronto 1:00 PM
154. Los Angeles at ... 7:00 PM
Saturday, ...
155. Buffalo at Bos... 7:30 PM
156. Winnipeg at ... 2:00 PM
157. Detroit at ... 5:00 PM
158. Pittsburgh ...
159. Dallas at ...landers
160. Calga... New Jersey
161. Va... iladelphia
162. T... San...
163. ...
164. ...
166. ...
167. ...dmonton
168. St. L...aheim

November

Tuesday, Nov. 1
169. Ottawa at ...burgh 7:30 PM
170. Tampa ... Quebec 7:30 PM
171. Hartford ...oit 7:30 PM
... islan...las 7:30 PM
...Calgary 7:30 PM
...Los Angeles 7:30 PM
Wednesday, Nov. 2
176. Chicago at Buffalo 7:30 PM
177. Boston at Ottawa 7:30 PM
178. Tampa Bay at Montreal 7:30 PM
179. Islanders at St. Louis 7:30 PM
180. Toronto at Winnipeg 7:30 PM
181. Florida at Edmonton 7:30 PM
182. Washington at Vancouver 7:30 PM
183. Rangers at Anaheim 7:30 PM
Thursday, Nov. 3
184. Pittsburgh at Boston 7:30 PM
Friday, Nov. 4
185. Philadelphia at Hartford 7:30 PM
186. Toronto at Detroit 7:30 PM
187. Winnipeg at Dallas 7:30 PM
188. Edmonton at Calgary 7:30 PM
189. Los Angeles at Vancouver 7:30 PM
190. New Jersey at Anaheim 7:30 PM
Saturday, Nov. 5
191. Chicago at Boston 7:30 PM
192. Hartford at Pittsburgh 7:30 PM
193. Montreal at Ottawa 7:00 PM
194. Buffalo at Philadelphia 7:00 PM
195. Quebec at Washington 7:30 PM
196. Islanders at Tampa Bay 7:30 PM
197. Detroit at Toronto 7:30 PM
198. Winnipeg at St. Louis 7:30 PM
199. Florida at Vancouver 7:30 PM
200. Rangers at San Jose 7:30 PM
... Nov. 6

Column 3

Monday, ...
204. Boston at Ottawa 7:30 PM
205. Dallas at Islanders 7:30 PM
206. San Jose at Vancouver
Tuesday, Nov. 8
207. Montreal at Hartford 7:00 PM
208. New Jersey at Pittsburgh 7:30 PM
209. Tampa Bay at Buffalo 7:30 PM
210. Philadelphia at Washington 7:30 PM
211. Edmonton at Detroit 7:30 PM
212. Winnipeg at Detroit 7:30 PM
213. St. Louis at Calgary 7:30 PM
214. Vancouver at San Jose 7:30 PM
215. Anaheim at Los Angeles 7:30 PM
Wednesday, Nov. 9
216. Hartford at Rangers 7:30 PM
217. Islanders at Florida 7:30 PM
218. Tampa Bay at Toronto 7:30 PM
Thursday, Nov. 10
219. Quebec at Boston 7:30 PM
220. Ottawa at Buffalo 7:30 PM
221. Montreal at Philadelphia 7:30 PM
222. Washington at Philadelphia 7:30 PM
223. Toronto at Chicago 7:30 PM
224. Pittsburgh at Dallas 7:30 PM
225. St. Louis at Winnipeg 7:30 PM
226. Anaheim at San Jose 7:30 PM
227. Calgary at Los Angeles 7:30 PM
Friday, Nov. 11
228. Islanders at Rangers 7:30 PM
229. Edmonton at Florida 7:30 PM
230. Vancouver at Anaheim 7:30 PM
Saturday, Nov. ...
231. Ottawa at Boston ...
232. Hartford at Islanders ...
233. Boston at ...
234. Philadelphia at Washington ...
235. Edmonton at Tampa Bay ...
236. Montreal at ...
237. Pittsburgh ...
238. Detroit at ...
239. Chicago at ...
240. Buffalo at St...
241. Vancouver at Los...
242. ...
243. ...
... at Phila...
...ton at Florida 6:00 PM
...uis at Anaheim 8:00 PM
...y at Anaheim 00 PM
...day, Nov. ...
...Winn...
Wednesday, Nov. 16
...ago at Anaheim 7:30 PM
...Louis at Hartford 7:00 PM
...tsburgh at Quebec 7:30 PM
...landers at Montreal 7:30 PM
...Dallas at New Jersey 7:30 PM
...Detroit at Tampa Bay 7:30 PM
...at Toronto 7:30 PM
...ver at Edmonton 7:30 PM
Thursday, Nov. 17
261. St. Louis at Boston 7:30 PM
262. Ottawa at Pittsburgh 7:30 PM
263. Montreal at Quebec 7:30 PM
264. Rangers at Philadelphia 7:30 PM
...6. Detroit at Florida 7:30 PM
266. Buffalo at Vancouver 7:30 PM
267. Buffalo at Los Angeles
Friday, Nov. 18
268. Islanders at New Jersey 8:00 PM
269. Toronto at Washington 7:30 PM
270. Winnipeg at Tampa Bay 7:30 PM
271. San Jose at Dallas 7:30 PM
272. Calgary at Edmonton 7:30 PM
Saturday, Nov. 19
273. Washington at Boston 7:00 PM

274. Islanders at Hartford 7:00 PM
275. Rangers at Ottawa 7:00 PM
276. Quebec at Montreal 7:00 PM
277. Pittsburgh at Philadelphia 7:30 PM
278. New Jersey at Tampa Bay 7:30 PM
279. Winnipeg at Florida 7:30 PM
280. St. Louis at Vancouver 7:30 PM
281. Calgary at Vancouver 7:30 PM
Sunday, Nov. 20
282. Detroit at Philadelphia 7:00 PM
283. San Jose at Edmonton 6:00 PM
284. Chicago at Anaheim 5:00 PM
Monday, Nov. 21
285. Pittsburgh at Hartford 7:00 PM
286. Hartford at Montreal 7:30 PM
287. Florida at Quebec 7:30 PM
288. Vancouver at Toronto 7:30 PM
289. Buffalo at Dallas 7:30 PM
Tuesday, Nov. 22
290. Los Angeles at Calgary 7:30 PM
291. Chicago at San Jose 7:30 PM
Wednesday, Nov. 23
292. Philadelphia at Hartford 7:00 PM
293. Rangers at Pittsburgh 7:30 PM
294. Boston at Buffalo 7:30 PM
295. New Jersey at Ottawa 7:30 PM
296. Florida at Montreal 7:30 PM
297. Tampa Bay at Islanders 7:30 PM
298. Vancouver at Washington 8:00 PM
299. St. Louis at Detroit 7:30 PM
300. Quebec at Dallas 7:30 PM
301. Toronto at Winnipeg 7:30 PM
302. Los Angeles at Edmonton 7:30 PM
303. San Jose at Anaheim 7:30 PM
Thursday, Nov. 24
304. Quebec at St. Louis 7:30 PM
305. Chicago at Calgary 7:30 PM
Friday, Nov. 25
306. Anaheim at Buffalo 1:00 PM
307. Vancouver at Buffalo 1:00 PM
... Philadelphia 1:00 PM

Column 4 (right)

Saturday, ...
312. Anaheim at Hartford 1:30 PM
313. San Jose at Pittsburgh 7:30 PM
314. Florida at Ottawa 7:30 PM
315. Los Angeles at Montreal 7:30 PM
316. Washington at Quebec 7:00 PM
317. Toronto at Islanders 7:00 PM
318. Tampa Bay at Philadelphia 7:00 PM
319. New Jersey at Detroit 7:00 PM
320. St. Louis at Dallas 8:30 PM
321. Calgary at Edmonton
Sunday, Nov. 27
322. Van... 7:00 PM
323. Tam... 7:00 PM
324 ... 7:00 PM
325 ...
Monday, Nov. ...
...les at Ottawa 7:30 PM
...at Montreal 7:30 PM
...troit 7:30 PM
329. W... 7:30 PM
330. Toron...
Tu...
331. ...gers at Ha... 7:00 PM
332. ...les at Pittsb... 7:30 PM
33... ...les at Quebec 7:30 PM
33...
Wedne... Nov. 30
...Washington... 7:30 PM
...stat... 7:30 PM
...ronto 7:30 PM
...pa Bay 7:30 PM
...s at Detroit 7:30 PM
340. M... at St. Louis 7:30 PM
341. Winnipeg at Edmonton 7:30 PM

December

Thursday, Dec. 1
342. Hartford at Boston 7:30 PM
343. Washington at Pittsburgh 7:30 PM
344. Quebec at New Jersey 7:30 PM
345. Islanders at Philadelphia 7:30 PM
346. San Jose at Florida 7:30 PM
347. Montreal at Chicago 7:30 PM
Friday, Dec. 2
348. Los Angeles at Buffalo 7:30 PM
349. Anaheim at Rangers 7:30 PM
350. San Jose at Tampa Bay 7:30 PM
351. Calgary at Detroit 7:30 PM
352. Dallas at Vancouver 7:30 PM
Saturday, Dec. 3
353. Boston at Pittsburgh 7:30 PM
354. Philadelphia at Ottawa 7:30 PM
355. Detroit at Montreal 7:30 PM
356. Hartford at Quebec 7:00 PM
357. Buffalo at Islanders 1:00 PM
358. Edmonton at New Jersey 1:00 PM
359. Tampa Bay at Washington 7:30 PM
360. Chicago at Florida 7:30 PM
361. Los Angeles at Toronto 7:30 PM
362. Winnipeg at Vancouver
Sunday, Dec. 4
363. Boston at Hartford 7:00 PM
364. Calgary at Ottawa 7:00 PM
365. Edmonton at Rangers 7:00 PM
366. Anaheim at Chicago 6:00 PM
367. New Jersey at Islanders
Monday, Dec. 5
368. Tampa Bay at Winnipeg 7:30
369. San Jose at Dallas 7:30
Tuesday, Dec. 6
370. Rangers at Pittsburgh 7:30
371. Calgary at Quebec 7:30
372. Edmonton at Islanders 7:30
373. Boston at Detroit 7:3
374. Toronto at Vancouver
Wednesday, Dec. 7
375. Detroit at Hartford 7:0
376. Pittsburgh at Buffalo
377. Calgary at Montreal
378. Ottawa at Tampa Bay
379. St. Louis at Dallas
380. New Jersey at Winnipeg
381. Toronto at San Jose
382. Washington at Anaheim
Thursday, Dec. 8
383. Edmonton at Boston
384. Islanders at Rangers
385. Montreal at Philadelphia
386. Ottawa at Florida
387. Vancouver at Chicago
388. Washington at Los Angeles
Friday, Dec. 9
389. Hartford at Buffalo
390. Detroit at New Jersey
391. Quebec at Tampa Bay
392. Chicago at San Jose
393. Anaheim at San Jose
Saturday, Dec. 10
394. Calgary at Boston
395. Edmonton at Pittsburgh
396. Buffalo at Pittsburgh
397. Philadelphia at Montreal
398. Ottawa at Islanders
399. Quebec at Florida
400. Dallas at St. Louis
401. Vancouver at Winnipeg
402. Washington at Ottawa
403. Toronto at Los Angeles
Sunday, Dec. 11
404. New Jersey at Philadel...
405. Florida at Chicago
406. Detroit at St. Louis
407. Toronto at Anaheim
Monday, Dec. ...
408. Calgary at Hartford
409. Los Angeles at Vanc...
Tuesday, Dec. ...
410. New Jersey at Ottaw...
411. Florida at Boston
412. Rangers at Islander...
  (at Portland).
413. Winnipeg at Washi...

Far right column (cut off)

  1:30 PM
417. Otta...
418. Bos...
419. Buf...
420. Ran...
421. Da...
422. Isl...
423. Fl...
424. W...
425. O...
427. F...
428.
429.
430.
431.
432.
433
433
434
43
43
43

238

XV

The Lockout

The front-page story in the Toronto *Telegram* on Wednesday, February 6, 1952, was short and to the point:

> George McCullagh, vice-president of the Maple Leaf Gardens, announced today that tonight's scheduled National Hockey League game between the Maple Leafs and New York Rangers has been cancelled out of respect to the memory of the late King George VI.
>
> Speaking on behalf of the executive committee of the board of directors of the Maple Leaf Gardens in the absence of Major Conn Smythe, president of the Gardens, Mr. McCullagh said it was the unanimous opinion of the Board that it would be most inappropriate for the game to be played when the Nation and the whole Commonwealth and Empire were in mourning for the King.
>
> The game will be played later in the season with the date to be announced.

More than 44 years later, on October 11, 1994, the Maple Leaf hockey club took out an advertisement in the *Toronto Star* to make this announcement:

> TICKETHOLDER NOTICE:
> Tonight's game versus the Ottawa Senators has been postponed.
> Please retain your October 11 tickets for use at a future date to be determined.
> Ticket Information Line: (416) 596–3365

To postpone a game in memory of the king is one thing; to abandon a season out of greed is quite another. The silence at the Gardens was eerie. October, November, December, and still nothing. Darkness.

Hockey may be a business, but that's not what makes it a great game. It may involve millions, billions of dollars, but that is not what brings crowds to the rinks or motivates parents in towns all across Canada to drive their kids to skating schools and games in the wee hours of the morning. The NHL may be comprised of 18 American-based teams and only eight Canadian teams, but make no mistake, the character of the game was, is, and always will be Canadian. Perhaps Bettman was well-intentioned, perhaps his manipulations during the lockout were what *he* thought were best for the game, but

he was still the wrong man for the job. Since Bettman's arrival, he has created a bitter officials' strike that didn't have to be, and then an owners' lockout that threw an entire year of hockey into turmoil. That's not all. He also instigated 70-second commercial breaks at set times during periods, destroying the tempo of the games and making tedious breaks for fans watching live. (Fans at home could practically cook a meal and not miss the next faceoff.) To sweeten the pot for Anaheim to join the NHL, he reduced the entry fee from $50 million to $25 million, with the other $25 million going directly to Los Angeles for infringement rights (which the Kings would have been entitled to anyway. Would Hamilton ever receive this perk if they were to join?). He gave the Mighty Ducks 100% of their merchandising profits, while other teams that have been around for 70 years still shared profits league-wide in accordance with NHL laws. He initiated tenths of seconds for the final minute of play (as in the NBA), and demanded that *two* Zambonis clean the ice between periods to allow for ridiculous games and promotions.

Bettman's handling of the Mike Keenan fiasco was nothing short of appalling: After leading the Rangers to the Stanley Cup in his first year as coach with the club, Keenan quit the Blueshirts July 15 citing unpaid bonuses as the reason for terminating his contract. Two days later he held a press conference in St. Louis to announce his defection to the Blues. Bettman fined Keenan and suspended him for 60 days, approved a "settlement trade" by way of reparation, and fined the Blues *and* the Red Wings $250,000 and $25,000 respectively for tampering. What suspending an NHL coach in the middle of the summer was supposed to accomplish remained a mystery. Why Detroit's tampering was only one-tenth as bad as St. Louis' tampering was also left to the gods to debate. (Did St. Louis tamper "more" because they wound up signing Keenan?) What a trade had to do with tampering is also precedent-setting in its confusion. Furthermore, Bettman's inaction in the Bob Probert case was equally unforgivable. Probert, signed by the Blackhawks as a free agent during the summer, crashed his motorcycle in an accident that involved cocaine and a blood-alcohol level three times the legal limit, the second time such an incident has occurred. Yet in eight months after the crash, Bettman did nothing more than place Probert on the league's inactive list. No ban, no suspension. Nothing.

Bettman has made a mockery of the league, and more important, of the men who continue to make hockey the greatest sport in the world. The first time he ever entered Maple Leaf Gardens was February 17, 1993. Could such a man understand the game? Was

hockey in his blood? Was he capable of ruling on events that came out of the emotion of the game, the players? (Was it possible for a cook to create a superb dish if he didn't know the tastes and importance of the various ingredients? Or for a conductor to create a great symphony without understanding the spirit of each musician and instrument?) The understanding of hockey doesn't come from meetings or textbooks or knowledge of other sports. It comes from childhood, from an experience ingrained in the culture of a nation. Just as all Americans of a certain age know where they were the day Kennedy was shot, so too do all Canadians know where they were the moment Henderson scored in Moscow. Bettman never grew up watching Harvey and Howe and Bentley and Mosienko. Hockey was Bettman's *job*, his *work*, his *obligation*. It was not his undying passion.

At the same time, it takes two to tango, and Bob Goodenow, who represented the players, received an almost equally rigid mandate from the NHLPA not to concede on any proposal that would limit salaries. For a long time, he didn't. The public will never know what went on during the months of sporadic meetings between the two men, but the end result was that the lockout wiped out half a season of hockey. Bettman failed miserably to do his job, and so did Goodenow. Each might call the other names or hold the other up to blame, but just as in playoff hockey, excuses at this level were unacceptable. The fact was that there was no hockey being played in the NHL for more than 100 days.

The '94–'95 season was full of hope and promise, not only for the Leafs but for many teams and for the NHL as a whole. The Rangers had won the Cup for the first time in half a century in a thrilling seven-game series and would enjoy playing the year as champions. The Blues signed Al MacInnis as a free agent, traded for Esa Tikkanen, and by hook and crook got Mike Keenan to leave his Cup in New York to coach St. Louis. Chicago had a brand new stadium. Vancouver was a goal away from calling themselves Stanley Cup winners. Quebec had a heart transplant with the trade for Wendel. The Islanders were hoping Brett Lindros would revive the franchise. Kirk Muller was the new captain in Montreal. San Jose was coming off a playoffs full of surprise and promise. Detroit finally had the goalie they were looking for in Mike Vernon. And the Leafs had a powerful, awesome lineup on paper that longed to be put to the test. They were that close to a Cup . . . maybe.

The league had expanded by five teams in the last three years, and their popularity and attendance were encouraging. The Fox network signed a deal worth more than $200 million for five years to televise games across the much coveted American airwaves, beginning with the All-Star game in San Jose on January 21, 1995.* And then came

---

* Of the approximately 25 games that Fox plans on showing, none involves a Canadian team.

the lockout. The owners went on strike, refusing to own such expensive stock as "players" who wanted to be less and less "owned" and better and better paid each year. The All-Star game was cancelled, the Rangers' hoisting of their Stanley Cup banner postponed, the Leafs' new roster left to gather dust.

It was not until Goodenow replaced Alan Eagleson as executive director of the NHLPA in January 1991 that full salary disclosure occurred. Up until that time Ray Bourque had no idea how much Al MacInnis or Paul Coffey or Phil Housley was making unless he was a good enough friend to phone and ask or the player was open enough to announce his contract through the press. Once all salaries became public, contracts shot sky high because players could compare what others on other teams at similar positions and skills were making and demand as much. Informal "levels" of pay evolved, based on league maximums.

The first level is reserved for the two most influential players in the league, Mario Lemieux and Wayne Gretzky. The other players accept and respect their incomparable value. The next level is the superstar, which consists of perhaps 10 men: Steve Yzerman, Mark Messier, Joe Sakic, Doug Gilmour, Brett Hull, Eric Lindros, Pierre Turgeon, Jeremy Roenick, Pat Lafontaine, Sergei Fedorov. All forwards, their presence is essential to the success of the team and the franchise. The next level is the offensive defencemen and highest ranked goalies such as MacInnis, Bourque, Housley, Coffey, Brian Leetch, Felix Potvin, Grant Fuhr, Ed Belfour, Chris Chelios, Bill Ranford, Scott Stevens, Mike Richter, Curtis Joseph, Kirk McLean, and Patrick Roy. Then comes the second rank of forwards, superb players who are, in all likelihood, third or fourth most important on a strong team or most important on weaker teams, players such as Adam Oates, Cam Neely, Alexander Mogilny, Gary Roberts, Joe Nieuwendyk, Mike Modano, Dino Ciccarelli, Dave Andreychuk, Alexandre Daigle, Mark Recchi, Mats Sundin, Mike Ricci, Brendan Shanahan, Pavel Bure, and Trevor Linden.

There are also levels for defensive defencemen such as Sylvain Lefebvre, Bob Rouse, Eric Desjardins, Mark Howe, Luke Richardson, Glen Wesley, and Marty McSorley. This group might even be divided according to fame and reputation. For instance, McSorley, who is better known but less skilled, would be in a higher salary bracket than Lefebvre. Another level is for fourth-line players, those checkers and penalty killers who are lesser lights but play a significant role nonetheless. Finally, there is another level for "enforcers."

Each player knows his role on the team and can demand a salary commensurate with anyone on another team who fills the same job description yet makes more money. The problem occurs when players judge their salaries against the highest in the league at their level or position, thereby boosting *every* salary to the highest level. Then when a contract expires, a team has to increase the high end of the salary in order to make a player feel wanted and more

important, as well as to prevent another team from taking him. Salaries increase again. Take, for example, Sergei Fedorov in Detroit. For the '92–'93 season he made $270,000, which was 18th on the *team* payroll led by Steve Yzerman with $1.5 million and Mark Howe with $1,050,000. During the year, Fedorov scored 34 goals and 87 points. In 1993–94, he made $295,000, 16th on the club's payroll led by Yzerman now making $3.2 million, Ciccarelli $1.4 million, and Coffey $1.3 million. But Fedorov had a phenomenal season, scoring 120 points and winning the Hart and Selke Trophies. His salary for '94–'95 shot through the roof to $2,750,000, second only to Yzerman's unchanged $3.2 million. From a superb, underpaid second-line centre he developed into a first-level superstar and his salary was raised accordingly. Fair is fair, but the tenfold increase is symptomatic of the unbelievable salary explosion that has occurred in just three years. The Leafs are a perfect example of the huge escalation, as their payrolls since Fletcher's arrival in 1991 attest:

1991–92		*1992–93*	
Ellett	$700,000	Fuhr	$1,600,000
Clark	600,000	Gilmour	1,000,000
Fuhr	503,750	Anderson	900,000
Leeman	460,000	Ellett	725,000
Krushelnyski	450,000	Clark	600,000
Marois	425,000	Macoun	550,000
Zezel	400,000	Rouse	475,000
Bullard	378,000	Krushelnyski	450,000
Anderson	350,000	Zezel	410,000
Gill	325,000	Wamsley	400,000
Petit	300,000	Osborne	400,000
Berube	290,000	Borschevsky	375,000
Foligno	280,000	Baumgartner	330,000
Linseman	265,000	Gill	325,000
Rouse	250,000	Mironov	309,000
Bradley	230,000	Foligno	280,000
Fergus	225,000	McLlwain	275,000
Shannon	200,000	Lefebvre	275,000
Halkidis	200,000	Halkidis	230,000
Loiselle	190,000	Shannon	225,000
Deblois	180,000	Sacco	225,000

Hannan	180,000	McGill	205,000
Godynyuk	160,000	McRae	185,000
Reese	145,000	Manderville	175,000
Cimetta	125,000	Berehowsky	175,000
Pearson	115,000	Potvin	145,000
		Eastwood	145,000
		Pearson	130,000
		Cimetta	130,000

1993–94		*1994–95*	
Gilmour	$3,000,000	Gilmour	$3,000,000
Anderson	1,250,000	Sundin	2,000,000
Potvin	1,200,000	Andreychuk	2,100,000
Andreychuk	1,200,000	Gartner	1,500,000
Clark	900,000	Potvin	1,400,000
Cullen	900,000	Ridley	1,000,000
Ellett	750,000	Ellett	1,000,000
Macoun	685,000	Butcher	750,000
Gill	675,000	Gill	725,000
Lefebvre	600,000	Craig	700,000
Zezel	530,000	Jonsson	700,000
Krushelnyski	475,000	Macoun	685,000
Osborne	425,000	Manderville	425,000
Rouse	425,000	Warriner	425,000
Berg	405,000	Mironov	404,000
Baumgartner	370,000	Borschevsky	380,000
Mironov	356,250	Baumgartner	370,000
Berehowsky	325,000	Berg	360,000
Borschevsky	300,000	Martin	325,000
Rhodes	300,000	Berehowsky	325,000
Govedaris	250,000	Eastwood	300,000
Perreault	225,000	Rhodes	300,000
Lacroix	200,000	Jablonski	250,000
Manderville	200,000	Lacroix	200,000
Eastwood	150,000		
Pearson	130,000		

Just four years ago, Dave Ellett was the highest paid Leaf with a salary of $700,000 a year. That figure would put him 10th on the Leafs' list in 1994–95 and 176th in the entire NHL.

The salary structure was further skewered by the Ottawa Senators when they signed Alexandre Daigle, the number one draft choice overall in 1993, to a five-year, $12.5 million contract before he had played even one game in the NHL. Number one draft picks in years to come would naturally want to use that salary as the basis for negotiation, and first- or second-year players already in the NHL would also want that kind of money if they outperformed Daigle. Up, up, and away go the figures. Where they stop, nobody knows.

Not unless the owners get their way. They felt the insanity must stop. While Bettman was doing his Bush-league bargaining (Read my lips: No salary cap), the owners were adamant about imposing some system whereby the team payroll is controlled. They claimed such a system was essential to their economic survival. The players did not believe that in a time of such prosperity their bosses could be in such dire straits. They argued that while the owners maintained they couldn't afford to shell out more money for huge contracts, they did so anyway. If the situation were so bad, how could St. Louis pay Al MacInnis $3.5 million a year, or Edmonton Bill Ranford $3 million, or Anaheim Paul (like Daigle, never played an NHL game) Kariya $2.8 million? The NHLPA said it would never accept a system that restricted salaries in any way.

However, the owners had no choice but to lure players by offering huge salaries. If a player became a free agent, and a team felt that he would help win the Stanley Cup, didn't the team owner owe it to the city, the fans, the other players on the club, to sign him? The owners *didn't* have a choice. If they lost a great player or refused to try to sign one, they were accepting mediocrity and cheating fans. Fans would stay away, the team would lose money, and then it wouldn't be able to afford *any* great players. Meanwhile, there would always be another team — Ottawa, Chicago, St. Louis — willing to sign those expensive superstars to absurd super-duper contracts, so no form of "unspoken collusion" would ever work.

In one way, the players took advantage of their situation. Not only were their salaries increasing, they were doing so artificially quickly because often players demanded that their contracts be *renegotiated*. They refused to show up to camp or they walked out during the year. Their displeasure was a veiled threat: "Give me more money or I'll play poorly and hurt the team." Or not play at all and hurt the team. Players as often *don't* honour the full term of their contract as do. If both players and owners were prohibited from renegotiating, then salaries would escalate (what the players want), but at a more acceptable pace (what the owners say they want).

Although they are often compared, baseball salaries and hockey salaries are as different as grass and ice. Most hockey rinks are close

to sold out each night of a season that has 40 home dates.* Extra revenue can be created almost exclusively by raising ticket prices. In baseball cities, where excellent crowds also attend each game, there are still often 5,000 or more seats empty because the stadiums are much bigger and the schedule has 81 home dates. To spend a huge sum on a free agent in baseball was worth it because a new star could generate thousands of added ticket sales by his very presence. Not so in hockey. There is more than a passing relationship between the "corporate boxes" that began to infest all hockey rinks during the last decade and the concurrent salary explosion. Boxes are sterile, ugly additions that detract from the thrill of appreciating the game close up, but they generate vast sums of money. In Toronto, for instance, Ballard *put in* more seats in the '60s to generate revenue, but Fletcher is now taking seats *out* to generate even more, through private boxes. Capacity at the Gardens is now down to 15,728 (13,000 season ticket holders) but there are 67 private boxes and 16 superboxes. The private boxes seat from 6 to 12 people; two of the superboxes hold 28, and the 14 others hold 14. All told, these hockey apartments are rented for between $45,000 to $185,000 a season and seat a total of 968 people. Where can teams go after boxes? Chicago, Boston, and Vancouver have one answer: build a new stadium and give the whole damn rink a sponsor. Chicago's United Centre, Boston's Shawmut Centre,** and Vancouver's General Motors Place, crass though the names may be, will provide the teams with millions of advertising dollars. Apparently, that's what the game has to be all about now. Forget character, atmosphere, tradition. Money now makes the hockey world go 'round.***

The very purpose of the NHLPA has been altered dramatically in the last few years. When Alan Eagleson began the association in 1967, players were mad as hell. They were underpaid, treated poorly, and had no pension to speak of, yet were the most important part of the game. All they really wanted was a raise and a modicum of respect. Today, the players have that and more, but they no longer want to

---

* Two other "home" dates are in neutral site arenas.

** Sponsored by the Shawmut Bank, which was bought out in March 1995 by the Fleet Bank. It might be renamed the Fleet Forum.

*** Even the dignified voice of the Leafs' public address announcer Paul Morris must now spit out promotions between play.

be paid well according to social standards and what they do; they want their salaries gauged by the owners' and league's profits. That's a completely different yardstick, and not entirely fair given the lucrative contracts they already receive. By hinging their salaries to team income, players want to create a win-win situation for themselves that is not enjoyed by the owners. Are players on teams that lose millions, for instance, prepared to help cover those losses? Would players on the Blackhawks, Bruins, and Canucks help pay for their new arenas?

During the lockout, it was almost exclusively the highest paid players who were at the bargaining table and news conferences. In the eyes of the media, they were, of course, the "desirables," the ones to be photographed and quoted. But they were also the men most affected by any salary or payroll restrictions. Would role players such as Bob Bassen be affected? Or Bob Errey or Cliff Ronning or Randy Burridge or Wayne McBean or Scott Thornton? Not nearly to the same extent as Gretzky, Messier, and Coffey. Of course, if the top-level salaries were capped, the trickle-down effect would also be noticeable, but on a much smaller scale. Could most people feel sorry for a player being "forced" to make no more than, say, $4 million a year, instead of $5 million or $6 million? Not likely.

Only the most élite players were offered contracts to play for teams in Sweden, Finland, Russia, Germany, and Switzerland, and while they were not making millions, the NHLers still lived very comfortably. On Wayne Gretzky's All-Star team that played club teams in Europe, for instance, each player received about $3,500 a game. For a seven-game series over two and a half weeks that's $24,500. But the NHL consists of 700 players. Only about 40 or so were playing for pay during the strike; the other 660 who don't make millions in the NHL (especially rookies and fringe players) were being deprived of half a year's salary.

What the players never lost sight of during the lockout was their simple love for the game. Many joined junior and university teams, played charity games with other NHLers, played because they missed it. While there were no league games, NHLers raised more than $1.5 million for charities, minor hockey, and community organizations, including $500,000 for Ronald McDonald's Children Charities from the four-on-four Challenge at Copps Coliseum in Hamilton. That was, finally, what hockey is all about. Playing.

As for the Leafs, only a handful of "stars" were active. Doug Gilmour played a dozen games for S C Rapperswil-Jona in Switzerland, earning about $3,000 a game (all of which he donated to the NHLPA); Todd Gill was part of Gretzky's European tour; Borschevsky went back to Russia and played eight games with Spartak and six more with a tour of stars from the former Soviet Union (only his insurance and plane ticket were paid for); Kenny Jonsson played eight games for his former club Rogle in Sweden until Christmas before rejoining the farm team in St. John's for six more after;

and Mats Sundin also played with his old club, Djurgarden.*

Why did these active players, the superstars, the best in the world, play for such small sums in Europe when they could have been earning 100 times that in the NHL? One reason: they looked behind them and saw many of the great players of yesterday living on skid row. For this disgrace, the owners had themselves to blame.

On October 22, 1992, Mr. Justice George Adams of the Ontario Court of Justice convicted the NHL owners of wrongfully "misdirecting" $25,000,000 from the players' pension fund, a decision that affected more than 700 NHLers who retired before 1982. The suit was originally filed by some of the biggest names in the game — Gordie Howe, Bobby Hull, Carl Brewer, Andy Bathgate, Allan Stanley, Eddie Shack, and Leo Reise. Only then did the public and current NHL players learn of just how little former greats received in pensions. Gordie Howe, who played 26 years in the league, was getting only $13,000 a year; Brewer, after 12 years, $6,200; Woody Dumart, 16 years, $5,500; Reggie Fleming, 12 years, $7,700; Andy Bathgate, 17 years, $10,200. The numbers were appalling, and were not indexed annually to inflation. In other words, Howe's $13,000 would be $13,000 next year, in five years, in 10 years, until the day he died. To make matters worse, instead of admitting their wrongdoing and trying to right a hideous wrong, the owners protracted the court battle and tried everything in their power to avoid the full payback. Not until February 1, 1995, did the NHL finally agree to remunerate the players, but the figure they came up with (including interest) was $33,301,000, some $9 million less than what the NHLPA was seeking ($42,160,251).** No wonder the present generation of skaters feels fear, animosity, even rage toward their bosses.

The owners' earning potential, unlike the players', is not restricted by time. The years of an NHLer's career resemble the birth and death of a child: Darryl Sittler, 1970–84; Bob McGill, 1981–93; Ian Turnbull, 1973–84. Players have only a few years to make their $3 million or $4 million a season. For the owners, only actual death and burial stop the money from coming in (at least in wealthy hockey towns). But what does a player do after the cheering has stopped and the millions of dollars are being paid to new, young stars? That's where the pension becomes so important.

Players are also cheated out of tens of millions of playoff dollars year after year, money they willingly sacrifice for a chance to play for the Stanley Cup. The money allocated for the 1994 playoffs is indicative of the monstrous monetary mistreatment that continues to this very day. The Leafs are unequivocally the most valuable team in the whole league come playoff time. *Hockey Night in Canada* draws

---

* Kent Manderville, because of his slow-healing wrist injury to his scaphoid bone, was the only Leaf to be paid by the club during the lockout until he was deemed fit on November 21, 1994. He "earned" $46,000.

** The Leafs have allocated $2.3 million for their share.

Mike Gartner at a press conference
during the 1994-95 owners' lockout.
PETER TYM / THE GLOBE AND MAIL

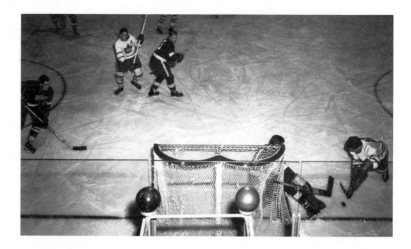

IMPERIAL OIL / TUROFSKY COLLECTION / HOCKEY HALL OF FAME

its biggest crowds by far when they play, generating untold sums from advertising revenues and other sources. Yet after they had played 18 games and lost to Vancouver in the semifinals, the entire Leaf team received only $550,000. Divide this by 20 — the number of players — and the figure is reduced to $27,500, or $1,430 per player per game. Even the Cup-winning New York Rangers got only $1,250,000 as a team, still less than $3,000 per man a game. To say that the players are underpaid in the playoffs is to underscore the unfairness of the revenue-salary relationship (during both the regular season and the playoffs) and to highlight how much the Cup means in symbolic terms.

For the owners, the lockout was about one thing: power. Power is how the owners became wealthy enough to pay $50 million to $100 million for a franchise in the first place, and that's how they're used to maintaining control — with an iron grip. What they refuse to accept is that while they may have gotten very rich through other business ventures, their prime assets in the NHL — hockey players — are not labourers and factory workers. They can't be "controlled." Monetarily the lockout made no sense since both sides lost huge sums. In Toronto, Gilmour lost more than $1 million in pay and the Gardens lost about $8.5 million in operating income,* which means a final loss of $1.9 million for shareholders of MLG Ltd. From the sickening perspective of dollars, it would have been better to play and disagree and make money than *not* to play and disagree and *not* make money.

But the only thing the players can't do that the owners can is *own*. That's what the money-men wanted to accomplish with the lockout, to show that they *own* the buildings, the teams, the players them-

---

* Including more than $5 million in refunds to subscribers.

selves. Retail sales of NHL merchandise were almost $1.5 *billion* in 1994, a 37% increase over the previous year and almost 10 times what sales were just four years earlier. With this figure in mind, $3 million or $4 million for Dougie or Messier seems like pretty small potatoes.

Arguments abound for both players and owners, but both sides should have wakened up long ago to the realization of just how good they have it. Players talked about "solidarity"? That was a Polish slogan for the pre-perestroika struggle against Communism. It was about putting bread on the table and making working conditions bearable. Bettman called the NHL a "business" and an "industry"? Those were terms appropriate for Ford, IBM, and Shell. Hockey is a game. It's fun to play, and it's fun to watch. Players are called players because they *play*. The Stanley Cup is a trophy and is coveted because of its history. All the rest is secondary. Bettman and Goodenow were most at fault for their nonchalance, their total lack of urgency in settling the dispute. A deal was reached only when the entire season was threatened. Until that time both sides were prepared to wait and do nothing. Had both men imposed a much earlier cancel-the-season deadline, fans would have had hockey much earlier and the owners a much longer (i.e., more profitable) schedule.

On the night of September 26, 1994, the Leafs played the Blackhawks at the Gardens in Toronto's 9th and final game of the preseason. The game was tied 1–1 and went into overtime. With less than half a minute to go, Mike Ridley drove to the net, and as Gill took a slap shot he was able to tip it past Belfour for the win. That was the last time the Leafs scored for 116 days. Time of the goal: 1994.

1917–18 Toronto St. Pats
(Stanley Cup Champions) salary list:

Harry Holmes	$700
Hugh Cameron	900
Harry Mummery	600
Ken Randall	550
Reg Noble	700
Samuel Crawford	700
John Adams	900
Corb Denneny	500
Alfie Skinner	450
Harry Meeking	450

The St. Pats beat the Vancouver Millionaires 3–2 in the best-of-five finals. As champions, each player received an additional $350.

The newest Leafs, May 1995.
GRAIG ABEL

XVI

What's Next?

On January 13, 1995, the owners finally unlocked the doors. They got a rookie salary cap, and free agency was increased to the ripe old age of 32 (the players had wanted 30). The deal would last until the year 2000, but both sides would have the option to re-open negotiations after the '96–'97 season (the owners most certainly will). But the strides made in "labour negotiations" were certainly not worth the scars that were left by the loss of 36 regular season games. Leaf tickets went on sale January 19 for a 48-game schedule that would be shoved into 105 days. The last time teams played 48 games (over a decent 139 days) was back in 1941–42. This time, the Leafs would not play the Habs, Bruins, or Rangers even once in this sickly amputated season. (In '41–'42, the Leafs played these three clubs *23* times.) Can such a schedule truly be called a hockey season?

Leafs' schedule: 1995

Jan. 20	at Los Angeles	Mar. 11	Chicago
Jan. 21	at San Jose	Mar. 13	Los Angeles
Jan. 25	Vancouver	Mar. 15	at San Jose
Jan. 27	at Chicago	Mar. 17	at Anaheim
Jan. 28	Calgary	Mar. 18	at Los Angeles
Jan. 30	at Dallas	Mar. 21	at Vancouver
Feb. 1	at Vancouver	Mar. 24	Winnipeg
Feb. 3	at Edmonton	Mar. 25	at Winnipeg
Feb. 4	at Calgary	Mar. 27	Edmonton
Feb. 6	San Jose	Mar. 31	at Chicago
Feb. 8	Dallas	Apr. 3	at St. Louis
Feb. 10	at Detroit	Apr. 5	St. Louis
Feb. 11	Los Angeles	Apr. 7	Detroit
Feb. 13	Chicago	Apr. 8	Winnipeg

Feb. 15	Edmonton	Apr. 14	Dallas
Feb. 18	St. Louis	Apr. 15	at Winnipeg
Feb. 20	Detroit	Apr. 17	at Chicago
Feb. 22	at Detroit	Apr. 19	Anaheim
Feb. 23	Anaheim	Apr. 21	at St. Louis
Feb. 25	Winnipeg	Apr. 22	at Dallas
Feb. 27	at St. Louis	Apr. 26	Vancouver
Mar. 2	San Jose	Apr. 29	at Calgary
Mar. 4	Calgary	May 1	at Edmonton
Mar. 8	Dallas	May 3	at Anaheim

During the ridiculous process of resolving the lockout, the atmosphere at the Gardens remained upbeat, thanks to the respect and trust between Steve Stavro, Cliff Fletcher, and Mike Gartner. Stavro did everything he could to get the game back on ice, and Fletcher's

Action during the Leaf home opener, January 25, 1995.
DOUG MACLELLAN / HOCKEY HALL OF FAME

was one of the few voices of reason during usually inane negotiations. Not surprisingly, he was eliminated from the resolution process by the owners during the endgame because he was seen as too conciliatory. Gartner, as the NHLPA's president, played his role between Leaf management and players diplomatically, so that by the time the season was back on, no acrimony was felt by either players or management. At the Gardens, if nowhere else in North America, the desire to play the game ruled supreme.

Training camp lasted but a few days and players began the season way out of game shape. The insane travel schedule merely exacerbated, or exposed, their way-out-of-shapeness. For the Leafs, the adjustment to the shortened year was going to be greater than any other top team in the league. Having made the most player changes, they were the team that most needed time to gel. But there was no time. New line combinations had to click quickly and players had to familiarize themselves with each other's moves and styles instantly. If this didn't happen, losses would mount. Playing half a schedule meant one loss was like two in a normal season since there was only half the time to recoup the points.

The fans had acclimatized themselves only too quickly to winning, thanks to Borschevsky's great goal in Detroit in Game 7 in 1993. But while the atmosphere at the Gardens and in the city was positive, the early season game results reflected more the players' unfamiliarity with each other than the union solidarity from the lockout. At first, none of the drastic changes Fletcher had made went smoothly for the Leafs. Burns spent much of the first half of the season changing lines, putting new players in and taking other new players out, trying to find the best possible matchups, and trying to *establish* a chemistry that had been so naturally present the last couple of years. (While they had at one time seven Stanley Cup winners on the team, they now had just two — Gilmour and Macoun.) Practice time was nonexistent, and player camaraderie was slow to develop because of the strain in the early part of the playoff-pace schedule — 21 games in 38 days. The 10–0 perfect start to the '93–'94 season seemed like eons ago as a new series of worries concerned the club.

Small deals and injuries played further havoc with Burns' team, as did the shift in roles that the established Leafs had to adjust to with this very new hockey club. Just days after the lockout ended, Fletcher claimed Randy Wood from Buffalo for $10,000 in the waiver draft.* To add insult, no sooner had the season started than the injuries came. Berg suffered a partial tear in the anterior cruciate ligament of his right knee, which in layman's terms meant eight weeks without hockey. Ken Baumgartner signed a new three-year contract and then

---

* In a more minor deal, Yanic Perreault was sent to the Kings for future considerations.

separated his shoulder in the second game of the half-year (gone three to four months), and Gartner's lung collapsed after a late, clean hit by Bryan Marchment in Edmonton, that ghost-hockey town where only Stanley Cup champions are supported (Montreal west). All of a sudden, Hendrickson and Warriner were playing in the Gardens, not on the Rock, and Fletcher traded with the Kings to get proverbial tough guy Warren Rychel for a 4th-round pick in '95. Later, Butcher missed some games with back spasms, Ellett cracked a bone in his foot after blocking a shot, Gill hurt his shoulder, and Mike Craig broke a finger. Ken Belanger and Matt Martin were also recalled from St. John's, and now more than half of the starting lineup had not been with the Leafs the night Vancouver eliminated them from the '94 playoffs.

Toronto opened the season with seven of their first nine games on the road, spread out over two trips out west. In the season opener, they let a 3–2 second period lead in Los Angeles fade into a 3–3 tie. The next night in San Jose the whole team played very well except for one player — new defenceman Kenny Jonsson. Twice he tripped out of context, just fell down in open ice, to give Ray Whitney and then Jeff Friesen breakaways. Both scored and San Jose won 3–2. The hasty consensus was that Jonsson needed to learn how to skate before he could play in the NHL. After sitting out the next two games, however, Jonsson atoned for his early misgivings. He and partner Dave Ellett (until he got hurt) proved to be far and away the Leafs' best defencemen, and by the halfway point in the schedule talk of "rookie of the year" was heard in the same sentence as "Kenny Jonsson."

With each game, the Leafs struggled to find their form. They consistently played inconsistent hockey that kept them in the middle of the standings, floundering at .500 — a now barely acceptable level of performance to Torontonians. They beat Vancouver 6–2, lost to Chicago 4–1, beat Calgary 2–1, lost to them 4–1. For every win there was a loss, for every step forward a step back. For every game the Leafs broke out and scored a few, they followed with a drought. Each time they played solid defence, they came back with a weak, run-ning-all-over-the-place effort.

And so the season went. A playoff spot was virtually certain, but the accomplishment was not achieved with the same confidence as the last two runs at the Cup. Potvin in goal was his usual great, idiosyncratic self, always on all fours, stick laid across the crease, forever looking behind him for shots everyone but he himself knew he had saved. He kept the Leafs in most games the team played, and although Trevor Kidd has now developed into a superb goalie in Calgary, no one in these parts can ever regret Floyd Smith's decision to choose the Cat in that great '90 draft. But Rhodes, too, was playing well, maybe even better than Potvin. He didn't make an appearance until the 12th game of the year, a 2–1 win in Detroit, but in mid-March he started four in a row as the Leafs put together a bit

of a streak. Always more technically skilled than Potvin, Rhodes was again proving his tremendous talent.* His average was lower than Potvin's, and his save percentage was second in the league.

Chemistry is like God. Once you've found it, all your problems are solved. But until then, the world is a confusing place to be. The Leafs' defence had yet to find that God on ice. The loss of the great defenders — Lefebvre and Rouse — had an enormous impact on the whole Leaf defensive unit. Garth Butcher's play was inconsistent — not tough enough in front of the net, easily eluded along the boards, too slow in open ice, not disciplined enough without the puck. To compensate, his partner Jamie Macoun tried to do too much, getting far away from his meticulously consistent game. As a result, this veteran defensive pairing didn't provide that solid, stabilizing nucleus that could be used in all important situations. Further, the weaknesses of Mironov became all the more glaring. On the power play point, he continued *not* to shoot the puck, even though that was his only talent. And Todd Gill looked around the dressing room and was too conscious of the fact that he was the most senior Leaf on the team. He played with a burden of responsibility far beyond what he had to do to be the excellent player he had been the last two years. Berehowsky found himself in a Catch-22 position. He didn't play particularly well, but he was being used only sporadically. He couldn't develop and mature from the press box or the end of the bench, but Burns couldn't risk giving him a regular shift; the season was simply too short to train inexperienced players.

The era of Dougie had begun inauspiciously. He was asked to shoulder even more responsibility than in his previous two years with the Leafs. Without the captaincy his role on the team and in the city was big enough. But without Wendel to act as comrade and buffer for all the various pressures, his job became a burden. He didn't become just the toast of the town; he was the jam, the plate, the table, the whole damn house. His face was on billboards everywhere; his "cow" legs, advertising milk, were as popular as cows themselves, and the line for the accompanying television commercial — "Hey, Dougieeee!" — uttered by a teammate in that macho/geeky hockey voice was as frequently coined as Lanny's gruff "Meeeoowww" was for Swanson TV dinners 18 years earlier. He was the captain, the leader, the focus.

During the short season Burns played him with just about every possible combination, at first to lukewarm effect. Andreychuk couldn't score for the longest time and was relegated to the second line. Gartner was put with Dougie, but his injury forced lineup changes until his return. Sundin, however, showed beyond all doubt his remarkable talent as Gilmour's left-winger. He was huge, strong,

---

* By this time, Pat Jablonski had been loaned to Team USA for the world championships in Stockholm.

physical. His hands were as soft as butter, his shot hard and deadly accurate. He was certainly not the physically intimidating force Wendel was, but Sundin's offensive contribution saved the team on a number of nights, most memorably against Dallas when he scored with 1.8 Bettman-seconds left in regulation to give the Leafs a 3–3 tie at the Gardens.

The problem with the other forwards, particularly Ridley and Craig (Fletcher's other major off-season moves), was consistency. In the Leafs' first visit to Vancouver in mid-January, Toronto fell behind 4–1 after two periods but rallied on goals by Craig, Gartner, and Ridley in the third to get a point. This was the kind of scoring outburst the Leafs were hoping they had acquired. But just like the rest of the team, for every explosion there was a span of three or four games without a goal, and the defensive intensity behind their own blueline was equally inconsistent. The great irony was that Fletcher had inadvertently created the same problem he had last year and the year before. As Dougie went, so went the team. And, since he was in mid-gear most of the year, so too was the team. Borschevsky was, sadly, playing himself off the team, and the other new faces weren't picking up the slack. Although they were still unaccustomed to each other, Gilmour, Sundin, and Gartner would be superb together by the playoffs, but Sundin was supposed to be a second centre, not another winger for Dougie. On the second line, though, he had no one to pass to and no one to pass to him. That left Andreychuk in the lurch on the second line and put extra pressure on his linemates Ridley and Wood. This trio could create a superb unit — on paper it certainly reads well — but Ridley was the key. He had to get the wingers the puck, but the wingers, primarily Andreychuk, had to play with the toughness and commitment needed to get those passes. As Burns repeated through much of the season, the "passion" just wasn't there yet, in the dressing room or on the ice, and the team's terrible road record — they didn't get their fifth win until mid-April — confirmed Burns' assessment.

The players had to want to win for themselves and their coach. In February, Burns' boys played without Potvin (he was being rested for the first time in a dozen games) and Dougie (a slight neck injury) and played a superbly inspired game that got them a 2–1 win in Detroit. This could have been used as a chance to establish momentum, but the next night they were blown away 5–2 by the Kings at the Gardens. It was a loss only too easily explained: the Leafs were playing their third game in four nights; the Kings, their first in six days. The next game two days later seemed to confirm the fatigue excuse. They beat the Blackhawks 4–2 in a thorough and impressive win. Sundin had two goals, Ridley one and an assist, and Potvin was excellent.

But two nights later they failed to build from those strong wins, losing handily to Edmonton 4–1. They played without fire, determination, character. The record slid back to .500. A 3–1 win over St.

Louis was followed by a 4–2 loss to Detroit. .500. Detroit won 4–1; Toronto beat Anaheim 3–1. .500. They beat Winnipeg 5–2, lost to the Blues 3–2. .500. And so went the games. (But a Montreal loss was almost as good as a Leaf win, so it was just as fun to watch the Habs lose five games in a row, including a 7–0 embarrassment to the Philly Flyers before a hostile Forum crowd.)

The Sundin-Clark trade took a rather bad public relations turn when Quebec and Wendel shot to the top of the league. The lockout had allowed Clark to recover from his head injury, and after 27 games he was averaging nearly a point a game and infusing in the team exactly the character he had provided in Toronto. Sundin started off equally well in a Leaf uniform, but the mediocre team results meant the deal was viewed with even greater scepticism, if not downright hostility. Too, the team fighting the Nordiques for first place overall was the Pittsburgh Penguins who were helped enormously by John Cullen's 30 points in 30 games. (Cullen had been released outright by the Leafs during the summer.)

The '95 Leafs had superb talent, but this talent had yet to cohere. While the media spread damaging gossip of dissension and trade (Berehowsky wanted out; Ridley was on the block; Rhodes was on his way), the team needed to become emotionally stronger. If this didn't happen, the chemistry of the club would be further eroded and the season all for nought. Perhaps the biggest loss of the season was the early absence of Berg, whose guts and determination were exactly what had been lacking. The first game back for Berg was also the first for Rich Sutter whom Fletcher had acquired from Tampa Bay for future considerations. (This spelled the end for Terry Yake, who cleared NHL waivers and was demoted to St. John's.) With Manderville, they formed a perfect fourth line that produced a much needed, grinding 2–1 win in San Jose, followed by a 3–3 tie in Anaheim and an impressive 5–3 win over Los Angeles. (Only a 3–1 loss to Vancouver soured an otherwise positive four-game western road trip.) With a fourth line that could check and move people off the puck, the games became a little more open for Gilmour, Sundin, and Ridley, all of whom started to play in mid-season form and develop the toughness needed for the playoffs. The next four games produced two more wins and ties, but then three consecutive losses put their record back to .500.

The shortened season meant less time — less time for the coach, less time for the players, and less time for the Silver Fox. The trade deadline was Friday, April 7, 3:00 p.m. EST and Fletcher was the most active in the league, making five deals: from the Islanders he obtained Benoit Hogue, a 3rd-round draft in 1995 and a 5th in '96 for superb goalie prospect Eric Fichaud; Borschevsky went to Calgary for a 6th-round choice in '96; Paul DiPietro came from Montreal for a 4th-rounder in '95, '96, or '97; tough guy Grant Jennings arrived from Pittsburgh for Drake Berehowsky; and Mike Eastwood was sent to Winnipeg with a 3rd-round choice in '95 for another

scrapper, Tie Domi.* For the second time in eight months, the starting roster had been dramatically altered, this time with only a dozen games left in the regular season. The first of those came the night of the deadline and saw the awesome Red Wings blow the newest Leafs away 4–2 at the Gardens. Gilmour broke his nose badly, and Domi pulled a thigh muscle, and the lineup looked a hodge-podge of great skill and total unfamiliarity. The addition of three tough players — Rychel, Domi, and Jennings — indicated just how much Wendel has been missed, but most confusing of all was the team's incredible scoring drought that lasted all season. With Gilmour, Andreychuk, Sundin, Gartner, Ridley, Hogue, Wood, and Craig, the team averaged less than three goals a game. This drought, however, was attributable as much to the Leafs' greatest weakness, its defence, as it was to any lost scoring touch of the scorers. Without Rouse and Lefebvre to get the puck quickly out of the Leaf end, the whole team played much more behind its own blueline. No one can score from there. Unfortunately, this was the one area Fletcher was not able to improve by the trading deadline, and his letting go of Berehowsky proved just how frustrating the position had been. The biggest problem of all was time. There was none of it for the 13 new faces to get used to each other.

On September 6, 1993, Fletcher made a three-year, $250,000 commitment to the International Hockey Centre of Excellence at the new Hockey Hall of Fame to help develop hockey at its earliest stages. This donation helped solidify a vital connection between the Hall and the Leafs, one that should become even stronger and closer. The new Hall is located at Yonge and Front Streets, just three subway stops from the Gardens, in and underneath the old Bank of Montreal building built in 1885–86. The Hall's revitalization has been a crucial factor in linking the new Leafs to the old tradition of Smythe and the virtues of the Original Six. It used to be located at the Canadian National Exhibition on lands donated by the City of Toronto. It was opened on August 26, 1961, by Prime Minister John Diefenbaker, and 43 players were inducted during the inaugural ceremony.** At first, it was only open during the three weeks of the "Ex," but later stayed open on weekends all year and finally, as its popularity grew and grew, opened daily. There was never an admission charge, and it had 7,000 square feet of display space for exhibiting artifacts and memorabilia.

As everything in hockey expanded in the '70s of Orr and the '80s of the Oilers, the Hall outgrew its location. It was inconvenient to

---

* Fletcher also signed free-agent right winger Jamie Heward to a two-year contract. Heward, Pittsburgh's first-round draft choice in 1989, is currently playing with the national team.

** Including the Leafs' Syl Apps, Charlie Conacher, Hap Day, and George Hainsworth.

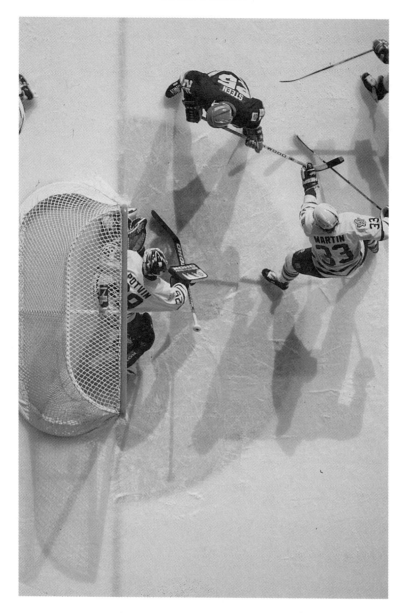

The Jets' Thomas Steen and Leafs' Matt Martin
battle in front of Potvin's crease.
DOUG MACLELLAN / HOCKEY HALL OF FAME

get to, and most of its collection was in storage as donations rapidly
exceeded space. A new building and better location were necessary.
In July 1988, with the support of Mayor Art Eggleton, Toronto City
Council approved a 99-year lease for the use of the Bank of Montreal, designated by the Toronto Historical Board for its architectural
significance. The new space would provide an incredible 51,000

square feet of display space and be located in the heart of Canada's largest city. Its success was inevitable.

The CNE Hall closed its doors forever on December 31, 1992. The new Hall opened its doors on June 18, 1993. It immediately established itself as one of the most popular attractions in the city, and the Great Hall that is the old bank area itself is the finest trophy room anywhere. Fletcher has used the Hall on a number of occasions for press conferences and other Leaf events, and the Hall in turn has set up a number of mini-displays during games at the Gardens. The connection is further enhanced by Ron Ellis, one of the key public relations men at the Hall and of course an integral part of the Leafs' Alumni.*

The new Hockey Hall of Fame.

By the time former Leaf president Donald Giffin lost his battle with cancer on March 20, 1992, he could see that the entire "institution" called the Toronto Maple Leafs had been reborn. Burns and Gilmour are extraordinarily popular figures in the city and can be seen on billboards and commercials left, right, and centre. Jerseys, hats, and licence plates bearing the Leaf emblem dot the downtown on a crowded Saturday afternoon, and bumper stickers boast "My Canada Includes Wendel." Burns' team motto of "DON'T JUST PLAY . . . COMPETE" is emblazoned on the walls of the Leaf dressing room and in the soul of each of the team's players. As is his explanation: "Ability and speed and muscle matter in this league as they always have, but the teams that show up and compete the most nights are the ones at the top of the ladder." Burns' ability to make hockey a

---

* For instance, in June 1993 he escorted 100 Booster Club members on a personal tour of the Hockey Hall.

DOUG MACLELLAN / HOCKEY HALL OF FAME

team game, to get the most out of each individual for the good of the club, is indisputably in the Imlach tradition of genius. To be sure, defeat does not rest lightly on his shoulders.

The lobby of Maple Leaf Gardens has a huge blue Leaf on the floor and a great Art Deco reproduction clock in front. Below the clock are glass doors through which you can see the ice and arena, and no more magical, spine-tingling view is there in any stadium. (Unfortunately, a computer pixelboard blunts the effect as yet more advertisements announce upcoming events.) Past the turnstiles is a Captain's Wall, where the 17 leaders from the team's 68 years are represented. Elsewhere superb vintage colour photographs of great Leafs enhance your walk through the most hallowed halls in hockey history. The Stanley Cup banners that grace the rafters look simple and elegant, and are warm testaments to the team, its achievements, its tradition, its glory. On March 11, 1995, before the game against Chicago, the Leafs celebrated the achievements of the great Turk Broda (1936–43 and 1945–52) and Johnny Bower (1958–70), raising their number 1 to the rafters to join Syl Apps and Ted Kennedy as "honoured" Leafs. Future honourees from the '67 Cup team are still many — Armstrong, Kelly, Keon, Baun, Stanley, Mahovlich, and perhaps most notably Tim Horton and his number 7,* if for no other reason than to complement Buffalo's plans to retire Horton's num-

---

* Also worn by Clancy, Bentley, Primeau, and McDonald.

ber in the Aud in the very near future. Horton still holds the Leafs' iron man record — 486 games — which lasted from 1961 to 1968, but perhaps the ultimate compliment came from Gordie Howe who called him the strongest player he ever saw (i.e., in the history of the game). The Leafs plan to honour two players a year, and after the '67 greats is a list equally long: Primeau, Davidson, Sittler, Salming . . .

The great Leafs of Imlach's '60s are now the great Alumni of the '90s. Armstrong is a scout, Ellis is at the Hall, and Harris is the old-timers' organizer. Darryl Sittler works at the Gardens, and everyone else is more than welcome to stop by and say hello. The game is different now. There are too many teams to know *all* the players, and teams in non-hockey towns have been awarded franchises that the owners will have to move in a few years once the novelty of the game has worn off. Commentators today no longer have the luxury of saying, "He shoots; he scores." The play is too quick to allow for such wordiness.

Players are in immaculate, flawless physical condition. Goalies have water bottles on top of their nets and cameras inside them. Instant replays decide goals after they've been scored, perhaps after another goal at the other end has been scored. The equipment the players wear is lighter, more sophisticated and stylish, like the latest fashions from Paris and Milan. Shiny sticks are all the vogue, and the bright lights of the television-exposed arenas cast a Hollywood pall over what was once just a simple rink, an icy battlefield. Ravina Gardens and the Mutual Street Arena have been reduced to photographs, and Alan Eagleson from prosecutor to defendant (after being charged with racketeering, fraud, and embezzlement by the U.S. government). But the Leafs, though of vastly different emotional and social stock from their boyhood idols, have been sitting on the same Leaf bench for 60 years, playing basically the same game, while the society they live in outside the midsummer night's Gardens has changed dramatically.

During the lockout, the CBC rebroadcast a small number of "classic" games, culminating in a playoff match from April 14, 1959, at the Gardens, Game 3 of the finals between the Habs and the Leafs. To watch that game was not so much a lesson in history as an eye-opener as to just how good the hockey was 35 years ago. Only the television cameras were ancient. Bill and Foster Hewitt were at the mike (they had to share), and the game featured players who could beat any team from this mid-'90s, 26-team league. Although they looked smaller and the rink proportionately bigger, the game was much faster. There was no hooking and grabbing and slashing to slow a player down, no cheap, expansion team "trap." If you wanted to catch your man, you had to *skate* to him.

To see the Big M wind up in his own end was to watch the origin of speed. When you saw Bower and Plante in the nets without masks, you winced and flinched at their poise and almost stupid bravery. You could *see* their emotions in their faces! You never knew Dick Duff

skated that quickly or Pulford that smoothly, and you understood why Harvey, that huge, cool enigma on the Montreal blueline, had the reputation of greatness he had. The players finished their checks and the checks were hard. There were very few offsides, play went on for minutes at a time, and when the puck was held in the corners the whistle blew before a scrum developed. The players, though without names on the back of their jerseys, became identifiable after one shift, one reference by the Hewitts, and even though you knew the Leafs had won 3–2 in overtime, the excitement was fantastic. When Duff ripped a slapper past a surprised Plante at 10:06 of the overtime, the noise from the crowd was deafening. The ending *defined* the Stanley Cup tradition.

New Leaf Paul DiPietro in action against the
Canucks during the final game of the regular season.
GRAIG ABEL

While Fletcher's tenure with the Leafs was very much up in the air when he first got to Toronto in 1991, his job is now the personification of secure. On October 4, 1994, he signed a new contract that will take him through to the summer of 1999, which he has said will be his last year in hockey: "Realistically, when this contract expires that will probably be it. I'll be 63. To finish my career as a Toronto Maple Leaf will just be terrific. There's so much going on here; it's rejuvenated my career. I'm just happy to be a part of it."* Ironically, Steve Stavro is in the other boat. If the Public Trustee gets its way, he could be legally forced to sell his tentative ownership of the Leafs. It will be a divisive battle that might well send the club into disarray, albeit through little fault of Stavro's.

Even as Fletcher builds a Cup-winning team for today, he is forever conscious of his long-term plans. In a March 1995 interview, he wrote down a number of Leaf names on a piece of paper. "This is what the team for the 1997–98 season should look like," he said, hiding the paper. "I can tell you that only seven players from this year's roster will be included. I'll give you three names from this season's team who I'm counting on. They are Potvin, Sundin, and Jonsson." The names connect only too clearly the past to the future. Leaf success has always hinged on great goalies, from Hainsworth to Chabot to Broda to Bower and now to Potvin. Too, the Swedish pair of Sundin and Jonsson eclipses in talent the ground-breaking discoveries of Salming and Hammarstrom more than 20 years earlier, and maintains a vital connection between Sweden and the Leafs that will only get stronger with Anders Hedberg as scout (although Ballard refused to sign him and Ulf Nilsson as players, Fletcher was only too happy to do so as scout).

In three years the Leafs have become once again a vital member of the Stanley Cup playoffs, and tradition and organizational professionalism have been resurrected by Stavro and Fletcher. The Leafs haven't won a Cup — they have no laurels upon which to rest yet — but the fans are eager and impatient and all signs point to "when," not "if." The Leafs no longer need to rely on Central Scouting or guesswork to determine the skill of a player. Fletcher's scouting staff is now 13 men strong and the most comprehensive in the NHL.** In the "Births" section of the *Toronto Sun* on December 6, 1994, the

---

* Six weeks later he joined the board of directors of Mackenzie Financial Corporation, a testament to his reputation as a businessman and as an ambassador for the Leafs.

** Floyd Smith is the Director of Player Development; George Armstrong and Doug Woods cover the OHL; Garth Malarchuk, the WHL; Dick Bouchard, the WHL Eastern Division, Manitoba, Saskatchewan, and Minnesota high schools; Ernie Gare, WHL Western Division and British Columbia; Bob Johnson, the QMJHL; Dan Marr, North American colleges and junior leagues; John Choyce, the pro leagues; Anders Hedberg, Europe; Peter Johnson, the U.S.; Jack Gardiner, U.S. colleges and New England high schools.

happy parents of a new son began their announcement this way: "Attn: Cliff Fletcher/A Future All-Star is Born!" If there's a grain of truth to that, you just know a Leaf scout in some Spadina Avenue suit will watch the kid play in some cold, small-time Scarborough arena in 15 or 16 years. Afterwards, he'll go to the dressing room and introduce himself to the pock-marked, teenaged child-star: "Kid, how'd you like to play for the Toronto Maple Leafs?"

"Sure, Mister."

24   JACK ADAMS
ST. PATRICKS - TORONTO
National Hockey League

HOCKEY HALL OF FAME

Appendix

Tim Horton.
HOCKEY HALL OF FAME

1977 —	Tim Horton (1949–70)
1978 —	Andy Bathgate (1964–65)
	Jacques Plante (1970–73)
	Marcel Pronovost (1965–70)
1980 —	Harry Lumley (1952–56)
1981 —	Allan Stanley (1958–68)
	Frank Mahovlich (1956–68)
1982 —	Norm Ullman (1968–75)
1984 —	Bernie Parent (1971–72)
1985 —	Gerry Cheevers (1961–62)
	Bert Olmstead (1958–62)
1986 —	Leo Boivin (1951–54)
	Dave Keon (1960–75)
1989 —	Darryl Sittler (1970–82)
1990 —	Fernie Flaman (1950–54)
	Bud Poile (1942–47)
1991 —	Bob Pulford (1956–70)
1992 —	Frank Mathers (1948–50, 1951–52)
	Lanny McDonald (1973–79)
1994 —	Harry Watson (1946–55)

APPENDIX

BUILDERS

1947 —	William A. Hewitt
1958 —	Conn Smythe
1960 —	Frank J. Selke
1965 —	Foster Hewitt
1977 —	Harold Ballard
1978 —	J.P. Bickell
1984 —	Punch Imlach
1985 —	Rudy Pilous

Retired Numbers

5 —	Bill Barilko (1946–51)
6 —	Ace Bailey (1927–34)

HOCKEY HALL OF FAME

Honoured Numbers

Sweater stays in use but is honoured by a banner in the
rafters and a special shoulder patch on the current jersey

1 —	Turk Broda (1936–43, 1945–52) and Johnny Bower (1958–70)
9 —	Syl Apps (1936–43, 1945–48)
10 —	Ted Kennedy (1942–57)

Stanley Cup Champions

1914: *Toronto Blueshirts* (National Hockey Association)

Harry Holmes, Jack Marshall (player/manager), Harry Cameron, Frank Foyston, Alan Davidson (captain), Jack Walker, Cully Wilson, Roy McGiffen, George McNamara, Con Corbeau, Frank and Dick Carroll (trainers)

1918: *Toronto Arenas* (first team from the NHL to win the Cup)

Harry Holmes, Harry Mummery, Harry Cameron, Reg Noble, Alf Skinner, Harry Meeking, Rusty Crawford, Corbett Denneny, Ken Randall, Jack Adams, Sammy Hebert, Jack Coughlin, Jack Marks, Charlie Querrie (manager), Dick Carroll (coach), Frank Carroll (trainer)

1922: *Toronto St. Pats*

> John Ross Roach, Bill Stuart, Harry Cameron, Eddie Gerard, Corbett Denneny, Cecil "Babe" Dye, Reg Noble, Ken Randall, Lloyd Andrews, Rod Smylie, Stan Jackson, Theodore Stackhouse, Nolan Mitchell, Charlie Querrie (manager), Eddie Powers (coach), Bill Popp (trainer)

The Toronto Maple Leafs outside the newly-built Maple Leaf Gardens, 1934.
HOCKEY HALL OF FAME

1932: *Toronto Maple Leafs*

> Charlie Conacher, Harvey Jackson, King Clancy, Andy Blair, Red Horner, Lorne Chabot, Alex Levinsky, Joe Primeau, Harold Darragh, Hal Cotton, Frank Finnigan, Hap Day, Ace Bailey, Bob Gracie, Fred Robertson, Conn Smythe (manager), Dick Irvin (coach), Tim Daly (trainer)

1942: *Toronto Maple Leafs*

> Reg Hamilton, Wally Stanowski, Syl Apps, Bob Goldham, Gord Drillon, Hank Goldup, Ernie Dickens, Dave Schriner, Bucko McDonald, Bob Davidson, Nick Metz, Bingo Kampman, Don Metz, Gaye Stewart, Turk Broda, Johnny McCreedy, Lorne Carr, Peter Langelle, Billy Taylor, Conn Smythe (manager), Hap Day (coach), Frank Selke (business manager), Tim Daly (trainer)

1945: *Toronto Maple Leafs*

> Don Metz, Frank McCool, Wally Stanowski, Reg Hamilton, Elwyn Morris, Johnny McCreedy, Tommy O'Neill, Ted Kennedy, Babe Pratt, Gus Bodnar, Art Jackson, Jack McLean, Mel Hill, Nick Metz, Bob Davidson, Dave Schriner, Lorne Carr, Conn Smythe (manager), Hap Day (coach), Frank Selke (business manager), Tim Daly (trainer)

1947: *Toronto Maple Leafs*

> Turk Broda, Garth Boesch, Gus Morston, Jim Thomson, Wally Stanowski, Bill Barilko, Harry Watson, Bud Poile, Ted Kennedy, Syl Apps, Don Metz, Nick Metz, Bill Ezinicki, Vic Lynn, Howie Meeker, Gaye Stewart, Joe Klukay, Gus Bodnar, Bob Goldham, Conn Smythe (manager), Hap Day (coach), Tim Daly (trainer)

1948: *Toronto Maple Leafs*

> Turk Broda, Jim Thomson, Wally Stanowski, Garth Boesch, Bill Barilko, Gus Morston, Phil Samis, Syl Apps, Bill Ezinicki, Harry Watson, Ted Kennedy, Howie Meeker, Vic Lynn, Nick Metz, Max Bentley, Joe Klukay, Les Costello, Don Metz, Sid Smith, Conn Smythe (manager), Hap Day (coach), Tim Daly (trainer)

1949: *Toronto Maple Leafs*

> Turk Broda, Jim Thomson, Gus Morston, Bill Barilko, Garth Boesch, Bill Juzda, Ted Kennedy, Howie Meeker, Vic Lynn, Harry Watson, Bill Ezinicki, Cal Gardner, Max Bentley, Joe Klukay, Sid Smith, Don Metz, Ray Timgren, Fleming Mackell, Harry Taylor, Bob Dawes, Tod Sloan, Conn Smythe (manager), Hap Day (coach), Tim Daly (trainer)

1951: *Toronto Maple Leafs*

> Turk Broda, Al Rollins, Jim Thomson, Gus Morston, Bill Barilko, Bill Juzda, Fern Flaman, Hugh Bolton, Ted Kennedy, Sid Smith, Tod Sloan, Cal Gardner, Howie Meeker, Harry Watson, Max Bentley, Joe Klukay, Danny Lewicki, Ray Timgren, Fleming Mackell, Johnny McCormack, Bob Hassard, Conn Smythe (manager), Joe Primeau (coach), Tim Daly (trainer)

1962: *Toronto Maple Leafs*

> Johnny Bower, Don Simmons, Carl Brewer, Tim Horton, Bob Baun, Allan Stanley, Al Arbour, Larry Hillman, Red Kelly, Dick Duff, George Armstrong, Frank Mahovlich, Bob Nevin, Ron Stewart, Billy Harris, Bert Olmstead, Bob Pulford, Eddie Shack, Dave

Keon, Ed Litzenberger, John MacMillan, Punch Imlach (manager/coach), Bob Haggert (trainer)

1963: *Toronto Maple Leafs*

Johnny Bower, Don Simmons, Carl Brewer, Tim Horton, Kent Douglas, Allan Stanley, Bob Baun, Larry Hillman, Dick Duff, Red Kelly, George Armstrong, Bob Nevin, Ron Stewart, Dave Keon, Billy Harris, Bob Pulford, Eddie Shack, Ed Litzenberger, Frank Mahovlich, John MacMillan, Punch Imlach (manager/coach), Bob Haggert (trainer)

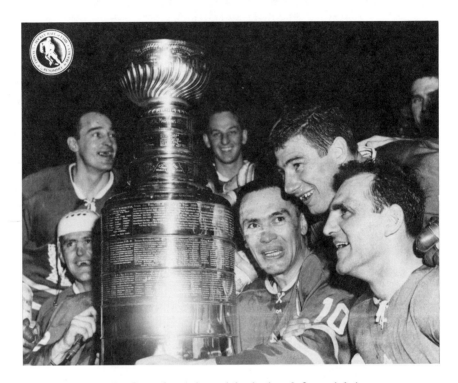

1964 Cup champions (clockwise, left to right):
Billy Harris, Frank Mahovlich, Jim Pappin, Bob Pulford,
Allan Stanley, Bobby Baun, and George Armstrong.
HOCKEY HALL OF FAME

1964: *Toronto Maple Leafs*

Johnny Bower, Carl Brewer, Tim Horton, Bob Baun, Allan Stanley, Larry Hillman, Al Arbour, Red Kelly, Gerry Ehman, Andy Bathgate, George Armstrong, Ron Stewart, Dave Keon, Billy Harris, Don McKenney, Jim Pappin, Bob Pulford, Eddie Shack, Frank Mahovlich, Ed Litzenberger, Punch Imlach (manager/coach), Bob Haggert (trainer)

1967: Toronto Maple Leafs

> Johnny Bower, Terry Sawchuk, Bob Baun, Tim Horton, Allan Stanley, Larry Hillman, Marcel Pronovost, Aut Erickson, Jim Pappin, Pete Stemkowski, Bob Pulford, Frank Mahovlich, Dave Keon, Mike Walton, Brian Conacher, Red Kelly, George Armstrong, Ron Ellis, Larry Jeffrey, Milan Marcetta, Eddie Shack, Punch Imlach (manager/coach), Bob Haggert (trainer)

Trophy Winners

O'BRIEN TROPHY

First presented by M.J. O'Brien in 1910 to the champion of the National Hockey Association until the NHL took the trophy over in 1917 when the NHA folded. In 1924 it was decided the Prince of Wales Trophy would go to the league champion so the O'Brien was not awarded. But in 1928 the O'Brien was given to the winner of the Canadian Division of the NHL. This was done until 1939 after which it was given to the loser in the Stanley Cup finals. The trophy was permanently retired after the 1949–50 season.

1918 —	Toronto Arenas
1922 —	Toronto St. Pats
1933 —	Toronto Maple Leafs
1934 —	Toronto Maple Leafs
1935 —	Toronto Maple Leafs
1938 —	Toronto Maple Leafs
1941 —	Toronto Maple Leafs
1942 —	Toronto Maple Leafs
1947 —	Toronto Maple Leafs

PRINCE OF WALES TROPHY

Awarded to the NHL champions from 1924 to 1927. From 1927 to 1938, it was given to the champions of the American Division and from 1938 to 1967 was once again awarded to the league champion of the six-team NHL.

| 1948 — | Toronto Maple Leafs |
| 1963 — | Toronto Maple Leafs |

ART ROSS MEMORIAL TROPHY

Since its inception in 1948, no Leaf has won this trophy. However, prior to 1948 these Leafs led the NHL in scoring:

1929 —   Ace Bailey
1932 —   Harvey Jackson
1934 —   Charlie Conacher
1935 —   Charlie Conacher
1938 —   Gordie Drillon

CALDER MEMORIAL TROPHY

1937 —   Syl Apps
1943 —   Gaye Stewart
1944 —   Gus Bodnar
1945 —   Frank McCool
1947 —   Howie Meeker
1958 —   Frank Mahovlich
1961 —   Dave Keon
1963 —   Kent Douglas
1966 —   Brit Selby

Al Rollins.
HOCKEY HALL OF FAME

HART MEMORIAL TROPHY

1944 —   Babe Pratt
1955 —   Ted Kennedy

LADY BYNG MEMORIAL TROPHY

1932 —   Joe Primeau
1938 —   Gordie Drillon
1942 —   Syl Apps
1952 —   Sid Smith
1955 —   Sid Smith
1961 —   Red Kelly
1962 —   Dave Keon
1963 —   Dave Keon

CONN SMYTHE TROPHY

1967 —   Dave Keon

APPENDIX

SELKE TROPHY

1993 — Doug Gilmour

JACK ADAMS TROPHY

1993 — Pat Burns

VEZINA TROPHY

1941 — Turk Broda
1948 — Turk Broda
1951 — Al Rollins
1954 — Harry Lumley
1961 — Johnny Bower
1965 — Johnny Bower and Terry Sawchuk

Toronto Maple Leaf Trophies

J.P. BICKELL MEMORIAL CUP

Awarded at the discretion of the Board of Directors to a Leaf for a
tremendous feat, one season of spectacular play, or remarkable
service over a number of years

1953 — Ted Kennedy
1954 — Harry Lumley
1955 — Ted Kennedy
1956 — Tod Sloan
1959 — George Armstrong and Bob Pulford
1960 — Johnny Bower
1961 — Red Kelly
1962 — Dave Keon
1963 — Dave Keon
1964 — Johnny Bower
1965 — Johnny Bower
1966 — Allan Stanley
1967 — Terry Sawchuk
1969 — Tim Horton
1971 — Bob Baun
1972 — King Clancy
1979 — Mike Palmateer
1993 — Doug Gilmour

Bower beats Howe to the puck.
IMPERIAL OIL / TUROFSKY COLLECTION / HOCKEY HALL OF FAME

MOLSON CUP

1974 — Borje Salming

1975 — Darryl Sittler

1976 — Darryl Sittler

1977 — Borje Salming

1978 — Borje Salming

1979 — Darryl Sittler

1980 — Borje Salming

1981 — Darryl Sittler/Wilf Paiement

1982 — Michel Larocque

1983 — Rick Vaive

1984 — Rick Vaive

1985 — Bill Derlago

1986 — Ken Wregget

1987 — Rick Vaive

1988 — Ken Wregget

1989 — Gary Leeman

1990 — Gary Leeman

1991 — Peter Ing

1992 — Grant Fuhr

1993 — Doug Gilmour

1994 — Doug Gilmour

1995 — Mats Sundin

General Managers

1927–57 — Conn Smythe
1957 — Hap Day
1958–69 — Punch Imlach
1969–79 — Jim Gregory
1979–81 — Punch Imlach
1981–88 — Gerry McNamara
1988–89 — Gord Stellick
1989–91 — Floyd Smith
1991– — Cliff Fletcher

Coaches

1927–30 — Conn Smythe
1930–31 — Art Duncan[1]
1931–40 — Dick Irvin[2]
1940–50 — Hap Day
1950–53 — Joe Primeau
1953–56 — King Clancy
1956–57 — Howie Meeker
1957–59 — Billy Reay
1959–69 — Punch Imlach[3]
1969–73 — John McLellan[4]
1973–77 — Red Kelly
1977–79 — Roger Neilson
1979–80 — Floyd Smith[5]
1980–81 — Joe Crozier
1981–84 — Mike Nykoluk
1984–86 — Dan Maloney
1986–88 — John Brophy
1988–89 — George Armstrong
1989–90 — Doug Carpenter
1990–92 — Tom Watt
1992– — Pat Burns

1) Conn Smythe was 1–0–1 in 1930
2) Art Duncan was 0–3–2 in 1931
3) King Clancy was 7–1–2 in 1967
4) King Clancy was 9–3–3 in 1970–71
5) Dick Duff was 0–2 and Punch Imlach was 5–5 in 1979–80

Conn Smythe (left) and Dick Irvin, Sr. (right).
HOCKEY HALL OF FAME

Captains

1927–37 — Hap Day

1937–38 — Charlie Conacher

1938–40 — Red Horner

1940–43 — Syl Apps

1943–45 — Bob Davidson

1945–48 — Syl Apps

1948–55 — Ted Kennedy

1955–56 — Sid Smith

1956–57 — Ted Kennedy and Jim Thomson

1957–69 — George Armstrong

1969–75 — Dave Keon

1975–81 — Darryl Sittler

1981–86 — Rick Vaive

1986–89 — no captain

1989–91 — Rob Ramage

1991–94 — Wendel Clark

1994– — Doug Gilmour

All-Star Games

Maple Leaf Gardens has hosted eight All-Star Games. The first one ever played was a benefit game for "Ace" Bailey after a hit by Eddie Shore on December 12, 1933, ended his career. It was held at Maple Leaf Gardens on February 14, 1934, and raised $23,000. There were two subsequent benefit games, in 1937 for Howie Morenz, and 1939 for Babe Siebert. In 1947, the game became an annual event and the format was standardized so that the Stanley Cup champions of the previous year played the best of the rest of the league (though not necessarily at the champions' home rink). The last time this format was used was in 1968, when the game was held midway through the season for the first time. This was the last time Toronto hosted the game:

1.	February 14, 1934	Toronto 7	All-Stars 3
2.	October 13, 1947	All-Stars 4	Toronto 3
3.	October 10, 1949	All-Stars 3	Toronto 1
4.	October 9, 1951	1st Team 2	2nd Team 2
5.	October 6, 1962	Toronto 4	All-Stars 1
6.	October 5, 1963	Toronto 3	All-Stars 3
7.	October 10, 1964	All-Stars 3	Toronto 2
8.	January 16, 1968	Toronto 4	All-Stars 3

"ACE" BAILEY BENEFIT GAME, TORONTO, FEB. 14, 1934, NATIONAL LEAGUE ALL-STARS VERSUS TORONTO MAPLE LEAFS

HOCKEY HALL OF FAME

Line-ups for the First All-Star Game

TORONTO MAPLE LEAFS

Coach: Dick Irvin

1.	George Hainsworth	G
2.	Red Horner	D
3.	Alex Levinsky	D
4.	Hap Day	LW
5.	Andy Blair	C
7.	King Clancy	D
8.	Baldy Cotton	LW
9.	Charlie Conacher	RW

10.	Joe Primeau	C
11.	Busher Jackson	LW
12.	Hec Kilrea	LW
14.	Bill Thoms	C
15.	Ken Doraty	RW
16.	Charlie Sands	RW
17.	Frank Boll	LW

ALL-STARS

Coach: Lester Patrick, New York Rangers

1.	Chuck Gardiner	G	Chicago Black Hawks
7.	Lionel Conacher	D	Chicago Black Hawks
12.	Red Dutton	D	New York Americans
6.	Ivan Johnson	D	New York Rangers
17.	Allan Shields	D	Ottawa Senators
2.	Eddie Shore	D	Boston Bruins
11.	Normie Himes	C	New York Americans
16.	Howie Morenz	C	Montreal Canadiens
10.	Hooley Smith	C	Montreal Maroons
9.	Nels Stewart	C	Boston Bruins
14.	Larry Aurie	RW	Detroit Red Wings
15.	Bill Cook	RW	New York Rangers
3.	Frank Finnigan	RW	Ottawa Senators
18.	Jimmy Ward	RW	Montreal Maroons
4.	Aurel Joliat	LW	Montreal Canadiens
5.	Herbie Lewis	LW	Detroit Red Wings

SCORING SUMMARY

First Period

1.	Toronto	Cotton (Blair, Doraty)	4:00
2.	Toronto	Jackson (Kilrea, Primeau)	7:11
3.	All-Stars	Stewart (Ward)	14:15

Penalties: none

Second Period

4.	Toronto	Jackson (Thoms)	1:33
5.	All-Stars	Morenz (Joliat)	8:24
6.	All-Stars	Finnigan (Stewart)	9:15
7.	Toronto	Day (unassisted)	11:13

Penalties: none

Third Period

8.	Toronto	Kilrea (Jackson)	4:05
9.	Toronto	Doraty (Blair)	18:26
10.	Toronto	Blair (unassisted)	18:41

Penalties: none

Referees: Bobby Hewitson, Mike Rodden
Attendance: 14,000

Leafs All-Stars

These Leafs have been selected to or competed for the All-Star team. The selection of All-Stars began in 1930–31 and was intended simply to identify and honour the best players in the league (until the All-Star game became an annual event). Since 1969 the best players from the NHL have made up both teams. Numbers in brackets indicate first- or second-team selection; where no number is given, players were picked by the coach as the team's representative or to fill the roster. Because the game was played at the beginning of the season, players were chosen All-Stars for one season (i.e.: '37–'38), but did not play the game until the next ('38–'39). Underneath each season is listed the date and venue for each All-Star game.

1930–31   King Clancy, defence (1st)
              Dick Irvin, coach (2nd)

1931–32   Harvey Jackson, left wing (1st)
              King Clancy, defence (2nd)
              Charlie Conacher, right wing (2nd)
              Dick Irvin, coach (2nd)

1932–33   King Clancy, defence (2nd)
              Charlie Conacher, right wing (2nd)
              Harvey Jackson, left wing (2nd)
              Dick Irvin, coach (2nd)

1933–34   FEBRUARY 14, 1934
              MAPLE LEAF GARDENS
              King Clancy, defence (1st)
              Charlie Conacher, right wing (1st)
              Harvey Jackson, left wing (1st)
              Joe Primeau, centre (2nd)
              Dick Irvin, coach (2nd)

1934–35   Charlie Conacher, right wing (1st)
              Harvey Jackson, left wing (1st)
              Dick Irvin, coach (2nd)

1935–36   Charlie Conacher, right wing (1st)
               Bill Thoms, centre (2nd)

1936–37   NOVEMBER 3, 1937
              MONTREAL FORUM
              Harvey Jackson, left wing (1st)
              Charlie Conacher, right wing
              Red Horner, defence

1937–38   Gord Drillon, right wing (1st)
              Syl Apps, centre (2nd)

1938–39   OCTOBER 29, 1939
              MONTREAL FORUM

Syl Apps, centre (1st)
Gord Drillon, right wing (1st)

1939–40   No Leafs selected

1940–41   Turk Broda, goal (1st)
Wally Stanowski, defence (1st)
Sweeney Schriner, left wing (1st)
Syl Apps, centre (2nd)

1941–42   Syl Apps, centre (1st)
Turk Broda, goal (2nd)
Bucko McDonald, defence (2nd)
Gord Drillon, right wing (2nd)

1942–43   Lorne Carr, right wing (1st)
Syl Apps, centre (2nd)

1943–44   Babe Pratt, defence (1st)
Lorne Carr, right wing (1st)
Paul Bibeault, goal (2nd)
Hap Day, coach (2nd)

1944–45   Babe Pratt, defence (2nd)

1945–46   Gaye Stewart, left wing (1st)

1946–47   OCTOBER 13, 1947
MAPLE LEAF GARDENS
Cup-winning Leaf team vs. NHL All-Stars
No Leafs selected
to All-Stars

1947–48   OCTOBER 10, 1949
MAPLE LEAF GARDENS
Cup-winning Leaf team vs. NHL All-Stars
Turk Broda, goal (1st)

1948–49   OCTOBER 10, 1949
MAPLE LEAF GARDENS
Cup-winning Leaf team vs. NHL All-Stars
No Leafs selected to All-Stars

1949–50   OCTOBER 8, 1950
OLYMPIA STADIUM
Gus Morston, defence (1st)
Ted Kennedy, centre (2nd)
Turk Broda, goal
Sid Smith, left wing
Jim Thomson, defence

The All-Star format changed for the 1951 game. The First Team Stars, supplemented by players from the four American clubs, played the Second Team Stars, with added players from the two Canadian clubs. As a result, for the 1952 game, Gus Morston played on the First All-Star team against five teammates on the Second team!

1950–51 OCTOBER 9, 1951
MAPLE LEAF GARDENS
Jim Thomson, defence (2nd)
Ted Kennedy, centre (2nd)
Sid Smith, left wing (2nd)
Max Bentley, centre
Gus Morston, defence
Tod Sloan, centre
Harry Watson, left wing
Joe Primeau (coach)

1951–52 OCTOBER 5, 1952
OLYMPIA STADIUM
Jim Thomson, defence (2nd)
Sid Smith, left wing (2nd)
Gus Morston, defence
Fern Flaman, defence
Tod Sloan, centre
Harry Watson, left wing

The NHL reverted to its previous format, the Stanley Cup champions versus the rest of the league.

1952–53 OCTOBER 3, 1953
MONTREAL FORUM
Sid Smith, left wing
Jim Thomson, defence
Harry Watson, left wing

1953–54 OCTOBER 2, 1954
OLYMPIA STADIUM
Harry Lumley, goal (1st)
Tim Horton, defence (2nd)
Ted Kennedy, centre (2nd)
Sid Smith, left wing
King Clancy (coach)

1954–55 OCTOBER 2, 1955
OLYMPIA STADIUM
Harry Lumley, goal (1st)
Sid Smith, left wing (1st)
Jim Morrison, defence
Ron Stewart, right wing

1955–56 OCTOBER 9, 1956
MONTREAL FORUM
Tod Sloan, centre (2nd)
George Armstrong, right wing
Hughie Bolton, defence
Dick Duff, left wing
Jim Morrison, defence

Goaler Harry Lumley and teammates.
HOCKEY HALL OF FAME

1956–57   OCTOBER 5, 1957
             MONTREAL FORUM
             George Armstrong, right wing
             Dick Duff, left wing
             Rudy Migay, centre
             Jim Morrison, defence

1957–58   OCTOBER 4, 1958
             MONTREAL FORUM
             Dick Duff, left wing
             Billy Harris, centre

1958–59   OCTOBER 3, 1959
             MONTREAL FORUM
             George Armstrong, right wing
             Carl Brewer, defence
             Frank Mahovlich, left wing
             Bert Olmstead, left wing
             Punch Imlach (coach)

1959–60   OCTOBER 1, 1960
             MONTREAL FORUM
             Allan Stanley, defence (2nd)
             Bob Armstrong, defence
             Red Kelly, defence
             Frank Mahovlich, left wing
             Bob Pulford, left wing
             Punch Imlach (coach)

The Leafs and Detroit, November 30,
1955, Maple Leaf Gardens.
IMPERIAL OIL / TUROFSKY COLLECTION / HOCKEY HALL OF FAME

1960–61   OCTOBER 7, 1961
CHICAGO STADIUM
Johnny Bower, goal (1st)
Frank Mahovlich, left wing (1st)
Allan Stanley, defence (2nd) (did not play)
Tim Horton, defence

1961–62   OCTOBER 6, 1962
MAPLE LEAF GARDENS
Cup-winning Leafs vs. NHL All-Stars
Carl Brewer, defence (2nd)
Dave Keon, centre (2nd)
Frank Mahovlich, left wing (2nd)

1962–63   OCTOBER 5, 1963
MAPLE LEAF GARDENS
Cup-winning Leafs vs. NHL All-Stars
Carl Brewer, defence (1st)
Frank Mahovlich, left wing (1st)
Tim Horton, defence (2nd)

1963–64   OCTOBER 10, 1964
MAPLE LEAF GARDENS
Cup-winning Leafs vs. NHL All-Stars
Tim Horton, defence (1st)
Frank Mahovlich, left wing (2nd)

1964–65   OCTOBER 20, 1965
              MONTREAL FORUM
              Carl Brewer, defence (2nd) (did not play)
              Frank Mahovlich, left wing (2nd)
              Bob Baun, defence
              Ron Ellis, right wing

For the first time since the Ace Bailey Benefit, the All-Star game was played at mid-season. Thus, there was no game during the calendar year 1966.

1965–66   Allan Stanley, defence (2nd)
              Frank Mahovlich, left wing (2nd)
              Dave Keon, centre

1966–67   JANUARY 18, 1967
              MONTREAL FORUM
              Cup-winning Leafs vs. NHL All-Stars
              Tim Horton, defence (2nd)

1967–68   JANUARY 16, 1968
              MAPLE LEAF GARDENS
              Tim Horton, defence (1st)

Starting with the '68–'69 season, the game matched All-Stars from one division against All-Stars from the other. As the game was played at mid-season, the All-Stars now played the same year as their selection to the team.

1968–69   JANUARY 21, 1969
              MONTREAL FORUM
              Tim Horton, defence (1st)
              Norm Ullman, centre

1969–70   JANUARY 20, 1970
              ST. LOUIS ARENA
              Ron Ellis, right wing
              Dave Keon, centre

1970–71   JANUARY 19, 1971
              BOSTON GARDEN
              Jacques Plante, goal (2nd) (did not play)
              Dave Keon, centre (2nd)

1971–72   JANUARY 25, 1972
              MET SPORTS CENTRE
              Paul Henderson, left wing

1972–73   JANUARY 30, 1973
              MADISON SQUARE GARDEN
              Paul Henderson, left wing
              Dave Keon, centre

1973–74 JANUARY 29, 1974
CHICAGO STADIUM
Jim McKenny, defence
Norm Ullman, centre

1974–75 JANUARY 21, 1975
MONTREAL FORUM
Borje Salming, defence (2nd) (did not play)
Darryl Sittler, centre

1975–76 JANUARY 20, 1976
PHILADELPHIA SPECTRUM
Borje Salming, defence (2nd)
Wayne Thomas, goal

1976–77 JANUARY 25, 1977
PACIFIC COLISEUM
Borje Salming, defence (1st)
Lanny McDonald, right
  wing (2nd)
Ian Turnbull, defence

1977–78 JANUARY 24, 1978
MEMORIAL AUDITORIUM
Borje Salming, defence (2nd)
Darryl Sittler, centre (2nd)
Lanny McDonald, right wing

1978–79 CHALLENGE CUP
FEBRUARY 8, 10, 11, 1979
MADISON SQUARE GARDEN
NHL All-Stars vs. USSR National
  Team
Borje Salming, defence (2nd)
Lanny McDonald, right wing
Darryl Sittler

MILES NADAL / HOCKEY
HALL OF FAME

1979–80 FEBRUARY 5, 1980
JOE LOUIS ARENA
Borje Salming, defence (2nd)
Dave Burrows, defence
Darryl Sittler, centre

1980–81 FEBRUARY 10, 1981
LOS ANGELES FORUM
Robert Picard, defence

1981–82 FEBRUARY 9, 1982
THE CAPITAL CENTRE
Rick Vaive, right wing
Bob Manno, defence

1982–83 FEBRUARY 8, 1983
NASSAU COLISEUM
Rick Vaive, right wing

1983–84	JANUARY 31, 1984 MEADOWLANDS ARENA Rick Vaive, right wing
1984–85	FEBRUARY 12, 1985 OLYMPIC SADDLEDOME Miroslav Frycer, right wing
1985–86	FEBRUARY 4, 1986 HARTFORD CIVIC CENTRE Wendel Clark, left wing
1986–87	RENDEZ-VOUS '87 FEBRUARY 11 & 13, 1987 LE COLISÉE NHL All-Stars vs. Soviet National Team No Leafs selected
1987–88	FEBRUARY 9, 1988 ST. LOUIS ARENA Al Iafrate, defence
1988–89	FEBRUARY 7, 1989 NORTHLANDS COLISEUM Gary Leeman, right wing
1989–90	JANUARY 21, 1990 PITTSBURGH CIVIC ARENA Al Iafrate, defence
1990–91	JANUARY 19, 1991 CHICAGO STADIUM Vincent Damphousse, left wing
1991–92	JANUARY 18, 1992 PHILADELPHIA SPECTRUM Dave Ellett, defence
1992–93	FEBRUARY 6, 1993 MONTREAL FORUM Doug Gilmour, centre
1993–94	JANUARY 22, 1994 MADISON SQUARE GARDEN Doug Gilmour, centre Dave Andreychuk, left wing Wendel Clark, left wing (did not play) Felix Potvin, goal
1994–95	JANUARY 21, 1995 SAN JOSE ARENA Owners' lockout — All-Star Game cancelled

King Clancy is the only man to play in (1934), coach (1954), and referee ('39 and '47) an All-Star game.
Only seven players have both played in and coached an All-Star game, three of them Leafs — Hap Day, Joe Primeau, and Clancy.

Dave Andreychuk.
GRAIG ABEL

Felix Potvin.
DOUG MACLELLAN / HOCKEY HALL OF FAME

Most Valuable Player

This honour began in 1962.

1962 — Eddie Shack
1963 — Frank Mahovlich
1968 — Bruce Gamble
1991 — Vincent Damphousse

Leafs' All-Time Leaders

MOST SEASONS

1.	George Armstrong	21
2.	Tim Horton	20
3.	Ron Ellis	16
4.	Borje Salming	16
5.	Dave Keon	15
6.	Bob Baun	14
7.	Turk Broda	14
8.	Ted Kennedy	14
9.	Bob Pulford	14
10.	Jim McKenny	14
11.	Hap Day	13
12.	Ron Stewart	13
13.	Bob Davidson	12
14.	Red Horner	12
15.	Jim Thomson	12
16.	Johnny Bower	12
17.	Frank Mahovlich	12
18.	Darryl Sittler	12
19.	Sid Smith	12
20.	Nick Metz	12

MOST GAMES, CAREER

1.	George Armstrong	1187
2.	Tim Horton	1185
3.	Borje Salming	1099
4.	Dave Keon	1062
5.	Ron Ellis	1034
6.	Bob Pulford	947
7.	Darryl Sittler	844
8.	Ron Stewart	838
9.	Bob Baun	739
10.	Frank Mahovlich	720
11.	Jim Thomson	717
12.	Ted Kennedy	696
13.	Allan Stanley	633
14.	Turk Broda	629
15.	Bill Harris	610

MOST POINTS, CAREER

1.	Darryl Sittler	916
2.	Dave Keon	858
3.	Borje Salming	768

Tim Horton's 1964
playoff stick.
DOUG MACLELLAN /
HOCKEY HALL OF FAME

Bob Pulford in his Marlie days.

MOST GOALS, CAREER

1. Darryl Sittler 389
2. Dave Keon 365
3. Ron Ellis 332
4. Rick Vaive 299
5. George Armstrong 296
6. Frank Mahovlich 296
7. Bob Pulford 251
8. Ted Kennedy 231
9. Lanny McDonald 219
10. Wendel Clark 208
11. Syl Apps 201
12. Charlie Conacher 200
13. John Anderson 189
14. Harvey "Busher" Jackson 186
15. Sid Smith 186
16. Ron Stewart 186

MOST ASSISTS, CAREER

1. Borje Salming 620
2. Darryl Sittler 527
3. Dave Keon 493
4. George Armstrong 417
5. Tim Horton 349
6. Ted Kennedy 329
7. Bob Pulford 312
8. Ron Ellis 308
9. Norm Ullman 305
10. Ian Turnbull 302
11. Frank Mahovlich 301
12. Jim McKenny 246
13. Lanny McDonald 240
14. Rick Vaive 238
15. Red Kelly 232

MOST SHUTOUTS, CAREER

1. Turk Broda 62
2. Harry Lumley 34
3. Lorne Chabot 33
4. Johnny Bower 32
5. George Hainsworth 19
6. Bruce Gamble 17

 7. Mike Palmateer 15
 8. Ed Chadwick 14
 9. Al Rollins 11
10. John Ross Roach 8

MOST WINS, CAREER

 1. Turk Broda 302
 2. Johnny Bower 220
 3. Mike Palmateer 129
 4. Lorne Chabot 108
 5. Harry Lumley 104
 6. Bruce Gamble 81
 7. George Hainsworth 79
 8. Alan Bester 69
 9. Felix Potvin 59
10. Ed Chadwick 57
11. Al Rollins 57

MOST PENALTY MINUTES, CAREER

 1. Tiger Williams 1670
 2. Tim Horton 1389
 3. Wendel Clark 1341
 4. Borje Salming 1292
 5. Red Horner 1266
 6. Bob Baun 1155
 7. Bob McGill 988
 8. Rick Vaive 940
 9. Carl Brewer 917
10. Jim Thomson 830
11. Frank Mahovlich 782
12. Darryl Sittler 763
13. Todd Gill 742
14. George Armstrong 721
15. Jim Korn 708

MOST POINTS, SEASON

 1. Doug Gilmour ('92–'93) 127
 2. Darryl Sittler ('77–'78) 117
 3. Doug Gilmour ('93–'94) 111
 4. Darryl Sittler ('75–'76) 100
 5. Dave Andreychuk ('93–'94) 99
 6. Darryl Sittler ('79–'80) 97

7. Wilf Paiement ('80–'81) 97
8. Darryl Sittler ('80–'81) 96
9. Gary Leeman ('89–'90) 95
10. Vincent Damphousse ('89–'90) 94
11. Lanny McDonald ('75–'76) 93
12. Rick Vaive ('83–'84) 93
13. Lanny McDonald ('76–'77) 90
14. Darryl Sittler ('76–'77) 90
15. Ed Olczyk ('89–'90) 90
16. Rick Vaive ('81–'82) 89
17. Ed Olczyk ('89–'90) 88
18. Lanny McDonald ('77–'78) 87
19. Darryl Sittler ('78–'79) 87
20. Doug Gilmour ('91–'92) 87

DOUG MACLELLAN / HOCKEY HALL OF FAME

MOST GOALS, SEASON

1. Rick Vaive ('81–'82) 54
2. Dave Andreychuk ('92–'93) 54
   (29 with Buffalo)
3. Dave Andreychuk ('93–'94) 53
4. Rick Vaive ('83–'84) 52
5. Rick Vaive ('82–'83) 51
6. Gary Leeman ('89–'90) 51
7. Frank Mahovlich ('60–'61) 48
8. Lanny McDonald ('77–'78) 47
9. Wendel Clark ('93–'94) 46
10. Lanny McDonald ('76–'77) 46
11. Darryl Sittler ('77–'78) 45
12. Errol Thompson ('75–'76) 43
13. Lanny McDonald ('78–'79) 43
14. Darryl Sittler ('80–'81) 43
15. Ed Olczyk ('87–'88) 42

MOST ASSISTS, SEASON

1. Doug Gilmour ('92–'92) 95
2. Doug Gilmour ('93–'94) 84
3. Darryl Sittler ('77–'78) 72
4. Borje Salming ('77–'78) 66
5. Borje Salming ('80–'81) 61
6. Doug Gilmour ('91–'92) 61
   (27 with Calgary)
7. Vincent Damphousse ('89–'90) 61
8. Borje Salming ('77–'78) 60
9. Darryl Sittler ('75–'76) 59
10. Ian Turnbull ('76–'77) 57
11. Darryl Sittler ('79–'80) 57
12. Wilf Paiement ('80–'81) 57
13. Lanny McDonald ('75–'76) 56
14. Borje Salming ('78–'79) 56
15. Dan Daoust ('83–'84) 56
16. Ed Olczyk ('89–'90) 56

MOST PENALTY MINUTES, SEASON

1. Tiger Williams ('77–'78) 351
2. Tiger Williams ('76–'77) 338
3. Brian Curran ('89–'90) 301
4. Tiger Williams ('75–'76) 299
5. Tiger Williams ('78–'79) 298

6. Wendel Clark ('86–'87) 271
7. Bob McGill ('81–'82) 263
8. Jim Korn ('83–'84) 257
9. John Kordic ('89–'90) 252
10. Bob McGill ('84–'85) 250
11. Luke Richardson ('90–'91) 238
12. Dave Hutchison ('78–'79) 235
13. Rick Vaive ('80–'81) 229
14. Wendel Clark ('85–'86) 227
15. Al Secord ('87–'88) 221

MOST WINS, SEASON

1. Johnny Bower ('59–'60) 34
2. Mike Palmateer ('77–'78) 34
3. Felix Potvin ('93–'94) 34
4. Johnny Bower ('60–'61) 33
5. Turk Broda ('47–'48) 32
6. Harry Lumley ('53–'54) 32
7. Johnny Bower ('61–'62) 32
8. Turk Broda ('46–'47) 31
9. George Hainsworth ('34–'35) 30
10. Turk Broda ('49–'50) 30

MOST SHUTOUTS, SEASON

1. Harry Lumley ('53–'54) 13
2. Lorne Chabot ('28–'29) 12
3. Harry Lumley ('52–'53) 10
4. Turk Broda ('49–'50) 9
5. George Hainsworth ('34–'35) 8
6. George Hainsworth ('35–'36) 8
7. Turk Broda ('38–'39) 8
8. Harry Lumley ('54–'55) 8
9. Lorne Chabot ('29–'30) 6
10. Lorne Chabot ('30–'31) 6
11. Turk Broda ('37–'38) 6
12. Turk Broda ('41–'42) 6
13. Turk Broda ('50–'51) 6

Gerry Cheevers as a Leaf during the '61-'62 season.
HOCKEY HALL OF FAME

Approaching Milestones

1200 points:	Mike Gartner, 1191
1000 points:	Doug Gilmour, 969 Dave Andreychuk, 946
500 points:	Dave Ellett, 486
500 assists:	Dave Andreychuk, 498
300 wins:	Pat Burns, 282

The photographer's flash reflects the face of a young spectator on the glass.
IMPERIAL OIL / TUROFSKY COLLECTION / HOCKEY HALL OF FAME

Left to right: Ted Lindsay (Detroit captain), Marc Reaume,
Harry Lumley, Eric Nesterenko, Jim Thomson, and Gordie Howe.
HOCKEY HALL OF FAME

HOCKEY HALL OF FAME